Palgrave Histories of Policing, Punishment and Justice

Series Editor
David G. Barrie, The University of Western Australia, Crawley, Australia

Since the 1960s, studies of police, punishment and the courts have been an integral and popular part of historical scholarship, and have followed in the historical trajectory of a more expansive criminal justice apparatus around the world. This international book series aims to examine and debate some of the most pressing issues and problems in the field, and to stimulate new directions in research. It will showcase the work of both emerging and leading scholars of the social, cultural and institutional histories of police, punishment and the judicial sphere, and welcomes work grounded in various disciplines including criminology, sociology, history, law, legal history and political science.

Caroline Ingram

Women on Trial

Criminal Trials in Colonial Western Australia

palgrave
macmillan

Caroline Ingram
University of Western Australia
Crawley, WA, Australia

ISSN 2946-6075 ISSN 2946-6083 (electronic)
Palgrave Histories of Policing, Punishment and Justice
ISBN 978-3-031-98071-8 ISBN 978-3-031-98072-5 (eBook)
https://doi.org/10.1007/978-3-031-98072-5

Cover credit: f8 archive/Alamy Stock Photo

This Palgrave Macmillan imprint is published by the registered company Springer Nature Switzerland AG
The registered company address is: Gewerbestrasse 11, 6330 Cham, Switzerland

Acknowledgements This book arose from research undertaken for my doctoral thesis. I enjoyed every minute of that time. It was all made possible by my supervisors Professor Jane Lydon, Associate Professor David Barrie, and Dr Jeremy Martens. Thank you. Your feedback and advice have been invaluable and your encouragement through my moments of self-doubt was very much appreciated.

I am also very grateful to the archivists at the State Records Office of Western Australia who retrieved archival items for me day after day and the librarians at the State Library of Western Australia. Particular thanks are due to Senior Archivist Damien Hassan who went out of his way to retrieve difficult to find items on many occasions.

I very much enjoyed being a part of the postgraduate student cohort at the University of Western Australia. I loved learning about other students' research and I am grateful for their interest in my own. My particular thanks to Janet Osborne for always being willing to discuss Western Australian history and research with me. Many thanks also to Emily Lanman and Mary Blight with whom I have also had many discussions on Western Australian history. My thanks also to Emeritus Professor Peter Handford for a fruitful discussion on the legal history of Western Australia and to Associate Professor Tiffany Shellam for her help with the Robert Neill sketch. Thank you also to John Ingram, whose willingness to keep everything running allowed me the time to concentrate on this research and to Jesse Ingram for listening, with apparent interest, to constant updates on the progress of my thesis.

This research was supported by a Jean Rogerson Postgraduate Scholarship, an Australian Government Research Training Program Scholarship, and a Patricia Crawford Research Award in History at The University of Western Australia, for all of which I am truly grateful. My grateful thanks also to the Australian Academy of the Humanities for the award of a Publication Subsidy grant towards the publication costs of this book.

Competing Interests The author has no competing interests to declare that are relevant to the content of this manuscript.

Contents

List of Figures

List of Tables

1

Analysing the Criminal Trials of Women in Western Australia

In 1832, Mary Cooke appeared in the Court of Quarter Sessions of Western Australia charged with stealing four quarts of wine and two pounds of butter from her employer, William Tanner.[1] Mary was the first woman to be tried in Western Australia's Court of Quarter Sessions and, like many of the woman who came after her, was from the working classes. She was judged by a judge and jury who were not only of the opposite sex, but also drawn from the class of her employer. Mary, her husband Jeremiah, and their ten children had been brought out to the colony from England by Tanner as indentured servants in February 1831.[2] Before the year was out, Jeremiah had died and Mary was left to support and care for her family by herself. In November 1831 she was charged, and later convicted, of theft and was sentenced to six months' imprisonment with hard labour.[3] Although Mary was the first woman to be tried in the colony for a "serious" crime, a further 128

[1] *R v Mary Cooke*, criminal indictment files, January 1832, S122 cons3472 7 21, State Records Office of Western Australia (SROWA); Minute book Court of Quarter Sessions, 1832, S204 cons3577 1, SROWA.

[2] William Tanner et al., *The Tanner Letters: A Pioneer Saga of Swan River & Tasmania, 1831–1845* (Nedlands, W.A: University of Western Australia Press, 1981), 2.

[3] *R v Mary Cooke*; Minute book Court of Quarter Sessions, 1832.

C. Ingram, *Women on Trial*, Palgrave Histories of Policing, Punishment and Justice,
https://doi.org/10.1007/978-3-031-98072-5_1

cases involving female defendants were to be tried in the upper courts of Western Australia (the Court of Quarter Sessions and the Supreme Court of Western Australia) before the end of 1890.

There has been little examination of women's crime in nineteenth-century Western Australia. The majority of the available research focuses on the general population of offenders, who were predominantly male, during the latter half of the century.[4] Yet women's lived experience was different to that of men and many of the primarily working-class female defendants were illiterate, with limited employment options and, like all women, were subject to gendered expectations of acceptable behaviour. This lived experience affected the type of crime they committed and their treatment in the courtroom.

This gap in the available research raises several questions: how were women treated in Western Australia's criminal justice system during the nineteenth century? How did the rate of conviction of women's crimes compare to the general population of accused in Western Australia and to trials in other Australian states? What effect did defendants' co-accused status and use of legal representation have on conviction rates? How, and by whom, were recommendations ofmercy applied to female defendants in the upper courts of Western Australia? How did a range of social axes, including gender, class, and race, influence the understanding of women in the criminal justice system? This book seeks to examine the experience of women tried in the upper courts of Western Australia, to explore the ways in which the trials were gendered, and to examine how legal institutions and rules affected the outcome of women's trials. Specifically, it aims to address these questions by using both quantitative and qualitative evidence to examine four factors in Western Australian women's trials:

---

[4] For example: Alana Jayne Piper, "'I Was a Man of Honour': Masculinities and Theft in Early Twentieth-Century Western Australia," *Australian Historical Studies* 51, no. 3 (2020): 282–98; Barry Godfrey and David J. Cox, "'The Last Fleet': Crime, Reformation, and Punishment in Western Australia After 1868," *Australian & New Zealand Journal of Criminology* 41, no. 2 (2008): 236–58; Mark Finnane and Andy Kaladelfos "Race and Justice in an Australian Court: Prosecuting Homicide in Western Australia, 1830–1954," *Australian Historical Studies* 47, no. 3 (2016): 443–61.

the use of defence counsel,multi-defendant trials, Aboriginal women defendants, and the prerogative of mercy.[5]

Significantly, this book shows how, and why, some women appeared to achieve a more lenient outcome in the upper courts, while others were less fortunate. I argue that although legal rules and institutions, such as co-accused status, representation and the use of mercy, affected the verdicts and sentencing of women's trials, the outcome of those trials, and the experience of the defendant, were often mediated by gender. Women appeared less often in the courts than men; they were indicted for different crimes than men, and the outcome was often linked to their adherence to, or deviance from, gendered expectations of feminine behaviour.

While this situation was sometimes mirrored in trials in Britain, and in other parts of Australia, the very different conditions existing in Western Australia could lead to a different experience, and might sometimes lead to different outcomes, for Western Australian women accused of crime. From the time of its inception in 1829, the colony of Western Australia was characterised by low population numbers, and a low ratio of women to men, in comparison to other colonies in Australia.[6] Although male convicts were transported to Western Australia from 1850, unlike some of the eastern colonies, Western Australia never accepted female

[5] The term "Aboriginal" is used in this book to refer to Aboriginal and Torres Strait Island people of Western Australia in line with the expressed preference of many Western Australian Aboriginal people. As Western Australia encompasses many different Aboriginal social and linguistic groups, where possible Aboriginal people are referenced by their group name. The term Indigenous is used to refer to the Aboriginal and Torres Strait Island people of Australia generally; see Law Reform Commission of Western Australia, "Aboriginal Customary Laws: The Interaction of Western Australian Law with Aboriginal law and Culture, Project 94," published September 2006, 1, https://www.wa.gov.au/system/files/2021-04/LRC-Project-094-Final-report.pdf; Katherine Roscoe and Barry Godfrey, "Postcolonial Churn and the Impact of the Criminal Justice System on Aboriginal People in Western Australia, 1829–2020," *Journal of Criminology* 55, no. 4 (2022): 545.

[6] In 1845 Western Australia's population was 4357, in contrast to the population in South Australia which despite having been colonised only five years earlier, had risen to of 22,860. In 1890 Western Australia's population was sitting at 48,502 compared with a population of 318,947 in South Australia. Blue Books Western Australia, 1845, CO 22/23, 98, The National Archives UK (TNA), Australian Joint Copying Project (AJCP), http://nla.gov.au/nla.obj-2006147012; Blue books South Australia, 1845, CO 17/18, TNA, AJCP, http://nla.gov.au/nla.obj-1341814275; Australian Bureau of Statistics, "Historical population," 2016, accessed 25 January 2024, https://www.abs.gov.au/statistics/people/population/historical-population/latest-release.

convicts.[7] Its population remained low until the goldrushes of the 1890s when an influx of immigrants from other colonies nearly quadrupled the population within a decade.[8]

These factors created a completely different set of conditions for examining female criminality. The small population meant that women committing crime often became well-known identities within their communities and may have been known, at least by reputation, to the limited number of men eligible for jury duty.[9] Western Australia's low population meant that the number of lawyers practising in the colony was small and that few judges were appointed.[10] During this period, Western Australia also created separate laws to apply only to Aboriginal defendants. Aboriginal women became subject to different laws to non-Aboriginal women, which could affect the outcome of their trial. For these reasons I have focused my research on the period between 1829, when the Swan River colony was established, to 1890, shortly before the Coolgardie gold rushes.

The case of Mary Cooke underscores another gap in the historiography. Unlike middle-class and upper-class women, who often wrote letters and kept diaries, working-class women left few written traces of their lives. Although these women, even if not illiterate, had little leisure time for writing, criminal records can provide a window into their lives. As Nancy Cushing notes: "Records created to document criminal proceedings inadvertently provide a way into past worlds, revealing details of occupations, relationships and daily life which are often not

---

[7] Joanne Hyland, "The Vilest and Most Degraded of Human Beings: An Investigation into why Female Convicts were not Transported to Western Australia," *Studies in Western Australian History* 34 (2020): 147.

[8] R.T. Appleyard, "Western Australia: Economic and Demographic Growth, 1850–1914" in *A New History of Western Australia*, ed. C. T. Stannage (Nedlands: University of Western Australia Press, 1981), 134.

[9] Leigh S.L. Straw, "'The Worst Female Character': Criminal Underclass Women in Perth and Fremantle, 1900–1939," *Journal of Australian studies* 37, no. 2 (2013): 209–10; Enid Russell, *A History of the Law in Western Australia and Its Development from 1829 to 1979* (Nedlands, W.A.: University of Western Australian Press, 1980), 137.

[10] Peter Handford, "Criminal Prosecutions in Western Australia: A View from the Nineteenth Century," *University of Western Australia Law Review* 43, no. 1 (2018): 143–71; Russell, *A History of the Law in Western Australia.*

otherwise written down."[11] Depositions created to hold women accountable for their actions, when read "against the grain," can also tell us about women's friendships, the strategies they used to survive, their children and institutionalisation.[12] Consequently, this research offers important insights into the way women were understood in the nineteenth century.

To understand modern debates about criminal justice, we need to examine the past. As Shani D'Cruze and Louise Jackson have written: "The 'newness' of recent patterns and trends can only be fully assessed by placing them in a broader historical context."[13] The history of female defendants in Australian courts is therefore required to inform more recent concerns about criminal justice, such as gendered differences in trial outcomes in Australian courts and the increase in the incarceration of women over the last few decades.[14] By examining how the criminal justice system was influenced by the social contexts of the past, it is possible to discern trends of continuity and change over time.

The Beginnings of the Legal System in Western Australia

Unlike the situation which had occurred in the older colonies of Australia, the legal system, and requisite court system, under which women, and men, were tried throughout the nineteenth century in

[11] Nancy Cushing, *A History of Crime in Australia: Australian Underworlds* (London: Routledge, 2023), 5.

[12] For reading "against the grain" see Antoinette Burton, "Introduction: Archive Fever, Archive Stories," in *Archive Stories: Facts, Fictions and the Writing of History*, ed. Antoinette Burton (Durham, NC: Duke University Press, 2005), 1–24.

[13] Shani D'Cruze and Louise A. Jackson, *Women, Crime and Justice in England since 1660* (New York: Palgrave McMillan, 2009), 1.

[14] Christine E.W. Bond and Samantha Jeffries, "Sentencing Indigenous and Non-Indigenous Women in Western Australia's Higher Courts," *Psychiatry, Psychology and Law* 17, no. 1 (2010): 70–78; Samantha Jeffries and Christine E.W. Bond, "Gender, Indigeneity, and the Criminal Courts: A Narrative Exploration of Women's Sentencing in Western Australia," *Women & Criminal Justice* 23, no. 1 (2013): 19–42; Lorana Bartels, Patricia Easteal and Robyn Westgate, "Understanding Women's Imprisonment in Australia," *Women & Criminal Justice* 30, no. 3 (2020): 204–19.

Western Australia was formed within the first few months of colonisation.[15] When Captain James Stirling anchored the *Parmelia* off the western coast of Australia on 31 May 1829, he had on board 152 people, household goods, plants, building materials, and animals. The ship was one of three which had set off from England with the intention of founding a colony, to be known as the Swan River colony, for its passengers and the several shiploads of colonists who were to follow. Colonists were to be granted land according to the amount of assets and the number of labourers brought with them.[16] Within weeks Stirling, as Lieutenant-Governor, had declared that British law would prevail in the new colony and that the "Protection of Law" should also apply to Aboriginal people within it.[17] In making this proclamation, Stirling ignored a system of law which was already in operation and which had been used by the Noongar people for tens of thousands of years.[18]

By January 1830, Stirling found himself obliged to set up a judicial system for the colony, although he had not yet received a commission to do so. Complaining of indentured servants, "whose habits were of the loosest description," he stated that a system of justice was needed to control the servants, protect the rights of their masters, and prevent theft and assault.[19] Accordingly, a Court of Petty Sessions was created to hear minor offences and a Court of Quarter Sessions for the more serious offences.[20] Continuing the British system of turning decommissioned ships into prison hulks, the wreck of the *Marquis of Anglesea* was pressed

[15] Alex C. Castles, *An Australian Legal History* (Sydney: The Law Book Company, 1993), 295.

[16] Valerie Fitch, *Eager for Labour: The Swan River Indenture* (Carlisle, W.A.: Hesperian Press, 2003), 32.

[17] Pamela Statham-Drew, *James Stirling: Admiral and Founding Governor of Western Australia* (Crawley: University of Western Australia Press, 2003), 131, 136; Russell, *A History of the Law in Western Australia*, 334; Geoffrey Bolton and Geraldine Byrne, *May it Please Your Honour: A History of the Supreme Court of Western Australia from 1861–2005* (Perth: The Supreme Court of Western Australia, 2005), 5.

[18] Neville Green, *Broken Spears, Aboriginals and Europeans in the Southwest of Australia* (Cottesloe: Focus Education Services, 1984), 18.

[19] Russell, *A History of the Law in Western Australia*, 11, 13.

[20] Russell, *A History of the Law in Western Australia*, 14.

into service as a temporary gaol.[21] The fact that Stirling did not express a concern that the justice system might be needed to protect the rights of indentured servants, many of whom were later to suffer severe hardship at the hands of their employers due to lack of food and wages, underscores the nature of the power structure existing between the landed classes and those brought to serve them.[22]

To preside over these courts, Stirling appointed eight justices of the peace who were selected, he wrote, from the "most wealthy and prudent" of the settlers. These men were to preside over both petty and quarter sessions but only two, William Henry Mackie and Alfred Hawes Stone, had legal training.[23] Stone was a qualified and practising solicitor when he arrived in the colony. Mackie had been educated at Cambridge but had never been called to the Bar.[24] This system of justice was based on the English system and, although trials at petty sessions did not involve a jury, those at quarter sessions utilised a grand jury to decide whether the indictment was a "true bill" and a petty jury to decide on the guilt or innocence of the defendant.[25] Jurors were initially selected from men entitled to grants of land, but by 1832, juror qualifications had changed to encompass male persons between the ages of twenty-one and sixty possessing property worth £50 or personal estate worth £100.[26] The system had one major and significant difference from that of England: justices were allowed to hearcapital offences at quarter sessions. Stirling justified this decision by appointing Mackie, "a gentleman learned in the law," to be Chairman of Quarter Sessions at a salary of £290, "to preside at and assist the Court," although the other justices were unpaid.[27] The colony was thus equipped with a justice system, modelled on English lines, which was composed entirely of men from the land-owning classes.

---

21 Katherine Ann Roscoe, "Island Chains: Carceral Islands and the Colonisation of Australia, 1824–1903" (PhD diss., University of Leicester, 2018), 40; Russell, *A History of the Law in Western Australia*, 16.

22 Statham-Drew, *James Stirling*, 178.

23 Russell, *A History of the Law in Western Australia*, 14.

24 Bolton and Byrne, *May it Please Your Honour*, 4, 7.

25 Castles, *An Australian Legal History*, 295.

26 Russell, *A History of the Law in Western Australia*, 15; *An Act for Regulating the Constitution of Juries; and the Office of Sheriff* 1832 (WA).

27 Russell, *A History of the Law in Western Australia*, 13.

At a time when women were considered to be the weaker sex, both physically and intellectually, and men were deemed to be responsible for the behaviour of their wives, this patriarchal system created a power imbalance within the criminal justice system.[28] While it is possible that the prejudices and biases brought into the court by these men may have sometimes resulted in a paternalistic benevolence for female defendants, it is equally true that those women whose behaviour was seen to threaten the strong social order of the time would have been viewed as objects for chastisement or correction.

The "Double Deviance" and "Chivalry" Theories

The "double deviance" theory hinges on the ideology of femininity and suggests that women were punished not only for deviating from the law, but also for deviating from the dominant discourse of femininity.[29] The feminine ideal in the Victorian period was closely tied to the home and family. Women were considered to be fragile and impressionable but they were also considered morally superior to men and their role was seen as that of the moral guardians of society. "Respectability" was a cultural construct that associated femininity with civilisation and domesticity, as opposed to masculinity which was associated with rationality, and was more a signifier of moral status than it was of social class.[30] Women deviating from gendered expectations of "respectable" feminine behaviour at this time, including traits such as passivity, piousness and modesty, were considered a danger to society and might be punished accordingly.[31]

---

[28] Lucia Zedner, "Women, Crime and Penal Responses: A Historical Account," *Crime and Justice* 14 (1991): 308; Penelope Hetherington, *The Marriage Knot: Marriage and Divorce in Colonial Western Australia 1829–1900* (Crawley, W.A.: UWA Publishing, 2013), 115.

[29] Frances Heidensohn, *Crime and Society* (London: Macmillan Education, 1989), 102; Frances Heidensohn, *Women and Crime* (London: Macmillan Press, 1985), 46–47.

[30] Woodruff D. Smith, *Respectability as Moral Map and Public Discourse in the Nineteenth Century* (London: Routledge, 2018), 4.

[31] D'Cruze and Jackson, *Women, Crime and Justice*, 63; Deirdre Palk, *Gender, Crime and Judicial Discretion in the English Criminal Justice System, 1780 to 1830* (Woodbridge, U.K.; Boydell Press, 2006).

However, because behaviour considered deviant is inextricably linked to the everchanging concepts of feminine ideology and cultural assumptions of gender roles, it too will change and shift over time.

An alternative theory, known as the chivalry theory, argued that women appeared less often in crime statistics due to chivalrous treatment by the male-dominated criminal justice system: "police officers dislike to arrest them, district attorneys to prosecute them, judges and juries to find them guilty."[32] This theory has been strongly criticised by criminologists who argue that it is racist, classist, and simplistic.[33] However, some historians and criminologists maintain that women were punished *less* harshly for similar crimes, due to a "civilising offensive" aimed at men in line with changing attitudes to violent masculinities.[34]

Other historians have called for the use of a more nuanced interpretation of the double deviance theory, arguing that women appearing in court were more likely to be convicted, and were given harsher sentences, when they were perceived to not meet gendered expectations of femininity and that women who used the courtroom to project an identity of respectable femininity could negotiate a lighter sentence.[35] Women whose lived experience transgressed patriarchal notions of acceptable feminine behaviour made them "dangerous" in the eyes of the courts.[36] In this book I argue that women appearing in the upper courts of nineteenth-century Western Australia who were able to present a persona

32 Otto Pollak, *The Criminality of Women* (Philadelphia: University of Pennsylvania Press, 1950), 152.

33 Dorie Klein, "The Etiology of Female Crime," in *The Criminology of Deviant Women*, eds Freda Adler and Rita James Simon (Boston: Houghton Mifflin Company, 1979), 73–75; Carol Smart, *Women, Crime and Criminology: A Feminist Critique* (London: Routledge and Kegan Paul, 1976), 46–53; Heidensohn, *Women and Crime*, 119.

34 Barry S. Godfrey, Stephen Farrall, and Susanne Karstedt, "Explaining Gendered Sentencing Patterns for Violent Men and Women in the late-Victorian and Edwardian period," *British Journal of Criminology* 45, no. 5 (2005): 696–720.

35 Andrew August, "'A Horrible Looking Woman': Female Violence in late-Victorian East London," *Journal of British Studies* 54, no. 4 (2015): 844–68.

36 Sandra Harding, "Conclusion: Epistemological Questions," in *Feminism & Methodology: Social Science Issues*, ed. Sandra Harding (Milton Keynes: Open University Press, 1987), 185; Anette Ballinger, "Dead Woman Walking: Executed Women in England & Wales, 1900–1955" (PhD diss., University of Sheffield, 1997).

of respectable femininity before the all-male judge and jury were more likely to receive leniency at the hands of the court.

Gender, Class, and Race

In recent decades, historians of crime have begun to use gender, class and race as categories of analysis.[37] Intersectionality, which describes how inequalities, such as gender, class and race, can intersect and overlap, is a way of understanding and analysing problems and situations using intersecting axes and mutually influencing systems of power.[38] This concept can be a useful tool for analysing criminal records which are particularly valuable for revealing insights into people who may have left few other traces, such as women, the working classes, ethnic minorities or Indigenous populations.

However, some scholars have disagreed with this approach, calling for historians to look beyond the intersection of gender, class and race as explanations in women's trials and arguing that the use and interpretation of legal institutions and rules, and the way those rules were applied, might be more significant to the trial's outcome.[39] Others have shown that the outcome of a trial could be dependent on several different variables, arguing that "studies which seek to understand the treatment of women … are hampered if gender is the sole focus for analysis."[40]

---

[37] For example: Alana Jayne Piper, "In Bad Company: Female Criminal Subcultures in Melbourne and Brisbane, 1860–1920" (PhD diss., University of Queensland, 2013); Daniel J.R. Grey, "'No Crime to Kill a Bastard-Child': Stereotypes of Infanticide in Nineteenth-Century England and Wales," in *Intersections of Gender, Class and Race in the Long Nineteenth Century and Beyond*, ed. Barbara Leonardi (Cham, Switzerland: Palgrave MacMillan, 2018), 41–66; Ray Evans, "Don't You Remember Black Alice, Sam Holt? Aboriginal Women in Queensland History," *Hecate* 8, no. 2 (1982): 7–21.

[38] Kimberlé Williams Crenshaw, "Demarginalising the Intersection of Race and Sex: A Black Feminist Critique of Anti-Discrimination Doctrine, Feminist Theory and Anti-Racist Politics," *University of Chicago Legal Forum* 1, no. 8 (1989): 139–67; Patricia Hill Collins and Sirma Bilge, *Intersectionality* (Oxford: Polity Press, 2016), 11.

[39] Carolyn Strange and Les Hetherington, "Murderess or Miscarriage of Justice? A Case of Husband Poisoning in Early Federation New South Wales," *Australian Historical Studies* 51, no. 3 (2020): 301.

[40] Rita Farrell, "Dangerous Women: Constructions of Female Criminality in Western Australia 1915–1945" (PhD diss., Murdoch University, 1997), 436.

In examining women's trials in pre-1891 Western Australia, this book adds to the growing body of literature concerned with the history of the criminal justice system and women's place within it. It also finds a place within histories concerned with the lives of people marginalised by society. By combining elements of social history with relevant concepts from criminology and the history of criminal justice, I hope to contextualise the way women's offending was understood by the criminal justice system and to identify patterns in the way that the system administered "justice" to women accused of crime.

Although this book is concerned with the treatment of female defendants in the criminal justice system, the context in which women's trials occurred is also examined. Gendered assumptions may have influenced women's behaviour during the nineteenth century, but they did not necessarily control it and the crimes women committed were highly dependent on the context in which they lived their lives. Social and economic factors also played a large part in shaping women's offending.[41] Consequently I also examine women's employment options, wage levels and poverty relief, in relation to the crimes for which they were charged, to gain a better understanding of women's patterns of offending and how this related to their trials.

Analysing the Data

The data for this study was retrieved mainly from two large online datasets, that is, the Prosecution Project, which contains data on serious, indictable offences across multiple Australian jurisdictions, Trove, which contains millions of digitised articles from Australian newspapers, and from numerous handwritten archival records.[42] It was interrogated to identify patterns of conviction or acquittal in the juries' verdicts, using a

[41] Sanne Muurling, Marion Pluskota, and Manon van der Heijden, "Introduction: Women and Crime in History," in *Women's Criminality in Europe, 1600–1914*, eds Manon Van der Heijden, Marion Pluskota, and Sanne Muurling (Cambridge: Cambridge University Press, 2020), 5.

[42] Mark Finnane, "Western Australia Criminal Trials 1830–1861" (ADA Dataverse, V1, 2019), https://doi.org/10.26193/OW6SR6; Mark Finnane, "Western Australia Supreme Court 1862–1899" (ADA Dataverse, V2, 2020), https://doi.org/10.26193/ESI64N; "Newspapers & Gazettes," Trove, accessed 7 May 2022, https://trove.nla.gov.au/newspaper/.

combination of quantitative and qualitative methods. When calculating offence category or rates of conviction in cases where the defendant was tried for more than one crime in the same trial, I have considered only the most serious of the charges. Some women appeared in the upper courts more than once and these have been included as separate cases. Likewise, when more than one offender was tried in the same trial for the same offence, the cases are counted separately in the statistics.

Case studies, used throughout the book to contextualise the findings drawn from the statistics, examine, not only the trial, but also the lived experiences of the women and the discourses surrounding women accused of crime. This mixed-methods approach provides a fuller and more nuanced methodology than would result from the use of either method alone and helps to provide possible explanations for patterns discerned in quantitative analysis.[43]

By using an intersectional methodology to analyse these case studies, I hope to determine not only the effect of representation, co-defendant status, Aboriginality and the use of mercy on the verdict and sentencing of the trial, but also the extent to which defendants were perceived to meet gendered expectations of respectable femininity and how this "feminine" identity contributed to the trial's outcome.

Structure

The book is arranged thematically and divided into seven chapters. This first chapter sets the context for the legal system of criminal justice in Western Australia and sets out the structure of the book. In the second chapter, I use four case studies to historically contextualise accounts of crime committed by women in Western Australia before 1891. By examining the lived experience of these women's lives we come closer to understanding their pathways to offending, the forces in society which propelled women down this path, and the survival strategies used by women living on the margins of society. These case studies show that

[43] John W. Creswell and J. David Creswell, *Research Design: Qualitative, Quantitative, and Mixed Methods Approaches* (Thousand Oaks, California: SAGE Publications, 2018), 4.

poverty, economic considerations, and lack of employment options can often be linked to women's crime. In some cases, such as those of infanticide, economic considerations might be entangled with women's shame, or fear of offending against society's expectations. In these situations, friendships between women could be a necessary survival strategy. Women on the margins of society might care for each other's children, support other women in court or look out for friends after sickness or injury.

In the third chapter, I examine the use of defence counsel to determine whether legal representation was advantageous to female defendants. The statistics are analysed to determine the percentage of defendants represented by counsel who received an acquittal or were convicted of a lesser charge, compared to those found guilty, and compared with similar percentages for defendants who appeared unrepresented. These figures are compared to published research on the general population of offenders in other states. The statistics are also interrogated to determine if counsel was more effective for different types of crime. Case studies are used to reveal the tactics and arguments used by counsel. The research shows that the use of defence counsel was a significant advantage for women accused of property theft but may have been less effective for defendants accused of interpersonal crimes. Although counsel used a variety of tactics to defend female clients, they would, where possible, emphasise the feminine characteristics of their female defendants to render them less dangerous in the eyes of the jury.

The fourth chapter examines the legal institution of trying two or more defendants together in the same trial. It has long been argued that joint trials are disadvantageous to defendants, but this claim has not been tested in regard to subgroups of defendants such as women. Here I ask whether being tried with a co-accused was prejudicial to the outcome of women's trials. Analysis of the statistics indicates that, although co-accused status was generally favourable for women tried in the upper courts, the effect was mediated by the category of offence, and women accused of violent crimes were less likely to gain an advantage from joint trials. These findings differ from recent research for the general population of defendants.

The fifth chapter examines cases of Aboriginal women tried in the upper courts of Western Australia and asks how the judicial system treated Aboriginal women accused of crime. The history of First Nations women as defendants in Australian courts is sparse but the question is all the more pertinent when we consider the high rate of incarceration of First Nations women today. In this chapter, I ask what types of crimes Aboriginal women were charged with, what the outcomes of their trials were, and how this compared to the general population of female defendants in the upper courts. The statistics and case studies examined indicate that Aboriginal women's experiences in the upper courts could be very different to that of non-Aboriginal women. Additionally, magistrates' ignorance of the law could adversely affect the course of the trial for women tried in rural areas under the *Courts of General Sessions Act 1845* (WA) and these women were more likely to receive a harsh sentence. Conversely, a degree of leniency appears to have been shown in the sentencing of some Aboriginal women.

The sixth chapter examines the concept of mercy, described by Douglas Hay as "the discretionary element of the law," and the manner in which it was used by those in positions of power in the court room.[44] Male judges and juries drawn from the land-owning classes determined the fate of the mainly working-class women tried in the upper courts but had the capacity to dispense mercy to defendants. This chapter examines which female defendants received mercy or leniency, and in what form. The research indicates that juries did exercise their prerogative to recommend mercy when they felt that women were deserving of it. Women received leniency in the form of mercy riders (recommendations to mercy) or partial verdicts (conviction of a lesser crime) from the jury for reasons such as family responsibilities, youth or provocation. Judges also exercised leniency in sentencing and women who were able to present a persona of respectable femininity, or young women accused of infanticide, were more likely to receive a lenient sentence.

[44] Douglas Hay, "Property, Authority and the Criminal Law," in *Albion's Fatal Tree: Crime and Society in Eighteenth-Century England*, eds Douglas Hay et al. (London: Penguin, 1975), 43.

In the last chapter, I determine what the analysis of this data tells us overall about the criminal trials of women in colonial Western Australia and suggest some avenues for further research.

The study of the history of crime and criminal justice can show us which behaviours and actions were valued by a society and which were deemed unacceptable. It can suggest why men and women deviated from accepted behaviours and what circumstances were considered to mitigate this deviancy. There is a need for research that looks beyond the concept of the sex of the defendant, or individual causal factors, and instead examines the complex and interwoven discourses, ideologies, and legal factors that operated in a holistic fashion to shape the way women were treated and understood in the legal system, and which ultimately influenced the outcome of the trial. By examining not only the women's trials, but also the pathways that led them to that point, and the effect the criminal justice system had on their lived experience, I hope that this study has given these women an identity and has contributed to a greater understanding of their lived experience.

This research suggests that, although legal rules and institutions were important to the outcome of women's trials, the concepts of gender and race were also considered by judges, juries, and counsel. The cultural construct of gender runs as a consistent thread throughout the trial accounts, often determining which women received leniency in the court. Aboriginal women, who were tried before judges and juries who had little understanding of Aboriginal lore or culture, could expect a different experience in the courts, and often a different outcome, to non-Aboriginal women. Aboriginal women appeared unrepresented in trials where they often could not understand the evidence given, where the rules of evidence were often disregarded, and where the chances of acquittal were lower than for non-Aboriginal defendants. Women's lived experience affected the types of crime they committed, and their experience as offenders during the early years of the Swan River Colony, and in many ways these patterns continue today. Only by understanding the way in which women were treated by the criminal justice system historically can we begin to understand how the legacies of that time continue to affect women's experience in the modern criminal justice system. In particular, an understanding of the ways in which First Nations female defendants were treated in the early years of the criminal justice system is of pressing concern given the overrepresentation of First Nations women incarcerated in Australian prisons today and the lack of scholarly research in this area.[45]

[45] "Corrective Services Australia," Australian Bureau of Statistics, accessed 14 April 2025, https://www.abs.gov.au/statistics/people/crime-and-justice/corrective-services-australia/dec-quarter-2024.

2

Who Were the Criminal Women of Nineteenth-Century Western Australia?

The case went dead against her,
The facts were all too plain;
Four months she got ('twas pretty hot),
This vagrant Mary Jane.

And so when they removed her,
She loudly did complain
In tones not mild, but protests wild,
Distressful Mary Jane.[1]

These lines appeared in a news report in 1898 and referred to a case of vagrancy heard in the police courts on Barrack Street, Perth. They exemplify not only the precarity of the lives of working-class women but also point towards the agency sometimes shown by women who challenged the authority of the courts. The defendant in this case was Mary Jane Hayes: a woman whose reputation was notorious in late-nineteenth-century Perth and Fremantle. During her lifetime she made at least eighty-five court appearances, three of which were in the Supreme

[1] "So fare Thee well, Poor Mary Jane," *Clare's Weekly*, 17 September 1898, 3.

C. Ingram, *Women on Trial*, Palgrave Histories of Policing, Punishment and Justice,
https://doi.org/10.1007/978-3-031-98072-5_2

Court, and was incarcerated in the Fremantle Lunatic Asylum five times for behaviour which transgressed the bounds of acceptable femininity.[2] On this occasion, she was accused of being an idle and disorderly person. In court the police accused her of drinking beer and sleeping in the open, and remarked on her lack of cleanliness.[3] Under laws targeting the poorer members of society, women, and men, could be charged with being idle and disorderly if they had insufficient means to maintain themselves or if found sleeping outdoors.[4] Was Mary Jane's life typical of women who appeared in the upper courts of Western Australia during the nineteenth century? To understand why women appeared in court charged with serious crime, it is necessary to first understand their lives. Who were the women who appeared in these courts? What can judicial records tell us about their lived experience and how that experience intersected with the criminal justice system?

This chapter aims to examine the lives of women accused of crime to historically contextualise the quantitative data on women's trials which is explored in the following chapters. It examines the lives and backgrounds of women indicted for serious crime in nineteenth-century Western Australia to gain a greater understanding of the social and economic forces which shaped their lived experience. I argue that lack of employment options for women, low wages, and poverty were part of the everyday lived experience for many working-class women and, together with the shame experienced by some women who conceived outside of marriage, were the driving forces behind much of women's crime in the colony.

I begin this chapter with a discussion of the use of case studies and microhistories and an examination of the nature and proportion of crime committed by the colony's women. This is followed by the case studies of four women brought before the upper courts in Western Australia. The case of Eliza Cook, a fifteen-year-old domestic servant indicted for the theft of clothing, illustrates some of the hardships faced by settler colonial women in the early years of the colony. Mary Woods's case

---

[2] Alexandra Wallis, "The Disorderly Female: Alcohol, Prostitution and Moral Insanity in 19th-Century Fremantle," *Journal of Australian Studies* (2019): 333–48.

[3] "News and Notes," *West Australian*, 13 September 1898, 4.

[4] *Police Ordinance 1849* (WA); *Police Ordinance 1861* (WA); *Police Act 1892* (WA).

exemplifies the precarity experienced by some of the wives and families of Enrolled Pensioner Guards, who arrived from 1850 onwards with the influx of convicts to Western Australia. The case study of Mary Goodall, one of the single women emigrants brought to Western Australia from the 1850s, exemplifies the cycle of poverty and institutionalisation experienced by some working-class women, and Edith Adams's case is illustrative of single women who appeared in court following the death of their newly born child.

Why Use Case Studies or Microhistories?

The cases of deviant women brought before the court can tell us much about the public discourses surrounding working-class women and the ways in which working-class women who failed to conform to gendered expectations of "respectable" behaviour were marginalised in the justice system. However, behaviour considered to be deviant changes throughout time in accordance with societal expectations, and the way in which deviant men and women are perceived also changes. It is therefore necessary, when investigating behaviour deemed to be criminal, to also examine the living conditions of those charged with, and convicted of, crime. Women who were known to have committed offences were often closely monitored by police, leading to more frequent arrests. Some women tried for crimes against good order, such as drunkenness or using obscene language, were also arrested for the more serious crimes of theft or violence. Recent research, which shows that these "versatile offenders" were the most frequent and difficult recidivists, challenges popular conceptions of women as committing mainly minor offences and argues that the use of historical methodologies, such as microhistories, combined with longitudinal criminological research, is more useful for the examination of crime than the more usual approach of using separate offence categories.[5]

[5] Alana Jayne Piper and Victoria Nagy, "Versatile Offending: Criminal Careers of Female Prisoners in Australia, 1860–1920," *Journal of Interdisciplinary History* 48, no. 2 (2017): 209–210.

In this chapter, I have used life histories of offenders to examine not only the "versatility" of some women's offending but also the impact that offending had on women's lives. To do so, I have supplemented criminal records with entries from employers' diaries and newspaper reports where available. Historians and criminologists who have engaged with the effect of news discourse in women's trials often refer to the framing of these reports—that is, the way information in news reports is selected, excluded or emphasised.[6] Most agree that the manner in which news reports portray women accused of crime influences public perception and legal responses to those acts although some research maintains that juries were capable of ignoring prejudicial news reports.[7] The framing of women who were accused of crime, as either "criminal" or "victim," also occurred in the newspapers of nineteenth-century Western Australia. It is undoubtedly true that these would have influenced society's understanding of women's crime and may also have influenced the jury's verdict in criminal cases.

The Nature and Proportion of Women's Crime in Western Australia

The women who appeared in the upper courts of Western Australia charged with indictable crime were overwhelmingly working class. Many had left friends and family behind in Britain to emigrate to Australia. Some came as wives and mothers, some as children, and a large number came as young, single women hoping to find marriage, security, and a better life. Some of these women had already been institutionalised as paupers in workhouses before they left Britain. Not all were able to improve their lives and, for some, the patterns of poverty, crime, and

[6] See Michael J. Carter, "The Hermeneutics of Frames and Framing: An Examination of the Media's Construction of Reality," *SAGE Open* 3, no. 2 (2013): 3.

[7] Patricia Esteal, Lorana Bartels, Noni Nelson and Kate Holland, "How Are Women Who Kill Portrayed in Newspaper Media? Connections with Social Values and the Legal System," *Women's Studies International Forum* 51 (2015): 31–41; David Plater and Victoria Geason, "The Prisoners Could Not Have That Fair and Impartial Trial Which Justice Demands': A Fair Criminal Trial in 19th Century Australia," *Canterbury Law Review* 25 (2019): 161–203.

interaction with the criminal justice system, seemingly left behind in Britain, were repeated in Western Australia.

As in other colonies in Australia, and in Britain, many more women were tried in the petty courts of Western Australia for crimes against good order, or for petty theft, than were tried for more serious crimes in the upper courts. For some women, an appearance in the upper court might be the only time they appeared in a court of law. For other women, their trial in the Court of Quarter Sessions or the Supreme Court of Western Australia was just one of a long string of appearances for crimes such as petty larceny, obscene language, drunkenness, or vagrancy, although these mostly occurred in the lower courts. Only six women appeared more than once in the upper courts of Western Australia between 1830 and 1890.

A total of 122 women, including eleven Aboriginal women, appeared before the Western Australian upper courts, in 129 cases, during this time period. They were charged with crimes such as larceny, receiving stolen goods, concealment of birth, arson, assault, and murder. The majority of cases (eighty-three) were for property crimes, thirty-seven were for interpersonal crimes, and a further nine women were tried for crimes against the State, such as perjury, harbouring an escaped prisoner, or giving a false statement to a registrar. Not all these women were found guilty by the jury. Of the 129 cases, just over half received a conviction (Table 2.1). In contrast, two-thirds of trials for the general population of offenders in the same period recorded a conviction.[8] The following chapters explore possible causes for this lower rate of conviction in women's trials.

The most common crime for which women were committed was simple larceny. This is a similar finding to analyses of statistics in other parts of Australia, and in Britain, at this time.[9] The most commonly

8 Computed from information in Mark Finnane, "Western Australia Criminal Trials 1830–1861" (ADA Dataverse, V1, 2019), https://doi.org/10.26193/OW6SR6; Mark Finnane, "Western Australia Supreme Court 1862–1899" (ADA Dataverse, V2, 2020), https://doi.org/10.26193/ESI64N.

9 Alana Jayne Piper and Lisa Durnian, "Theft on Trial: Prosecution, Conviction and Sentencing Patterns in Colonial Victoria and Western Australia," *Australian & New Zealand Journal of Criminology* 50, no. 1 (2017): 10, 12; Alana Jayne Piper, "In Bad Company: Female Criminal Subcultures in Brisbane and Melbourne, 1860–1920" (PhD diss., University of Queensland,

Table 2.1 Verdicts of women's trials in the upper courts of Western Australia, 1830–1890

	Property	Person	State	Total
Convicted	41	14	6	61 (47%)
Convicted (of a lesser crime)	1	5		6 (5%)
Acquitted	37	14	3	54 (42%)
Nolle prosequi	1	1		2 (2%)
Discharged	2	2		4 (3%)
Not fit to plead		1		1 (1%)
No case	1			1 (1%)
Total	83	37	9	129

Compiled from data in Mark Finnane, "Western Australia Criminal Trials 1830–1861" (ADA Dataverse, V1, 2019), https://doi.org/https://doi.org/10.26193/OW6SR6; Mark Finnane, "Western Australia Supreme Court 1862–1899" (ADA Dataverse, V2, 2020), https://doi.org/https://doi.org/10.26193/ESI64N; "Search Trials," The Prosecution Project, accessed 10 January 2023, https://app.prosecutionproject.griffith.edu.au/web/public-search; Record of Court Convictions, 1861–1914, S5072 cons1156 v23, SROWA; Correspondence inwards, 1828–1878, S2941 cons36, SROWA; Correspondence files, 1883, S675 cons527, SROWA; "Newspapers & Gazettes," Trove, accessed 7 May 2022, https://trove.nla.gov.au/newspaper/

stolen item was money, followed by clothing, but women were also charged with the theft of food, jewellery, household items, and livestock. From 1856, the number of larceny cases appearing in the upper courts dropped due to the introduction of the *Larceny Summary Conviction Ordinance 1856*. This allowed defendants the choice of being tried either summarily before a magistrate or at the Court of Quarter Sessions, if charged with the theft of items under the value of £5. The Act was passed not only to avoid incarcerating defendants for long periods of time while awaiting trial, but also so that the government could avoid the expense of sending witnesses to the Quarter Sessions in Perth.[10] This option meant that defendants were not remanded in gaol for periods of up to three months while awaiting trial, and many women did choose to be tried before a magistrate.

2013), 80; Shani D'Cruze and Louise A. Jackson, *Women, Crime and Justice in England since 1660* (New York: Palgrave McMillan, 2009), 31.

[10] *Larceny Summary Conviction Ordinance 1856* (WA).

I was able to determine the ages of 102 of the defendants using birth and death records, prisoner returns, Fremantle Lunatic Asylum case files, passenger lists, and newspaper reports. They ranged between eleven and fifty-six years old with the average age being twenty-nine years old. The largest group of women were those in their twenties (Chart 2.1). The majority of those charged with serious crime were in their twenties or thirties, suggesting a link between poverty, marital status, and women's crime. Similarly to findings by historians of women's crime in Britain, it appears that women were more likely to commit crimes such as theft when they had families to provide for and when family responsibilities created difficulties in obtaining, and keeping, paid employment.[11]

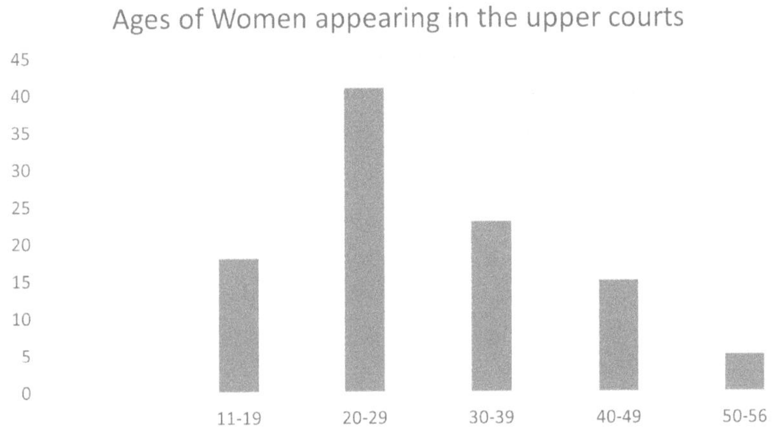

Chart 2.1 Information sourced from: Correspondence inwards, S2941 cons36, SROWA; Correspondence files, S675 cons527, SROWA; Quarterly Returns of Prisoners, S270 cons3676, SROWA; "Online Index Search Tool," Department of Justice, accessed 7 May 2022, https://www.wa.gov.au/organisation/department-of-justice/online-index-search-tool; Case books, 1865–1908, S2219 cons2724 and cons5759, SROWA

[11] See Deidre Palk, *Gender, Crime and Judicial Discretion, 1780–1830* (Woodbridge, U.K.: Boydell Press, 2006), 57; Peter King, "Female Offenders, Work and Life-cycle Change in Late-eighteenth-century London," *Continuity and Change* 11, no. 1 (1996): 61–90.

The Early Years

During the first twenty years of settlement, the amount of crime in the colony was small. The non-Aboriginal population of Western Australia remained low and only twenty-two women were tried in the upper courts. Most were working-class women from Britain who had come to the colony as the wives or children of indentured labourers, although a few were family members of soldiers who had been sent to the colony, and three were Aboriginal women. Five were children aged fifteen years or younger. Although it was not possible to determine whether all the women worked outside the home, ten worked as domestic servants and two took in laundry. The majority were charged with larceny or receiving stolen goods, although two were charged with perjury, another two with the murder, or concealing the birth, of their child, and two with the theft of livestock. Many of the thefts appear to have been opportunistic, with women taking washing left out to dry, or picking up items in their employers' houses.

The colony was founded by the mass emigration of indentured labourers, and their employers. These labourers were often sourced from parish poorhouses in England. Hoping to better themselves, and to eventually acquire their own land, they, and their families, were indentured to their masters for periods ranging from five to seven years. They signed an indenture specifically drawn up for tying servants to Swan River masters and the cost of their passage was deducted from their wages.[12] As there was little money circulating in the new colony, many servants were paid partly in kind. This took the form of food, fuel, "grog," and sometimes clothing. The amount of food, although supposedly regulated by the government, varied in amount and quality depending on the fortunes of their masters and, from 1833, employers living in rural areas were entitled to pay up to one-third of their servants' wages in spirits.[13] If

[12] Valerie J. Fitch, *Eager for Labour: The Swan River Indenture, 1829–1832* (Carlisle, W.A.: Hesperian Press, 2003), 52, 65, 80, 69, 72.

[13] Pamela Statham-Drew, *James Stirling: Admiral and Founding Governor of Western Australia* (Crawley: University of Western Australia Press, 2003), 159; Fitch, *Eager for Labour*, 72; Simon Stevens, "A Social Tyranny: The Truck System in Colonial Western Australia, 1829–99," *Labour History*, no. 80 (2001): 88.

their masters were unable to pay them at all they might be released from their indentures, although possibly still owing their passage money.[14] This meant that many servants found themselves in a precarious position with little money to support themselves or their families.

Case Study: Eliza Cook

The case of Eliza Cook is typical of some of the crime committed by women during the early years of the colony. It illustrates the opportunistic nature of much of the theft and the high value placed on food and clothing by a colony which was struggling to survive. In 1837, fifteen-year-old Eliza Cook was convicted of the larceny of a dress and collar and sentenced to six months' imprisonment with hard labour. William Drake complained that his family's clothes, which had been washed and draped over bushes in his yard to dry overnight, had been stolen. The missing clothes consisted of his wife Louisa's muslin dress, a pelerine (a woman's short cape), a lace habit shirt, a pair of sleeves, a baby frock, and a pair of stockings belonging to his servant, Caroline Flaherty. Clothing was difficult to come by in the early days of the settlement and was valued accordingly. Colonists might be required to wait until a ship arrived with goods from Britain before they could purchase new clothes.[15] Women's dresses were expensive, often taking up to twelve yards of fabric to make, and worn-out clothing was repaired, dyed or cut down to make pinafores and children's clothes.[16] Eliza was accused of the theft when she was seen, wearing Louisa's dress, and the collar of the pelerine, a few days later. Eliza claimed that she had found the dress and collar under a bush between Drake's house and the Commissariat store

[14] Fitch, *Eager for Labour*, 72, 108, 112.

[15] John Ramsden Wollaston, *Wollaston's Picton Journal (1841–1844)*, eds A. Burton and Percy U. Henn (Perth, W.A.: Paterson Brokensha, 1955), 34; "Classified Advertising," *Perth Gazette and Western Australian Journal (PGWAJ)*, 29 June 1833, 101; Alexandra Hasluck, *Royal Engineer: A Life of Sir Edmund DuCane* (Sydney: Angus and Robertson, 1973), 45.

[16] Damayanthie Eluwawalage, "History of Costume: The Consumption, Governance, Potency and Patronage of Attire in Colonial Western Australia" (PhD diss., Edith Cowan University, 2004), 191, 150.

but had no knowledge of the other items.[17] She was found guilty and served a six-month sentence in the Fremantle Gaol, a small, twelve-sided stone building also known as the Roundhouse, where Gaoler Henry Vincent complained of her "bad" behaviour, writing that he was unable to keep her away from the male prisoners.[18]

Eliza came from a background of poverty and her family's start in Australia was not easy. She was the daughter of Henry Cook who had arrived with his wife and children in 1830 as an indentured servant to Thomas Peel.[19] Peel brought 400 indentured servants with him to the colony, sourced from the poor of various British parishes, in order to claim a large amount of land. Through a series of mishaps, Peel was unable to claim the land he had hoped for and instead was granted land further south at Clarence. He was also unable to pay his servants and often unable to provide them with food. Many were in great distress and twenty-nine were reported to have died, including Eliza's mother.[20] In late 1830, the government was obliged to rescue Peel's labourers, releasing many from their indentures so that they were free to find work elsewhere in the colony, and providing them with stores until they were able to do so.[21] As a fifteen-year-old in 1837, Eliza may have been able to earn £10 per annum with board but would have had to buy her own clothes.[22] Her earnings would not have been enough to pay for more than a few dresses, undergarments, boots, and hats. The clothing taken was valued at £3.25; the dress alone worth £1.10.[23]

---

[17] *R v Eliza Cooke*, 3 April 1837, S122 cons3472 29 case 158, SROWA.

[18] James Thomas and Alex Stewart, *Imprisonment in W.A.: Evolution, Theory and Practice* (Crawley: University of Western Australia Press, 1978), 4; Emily Lanman, "Prisoners, Power and Panopticon: Investigating Fremantle Gaol, 1831–1841" (master's thesis, University of Notre Dame Australia, 2021), 44; Criminal indictment files, April 1837, S122 cons3472 29, SROWA.

[19] Rica Erickson, ed., *The Bicentennial Dictionary of Western Australians, pre-1829–1888*, vol. 1 (Nedlands: University of Western Australia Press, 1987), 637; Passenger list *Rockingham*, correspondence inwards, 22 May 1830, S2941 cons36 6 155, SROWA.

[20] Fitch, *Eager for Labour*, 119–23; Erickson ed., *The Bicentennial Dictionary*, 1:637; Ian Berryman ed., *A Colony Detailed: The First Census of Western Australia, 1832* (North Perth: Creative Research, 1979).

[21] Fitch, *Eager for Labour*.

[22] William Tanner et al., *The Tanner Letters: A Pioneer Saga of Swan River & Tasmania, 1831–1845* (Nedlands: University of Western Australia Press, 1981), 30.

[23] *R v Eliza Cooke*.

There is no record that Eliza ever offended again. The following year, at age sixteen, she married William Thacker, a convict who had been sent to King George's Sound in 1826 and had remained in Western Australia after his sentence expired.[24] While they may have had some rocky moments in their marriage, William twice advertising that he would not be responsible for his wife's debts, they raised a family of six children, and newspaper reports show that they were still living together in 1851.[25] Eliza's case typifies many of the cases of women's offending heard in the Court of Quarter Sessions at this time. Most were working-class women who did not offend again and usually followed the path of marriage and children expected of "respectable" women. Most were unmarried, widowed, or living apart from their husbands at the time of their offending. The fact that many of the women, like Eliza, came from a background of poverty, and were charged with the theft of food or money, points to a link between poverty, marital status, and women's crime in this period.

Pensioner Guards, Wives, and Children

By 1850, the non-Aboriginal population of Western Australia was still low, at less than 5,000 people, men outnumbered women two to one, and colonists were still finding it difficult to find enough men and women to fill their labouring requirements.[26] In an attempt to resolve some of these problems, Western Australia agreed to accept convicts from Britain and nearly 9,700 convicts were transported to Western Australia

[24] Denise Young, "Layers of Visibility: Convict Discipline, Crime and Punishment, King George's Sound, Western Australia, 1826–1831," *Studies in Western Australian History* 34 (2020): 42, 50.

[25] "Quarter Sessions—July 2," *Inquirer*, 9 July 1851, 1; Births, Agnes Thacker no. 4867, 1859, Middle Swan; Elizabeth Thacker no. 3183, 1856, Middle Swan; Fanny Thacker, no. 2432, 1854, Middle Swan; Frances Thacker no. 1448, 1850, Upper Swan; Mary Thacker no. 7321, 1863, Middle Swan; William Thacker no. 1091, 1848, Middle Swan, "Online Index Search Tool," Department of Justice, accessed 7 May 2022, https://www.wa.gov.au/organisation/department-of-justice/online-index-search-tool.

[26] Rica Erickson, *The Bride Ships: Experiences of Immigrants Arriving in Western Australia 1849–1889* (Carlisle, W.A: Hesperian Press, 1992); Geoffrey Bolton, *Land of Vision and Mirage: Western Australia since 1826* (Crawley: University of Western Australia Press, 2008), 22.

between 1850 and 1868.[27] With the convicts came pensioner guards and their families. These retired soldiers were employed to guard the convicts on their journey to Western Australia in return for a free passage to the colony for themselves and their family.[28] Although the pensioner guards were often employed for some years after their arrival, many of their wives found themselves thrust into poverty when their husband abandoned them or died.[29] Some wives left their husbands due to assault.[30] Many of these wives, and their daughters, then found themselves joining the communities living in the poorer areas of Perth or Fremantle, such as "the Old Establishment Yard" situated between Collie and Essex Streets or Fiddler's Cottages in Cantonment Street, Fremantle.[31] The Old Establishment Yard was notorious as a "disreputable rookery" where "vice and squalor were rampant."[32] In 1919, Joseph Hitchcock remembered the area as "tenements, which were little more than hovels which … became the slum quarters of the Fremantle of that day, the tenants being mostly ticket-of-leave men and their consorts—the demi-monde—always to be found in a seaport town." The people living in these areas were marginalised by poverty and unemployment. As Hitchcock noted, "To reside in the 'Old Establishment Yard' was to be branded as outside the pale."[33]

Many of the women living on the margins of society were recidivists, appearing time after time in the lower courts for crimes against

[27] Bolton, *Land of Vision and Mirage*, 25.

[28] Geoffrey Bolton, "Who Were the Pensioners?," *Studies in Western Australian History* 4 (1981): 84.

[29] For example, Pensioner Guard Bernard McGarvie abandoned his wife, Mary Ann, and family in 1857. See Frank H. Broomhall, *The Veterans: A History of the Enrolled Pensioner Force in Western Australia 1850–1880* (Carlisle, W.A.: Hesperian Press, 1989), 186.

[30] For example, Agnes Arbuckle's pensioner guard husband left the colony after repeatedly assaulting her. See "Police Court, Perth," *Perth Gazette and West Australian Times (PGWAT)*, 7 February 1868, 2.

[31] Joseph Keane Hitchcock and J. W. B. Stevens, *The History of Fremantle: The Front Gate of Australia, 1829–1929* (Fremantle, W.A.: Fremantle City Council, 1929), 34; "Supreme Court—Civil Sittings," *Inquirer and Commercial News (ICN)*, 20 June 1888, 4.

[32] "Friday, April 7," *ICN*, 12 April 1876, 2 (Supplement to the *Inquirer*); "Early Days of Fremantle," *Fremantle Times (FT)*, 23 May 1919.

[33] "Early Days of Fremantle."

good order, such as vagrancy, drunkenness, or abusive language.[34] Society expected criminal behaviour from these women and the discourses surrounding them positioned them as belonging to a "criminal class."[35] Although scholars no longer subscribe to the idea of a "criminal" class, research suggests that many of these women may have belonged to a distinct social class which was separated from the "respectable" working class by poverty and unemployment and which had its own discrete culture.[36] Modern scholarship refers to this as an "underclass." Robert MacDonald has defined this as:

> a social group or class of people located at the bottom of the class structure who, over time, have become structurally separate and culturally distinct from the regularly employed working-class and society in general ... and almost permanently confined to living in poorer conditions and neighbourhoods.[37]

Women who formed part of the underclass of Perth and Fremantle lived precarious lives. Many were recidivists and were imprisoned multiple times. Furthermore, the poverty that kept women in this subculture also required relief from the State. By the 1860s, the colony of Western Australia was dealing with an increasing number of destitute people. The increase in population was made up largely of convicts and young women hoping to work as domestic servants, who had no resources to fall back on. It is a fact that the lived experience of some women involved both the prison and the Perth Poor House. A comparison of court reports and prison records with Colonial Secretary's Office correspondence shows that women charged with crimes such as drunkenness, theft, or abusive language also often requested poor relief from the State and their children were admitted to the Poor House, or to an orphanage,

34 Leigh S.L. Straw, *Drunks, Pests and Harlots: Criminal Women in Perth and Fremantle, 1900–1939* (Kilkerran: Humming Earth, 2013); "Trove," National Library of Australia, accessed 26 May 2022, https://trove.nla.gov.au/.

35 Piper, "In Bad Company," 8.

36 Piper, "In Bad Company".

37 Robert MacDonald, "Dangerous Youth and the Dangerous Class," in *Youth, the "Underclass" and.*
Social Exclusion, ed. Robert MacDonald (London: Routledge, 1997), 4.

when their mothers found themselves unable to care for them.[38] Residents of the Poor House included women whose husbands were in gaol, women and children who had been abandoned, young pregnant single women, and women and children escaping violence and abuse in the home.[39] The Poor House represents another form of incarceration for working-class women and the strict rules and regulations which applied to inmates may have made it a place of last resort for some destitute women.[40]

This precarity meant that friendships between underclass women might be a necessary survival strategy, providing much-needed support networks.[41] Many women had left family and friends behind them in Britain and had no family to provide support when they found themselves in difficulty. Women formed friendships to support each other's testimony in court, care for each other's children, and provide refuge when required. Drinking together was a social ritual which helped cement these bonds, but alcohol was also the cause of addiction for some women and withdrawal symptoms could be life threatening if incarcerated.[42] Women supported each other in petty crimes, working in pairs to rob unsuspecting men visiting the hotels of Perth and Fremantle, or looking out for each other on the streets.

Judicial records and reports of crime can shed light on the ways in which these support networks were used. The testimony of Christina Burkinshaw, the daughter of a pensioner guard who appeared as a witness in a case of assault on 6 January 1872, is one example of this.[43]

---

[38] Correspondence inwards, S2941 cons36, SROWA; Correspondence files, S675 cons527, SROWA; Record of court convictions, 1861–1914, S5072 cons1156 v23, SROWA; Quarterly Returns of Prisoners, S270 cons3676, SROWA; "Newspapers & Gazettes," Trove, accessed 7 May 2022, https://trove.nla.gov.au/newspaper/.

[39] Penelope Hetherington, *Paupers, Poor Relief and Poor Houses in Western Australia, 1829 to 1910* (Crawley, W.A: UWA Publishing, 2009).

[40] Hetherington, *Paupers, Poor Relief and Poor Houses*, 115.

[41] Piper, "In Bad Company".

[42] Alana Jayne Piper, "'A Growing Vice': The *Truth* about Brisbane Girls and Drunkenness in the Early Twentieth Century," *Journal of Australian Studies* 34, no. 4 (2010): 492; For examples see "Inquest on the Body of Edward Holmes," 5 March 1891, S675 cons527 1891/0554 1–5, SROWA; Case Book - Female Patients, 22 May 1889, S2219 cons2724 3 136, SROWA.

[43] *R v Frederick Johnson*, 3 February 1872, S122 cons3473 58 case 490, SROWA; Erickson ed., *The Bicentennial Dictionary*, 1:454.

Christina, whose husband was imprisoned, had been described in a recent newspaper report as "a good-looking woman, neatly attired," and had been living with Frederick Johnson and his pregnant wife Elizabeth in Fremantle. Christina was a recidivist, appearing throughout her lifetime for various charges of theft, conspiracy to defraud, and creating a disturbance.[44] Elizabeth accused Frederick of beating her with a rope and a stick, dragging her outside by the hair, and throwing buckets of water over her after he had come home for his evening meal to find that she had been drinking and was asleep on the sofa. Christina testified that she had prepared the meal herself after Elizabeth had told her that she was not well: "The tea was by the fire and the tea things were ready. I prepared the tea myself." She stated that Frederick had also hit and kicked his wife and added that neither she nor Elizabeth had been drinking. However, other witnesses who testified as to Elizabeth's "bad character," and Dr Mayhew's dismissal of Elizabeth's injuries as "scarcely noticeable," resulted in Frederick being discharged, the judge stating that "there had been faults on both sides."[45] Although Elizabeth had made the complaint against her husband, in the courtroom her role as a wife was judged and her femininity was on trial. It is clear that Christina had not only attempted to help Elizabeth by preparing the meal but was also anxious to protect Elizabeth's reputation as a "good" wife when she stated that they had not been drinking and that the evening meal had been prepared. Sadly, there was no one to support Christina or to protect her from Charles Cole, ten years later, when she was murdered, and probably raped, at New Norcia.[46]

Although historians have shown that violence against women was not limited to the working classes, assault and murder added to the precarity of the lives of many working-class women, and violence was often cited in depositions.[47] It was considered allowable for men to "chastise" or

---

[44] "Newspapers and Gazettes," Trove, accessed 29 August 2022, https://trove.nla.gov.au/newspaper/.

[45] "Supreme Court," *PGWAT*, 12 January 1872, 3.

[46] "Law Intelligence," *Daily News (DN)*, 11 January 1883, 3; "Occasional Notes," *West Australian*, 16 January 1883, 3.

[47] Kay Saunders, "The Study of Domestic Violence in Colonial Queensland: Sources and Problems," *Australian Historical Studies* 21, no. 82 (1984): 73.

"punish" their wives although violence which exceeded socially acceptable limits could be deemed as "cruelty."[48] Women often had little recourse to prevent this and were seldom in a position to bring a charge of violence against their intimate partner in a court of law, as any personal resources they owned became their husband's property upon marriage.[49] Some women did separate from their husbands, although this might mean that they needed to find a means to support themselves and their children: a difficult task at a time when employment opportunities for women were limited and remuneration low.[50] A network of female friends could provide refuge for women escaping violence, support women's testimony in court, and provide support during times of illness.

Criminal records and newspaper reports of trials also provide other instances of women providing support to each other. When Mary Fannon was injured in a dispute with Kate Taaffe and Eliza Bell in their yard in Adelaide Street, Fremantle, it was her neighbour, Mary Jane Hayes, a woman who appeared time and again in the Western Australian courts, who took her inside and washed her wounds.[51] When Lydia Dysart was hit over the head with a bottle by Louise Hearne outside Lydia's home in Suffolk Street, Fremantle, she sought help from Annie Green and Joanna Thompson in the Old Establishment Yard. They then called the police and helped Lydia to the doctor's house.[52] These records suggest a working-class community living crowded together in tenements and dwellings where friendships and support networks were formed between women but where women's disputes might also be "settled" by the time-honoured method of assault.

---

[48] William Blackstone, *Commentaries on the Laws of England*, vol. 1 (Oxford: Clarendon Press, 1765), 442–45; Martin J. Wiener, *Men of Blood: Violence, Manliness, and Criminal Justice in Victorian England* (West Nyack: Cambridge University Press, 2004), 174.

[49] Penelope Hetherington, *The Marriage Knot: Marriage and Divorce in Colonial Western Australia 1829–1900* (Crawley, W.A.: UWA Publishing, 2013), 109.

[50] Hetherington, *The Marriage Knot*, 114.

[51] "Fremantle Police Court," *DN*, 29 January 1887, 3.

[52] *R v Louise Francis Hearne*, 3 July 1878, S122 cons3473 93 case 843, SROWA.

Case Study: Mary Woods

The case of a pensioner guard's daughter, Mary Woods, illustrates the lives experienced by many underclass women in nineteenth-century Western Australia which were made precarious by events such as imprisonment, abandonment, and ill-health. In 1851, Enrolled Pensioner Guard Daniel McIntyre, and his wife Jane, left Ireland to sail to Western Australia on board the *Mermaid* with their three children. The youngest, Mary, was just three months old.[53] Daniel had served as a soldier for twenty-one years, eighteen of which had been spent in the East Indies. In 1831 he married Jane White in Dinapore, India.[54] Jane and Daniel separated soon after arrival in Western Australia and it is possible that Jane then began to cohabit with expiree Thomas Hudson, whom she later married.[55] Certainly, Jane's next daughter, Elizabeth, used the Hudson surname.[56] In 1857 Daniel left Western Australia, eventually returning to Ireland.[57] Mary grew up to be a tall woman, five feet six inches in height, with black hair, blue eyes, and a fair complexion.[58] When she was fifteen years old, she married convict Peter Rourke and their daughter Julia was born the next year.[59] Within a few months Peter, a tanner by trade, had been imprisoned for stealing kangaroo skins at the Vasse, south of

---

[53] M.S. James, *A Superior Body of Men* (Bloomington: Authorhouse, 2014), 833; A return of the number of Pensioners, their wives and children onboard the *Mermaid*, May 1851, S2941 cons36 221 152, SROWA.

[54] James, *A Superior Body of Men.*

[55] "Advertising," *Inquirer*, 18 August 1852, 2; Marriage, Thomas Hudson and Jane McIntyre, no. 3743, Fremantle, 1874, "Online index search tool," Department of Justice, accessed 4 January 2023, https://www.wa.gov.au/organisation/department-of-justice/online-index-search-tool.

[56] James, *A Superior Body of Men*, 833; Marriage, Matthew Bateman and Elizabeth Hudson no. 4048, Pinjarra, 1876, "Online Index Search Tool," Department of Justice, accessed 7 May 2022, https://www.wa.gov.au/organisation/department-of-justice/online-index-search-tool.

[57] James, *A Superior Body of Men*, 833.

[58] *Police Gazette Western Australia (PGWA)*, November 1880, 187, SLWA.

[59] Marriage, Peter Rourke and Mary Mcintyre no. 2320, Fremantle, 1865, "Online Index Search Tool," Department of Justice, accessed 4 January 2023, https://www.wa.gov.au/organisation/department-of-justice/online-index-search-tool; Birth, Julia Ann Rourke no. 9616, Fremantle, 1866, "Online Index Search Tool," Department of Justice, accessed 4 January 2023, https://www.wa.gov.au/organisation/department-of-justice/online-index-search-tool.

Perth, and Mary and Julia were left destitute.[60] They were approved for admission to the Perth Poor House, in Goderich (now Murray) Street, on the condition that Mary took a job in service to pay for her child's expenses.[61] Mary's experience of destitution and state relief was common among many underclass women. The biggest group to gain access to the Poor House were women with children whose husbands were imprisoned. Women who had no home or means of support could be admitted to the Poor House but the Government was eager to reclaim the expense wherever possible.[62]

In 1874, at age twenty-four, Mary married again: this time to expiree James Woods (Fig. 2.1).[63] It is not known what happened to her first husband. There is no further mention of Peter Rourke in the convict records after he received his certificate of freedom in Bunbury in 1873, and no death was registered, although a Peter Rourke was recorded as travelling to South Australia in 1876.[64] It is possible that Mary married Woods bigamously.

Mary's criminal activities appear to have begun a couple of years after this second marriage. When she was charged with pawning stolen clothing in 1876, Mary told policeman Corporal John McKay, that she did so as "there was nothing in their house."[65] Over the years Mary was accused of stealing clothing, boots, sheets, blankets, kettles, tumblers, and occasionally small amounts of money. The thefts were often opportunistic and mainly took place in dwelling houses or shops.[66] On at least two occasions, she sold the items to her brother-in-law, Mathew

---

60 General register, convict registers, S5056 cons1156 R28, SROWA.

61 Resident Magistrate Fremantle to Colonial Secretary, 26 November 1867, S2941 cons36 597 163, SROWA; Colonial Secretary to Resident Magistrate Fremantle, 27 November 1867, S2755 cons49 726, SROWA; Hetherington, *Paupers, Poor Relief and Poor Houses*, 53.

62 Hetherington, *Paupers, Poor Relief and Poor Houses*, 51–53.

63 Marriage, Mary Rourke and James Woods, no. 3792, Fremantle, 1874, "Online Index Search Tool," Department of Justice, accessed 4 January 2023, https://www.wa.gov.au/organisation/department-of-justice/online-index-search-tool.

64 General register, convict registers, S5056 cons1156 R28, SROWA; Rica Erickson ed., *Dictionary of Western Australians*, vol. 2. *Bond, 1850–1868* (Nedlands: University of Western Australia Press, 1979), 476.

65 *R v Mary Woods*, 5 July 1876, S122 cons3473 85 case 762, SROWA.

66 For example, *PGWA*, September 1876, 113, SLWA; *PGWA*, October 1893, 168, SLWA; "Fremantle Police Court," *West Australian*, 31 December 1892, 3.

Fig. 2.1 Photograph of James Woods, Mary's second husband, c. 1896. This photo is attached to his Fremantle Prison record which shows that James was a recidivist, arrested ten times in the late 1880s and 1890s, mostly for vagrancy. Courtesy SROWA, Registers local prisoners (male), S672 cons4173 1

Bateman, who had a shop in High Street, Fremantle.[67] Most of Mary's cases were tried in the lower courts, the goods stolen being valued at under £5, although two were tried in the Supreme Court. Unlike many other recidivist women, Mary usually pleaded guilty to these crimes in court. She was sentenced to fourteen days for that first larceny charge and spent much of her time, between 1867 and 1895, in and out of prison with sentences ranging from eight days to two years.[68]

From the archival records, we can see how Mary's prison sentences mediated and intersected with her role as a mother. Mary had at least three known children with James: Theresa, George, and a stillborn daughter. By February 1880 James had left Mary and was charged for deserting his wife "without reasonable cause, thereby leaving her without any means of support."[69] Two years later Mary gave birth to Amy, with another expiree, Edward Mowbray. Mary spent the rest of her life with

---

67 "Friday, April 1," *DN*, 1 April 1887, 3; *R v Mary Woods*; "The Supreme Court.—Criminal Sittings," *Western Mail*, 24 December 1887, 16.

68 Record of Court Convictions, 1861–1914, S5072 cons1156 v23, SROWA.

69 *PGWA*, February 1880, 26, SLWA.

Mowbray and had two more children, Louisa Jane, and Ada Maria.[70] When she was first sentenced in July 1876, Mary was over seven months pregnant with her second known child, Theresa. On the eighth day of her sentence, she was visited by the medical officer, and the next day was discharged by the Governor's orders.[71] In September she was again charged with larceny, this time for stealing numerous items from the Freemasons Hotel and the Emerald Isle Hotel (Fig. 2.2). This time Mary was sentenced to three months in prison but she was able to take four-week-old Theresa into the prison with her.[72] While there, Mary's baby was taken to be baptised by the Sisters of Mercy, who often visited the Roman Catholic prisoners, but Mary was unable to attend her baby's baptism. Theresa was taken from her mother by the Sisters and returned later that day.[73]

A similar situation arose in 1884 when Mary was sentenced to six months' imprisonment for stealing boots from Pearse's shop in High Street, Fremantle (Fig. 2.3). Amy, who was one year and nine months old, went with her into prison, but her presence there caused tension. The sheriff, James Roe, wanted to admit Amy to the Poor House but Mary argued strongly to keep her child with her, stating that she was still breastfeeding, that Amy was not strong, and that Mary's mother would not care for the child.[74] Mary's first child, Julia, who by now might have been considered old enough to care for Amy, had died four years earlier from an aneurism of the heart.[75] William Dale, Supervisor of the Poor House, also objected to admitting a young child, and Jane Hudson supported her daughter's statement by declining "to have anything to do with the child or any of the children as she has had enough of them."[76]

---

[70] *PGWA*, August 1884, 132, SLWA; Birth, Amy Wood no. 22949, Jarrahdale, 1882, "Online Index Search Tool," Department of Justice, accessed 7 May 2022, https://www.wa.gov.au/organisation/department-of-justice/online-index-search-tool.

[71] Record of court convictions, 1861–1914, S5072 cons1156 v23, SROWA; Reports and occurrences, 13–14 July 1876, S690 cons1156 occ26, SROWA.

[72] Reports and occurrences, 12 September 1876, S690 cons1156 occ26, SROWA.

[73] Reports and occurrences, 2 October 1876, S690 cons1156 occ26, SROWA.

[74] *PGWA*, August 1884, 131, SLWA; Gaoler Fremantle to the Sheriff, 29 July 1884, S675 cons527 1884/4667, SROWA.

[75] Death certificate, Julia Rorke, 28 December 1879, no. 1761.

[76] Gaoler Fremantle to the Sheriff, 29 July 1884, S675 cons527 1884/4667, SROWA.

Fig. 2.2 High Street, Fremantle looking west c1880. Although not a clear photograph, this shows High Street as Mary would have known it. Many of the town's shops and hotels lined this street. The second building on the left is the Emerald Isle Hotel from where Mary was charged, in September 1876, with the theft of two blankets and two sheets. Opposite is the Crown and Thistle Hotel, formerly run by Elizabeth Pace as the Boarding House. Fremantle Gaol can be seen at the end of the street on Arthur's Head. Courtesy City of Fremantle History Centre, LHC 2044A

Mary won that fight and was allowed to keep Amy with her in gaol. The two older children, George and Theresa, stayed with Mowbray until he was also charged with theft and remanded in gaol, when Mary Jane Hayes took care of them.[77]

In 1887, Mary Woods gave birth to her last known child, Ada Maria, in Perth Gaol.[78] Mary's role as a mother, and her ability to feed and care for her children, was affected by her husbands' desertions, by the periods during which Peter Rourke, James Woods and Edward Mowbray were imprisoned, and by the time she herself spent in prison. Nonetheless, Mary was more fortunate than some women whose families had been left behind in Britain and who found themselves without support in times of need. Her mother and sister also lived nearby and it is clear from Jane Hudson's statement that she had, at times, cared for Mary's children.[79]

---

[77] Sub Inspector E.G. Back to Superintendent of Poor House, 1 August 1884, S2126 cons430 1884/1337, SROWA.

[78] Medical journal, 21 June 1888, S701 cons1156 M24, SROWA.

[79] Gaoler Fremantle to the Sheriff, 29 July 1884, S675 cons527 1884/4667, SROWA.

Fig. 2.3 Pearse Brothers boot shop, High Street, Fremantle, 1892. On 26 July 1884, Mary stole two pairs of boots from Pearse's shop and received a sentence of six months' imprisonment. SLWA, *West Australian*, 22 December 1892, colour advertising supplement

At various times in her life, Mary also contended with sickness and ill-health. On 27 December 1885, the store of Davies Brothers in High Street, Fremantle, was consumed by fire and the contents of Daniel Congdon's adjoining store were bundled out onto the pavement to avoid a similar fate. Mary took advantage of the resulting chaos to pick up a packet containing five pairs of socks. She was tried summarily the next day and sentenced to three months' imprisonment.[80] Two weeks later the medical officer, James Hope, recommended that Mary be released from gaol due to an injury to her left hand.[81] The cause of the injury is unknown but it seems reasonable to assume that it may have occurred

[80] "Conflagration at Fremantle," *DN*, 28 December 1885, 3; "News and Notes," *West Australian*, 29 December 1885, 3; *PGWA*, December 1885, 211, SLWA.

[81] Authorities book, 11 February 1886, S5072 cons1156 V21, SROWA; Official correspondence, which may have given the circumstances of the injury, cannot be found in the State Records Office and may no longer exist.

during her time in gaol. A week later, Mary was discharged to the Colonial Hospital.[82] Although the affluent landed classes would usually be treated by a doctor in their homes, the destitute were treated in the Colonial Hospital on Goderich Street, Perth.[83] Aboriginal patients were even less fortunate as they were not admitted to the hospital at all, but could be treated as outpatients.[84] The treatment Mary received there is unknown, but at some stage before 1889, she had part of the hand amputated and it continued to cause her pain.[85] In August 1890 she was sent to the Colonial Hospital again, this time suffering from a tumour on the neck which the Colonial Surgeon, Dr Henry Barnett, stated would cause suffocation unless treated, possibly by an operation.[86] Although illness and ill-health might happen to any of the colonists, working-class men and women were more likely to become sick from overcrowding, contaminated public wells used for drinking water, and accidents or injuries related to labouring work.[87]

Incarcerated prisoners had the opportunity to improve their situation through the use of petitions, and many women did so. Prisoners might be considered for early release as a result of petitioning the Governor or by asking others to do this on their behalf. On at least two occasions, Mary used petitions in an attempt to gain her freedom. In their petitions, women would often cite reasons that emphasised their adherence to gendered understandings of femininity that made them appear less threatening. In September 1884, nearly two months into her six-month sentence for the theft of the boots, Mary petitioned the Governor, Sir Frederick Broome, for her release. In this petition she cast doubt on the

---

82 *PGWA*, March 1886, 39, SLWA; Authorities book, 11 February 1886, cons1156 V21, SROWA; Receipts and discharges, 22 February 1886, S5073 cons1156 R&d9b-R&d10, SROWA.

83 Geoffrey Bolton and Prue Joske, *History of the Royal Perth Hospital* (Perth, W.A.: Royal Perth Hospital, 1982), 14, 16.

84 Bolton and Joske, *History of the Royal Perth Hospital*, 22.

85 Medical Officer Fremantle Prison, 9 June 1888, S675 cons527 1888/1705, SROWA.

86 Colonial Surgeon to Resident Magistrate Fremantle, 28 July 1890, S675 cons527 1890/2150, SROWA.

87 Bolton and Joske, *History of the Royal Perth Hospital*, 29; Catie Gilchrist, *Murder, Misadventure and Miserable Ends: Tales from a Colonial Coroner's Court* (Sydney: HarperCollins, 2019), 165.

veracity of the main witness's testimony, stating that he had recently been convicted of larceny, but also emphasised her femininity by presenting herself as a mother with four children, pregnant with a fifth, and asking to be allowed to "return to her children and the comforts required by her condition."[88]

In 1888, while serving a two-year sentence for theft Mary again cited impending birth and her role as a mother in a petition, stating that she had four young children "who are left wholly unprovided for, except by casual charity." She also cited evidence of ill-health, explaining that part of her left hand had been amputated and that the hand would later need to be amputated at the wrist. In an appeal for sympathy, Mary wrote that "she dreads the coming events feeling assured that in either case her life would be imperilled."[89] It appears that Mary used petitions to effect early release in circumstances where she was incarcerated for an extended period or when she was due to give birth to a child in prison. However, Mary's petitions, as with those written by other female prisoners, were not always successful.

A prisoner's character might be considered when deciding on the merits of a petition. Thus, although Mary cast doubts on the witness's testimony in 1884, Magistrate John Slade, when asked for a report on the trial, commented instead on Mary's character writing: "This woman is a notorious thief. … She is married to a man named Woods but lives with Edward Mowbray, her husband being yet alive," and Mary's petition was refused.[90] A second petition that year by Mary's mother, stating that she would "do my utmost to cause her [Mary] to lead an honest and sober life" was more successful and Mary was released, Chief Justice Alexander Onslow citing the combination of time served with the imminent birth of her child as sufficient reason.[91] Mary's petition in 1888 was similarly unsuccessful and this time, a second petition, written by

[88] Mary Woods to the Governor, 22 September 1884, S675 cons527 1884/5630, SROWA.

[89] Mary Woods to the Governor, 23 May 1888, S675 cons527 1888/1705, SROWA.

[90] Alexander Onslow to Colonial Secretary, 8 October 1884, S675 cons527 1884/5630, SROWA; J.G. Slade to Colonial Secretary, 9 October 1884, S675 cons527 1884/5630, SROWA; J.G. Slade to Colonial Secretary, 9 October 1884, S675 cons527 1884/5630, SROWA.

[91] Jane Hudson to Colonial Secretary, 7 November 1884, S675 cons527 1884/5630, SROWA; Alexander Onslow to Colonial Secretary, 14 November 1884, S675 cons527 1884/5630, SROWA.

her twelve-year-old daughter Theresa, also failed. Theresa gave as a mitigating circumstance that her mother was "under the influence of liquor" when she committed her crime but added that she firmly believed that Mary would "refrain from intoxicating drinks" if released. She also gave evidence of Mary's femininity, stating that Mary was the mother of five children "all of whom are respectable."[92] Several women incarcerated in this time petitioned the Governor for early release and sometimes these petitions *were* successful.[93] The use of petitions exemplified one way in which women were able to use the criminal justice system to their advantage in order to change the course of their lives and to challenge the authorities responsible for their incarceration.

In January 1892, Mowbray experienced a serious accident, which marked a change in the pattern of offending for both himself and Mary. The family had just returned from Jarrahdale, where Mowbray had been working. The town of Jarrahdale at this time was the centre of a thriving timber industry which provided employment for many men.[94] On his return Mowbray had found work in Fremantle at Roby, Woods, Watson and Co's warehouse and was loading goods on a railway truck when a collision knocked him off, causing him to hit his head on the rail. The resulting concussion was so bad that he was taken to hospital suffering from "delirium," and several days later was reported to be "a little better."[95] From that point onwards Mowbray began to appear in the police courts, charged with crimes such as drunkenness and vagrancy.[96] In October, Mary was evicted from her home.[97] She continued to be imprisoned on larceny charges but also appeared a few times charged with drunkenness or obscene language.[98] At a time when

---

[92] Theresa Woods to the Governor, 13 May 1889, S675 cons527 1888/1705, SROWA.

[93] For example, see Elizabeth Smith to the Governor, 21 June 1886, S675 cons527 1886/2595, SROWA; Jane Dyson to the Governor, 15 April 1885, S675 cons527 1885/1505, SROWA.

[94] Victor George Fall, *The Mills of Jarrahdale, a Century of Achievement 1872–1972: A History* (Nedlands: Royal Western Australian Historical Society, 1972), 33.

[95] "General News," *ICN*, 6 July 1892, 5.

[96] *PGWA*, March 1893, 36, SLWA; *PGWA*, April 1893, 62, 68, SLWA.

[97] "Fremantle Local Court," *West Australian*, 10 October 1893, 7.

[98] For example, see "September 15," *ICN*, 22 September 1893, 22; "Police Intelligence," *West Australian*, 15 June 1893, 2.

women's options for employment were both limited and poorly remunerated, an accident such as this, which limited a man's ability to find work, could be an economic disaster for his family.

Mary continued to steal objects from shops. In 1893, when tried summarily for the theft of two kettles from Davies's shop she admitted the theft but stated that she had taken the objects in repayment of a debt. In the following trial, Mowbray was convicted of vagrancy and sentenced to six months' imprisonment.[99] By August 1895, Mary and Mowbray, now forty-five and sixty-seven years old, respectively, were living in a tent in Green's Valley in a state of destitution. Mary had been released from prison three months earlier but was bedridden through illness. Mowbray had vertigo, falling over when he bent down, and was unable to work. They were approved to receive outdoor rations. It was expected that family members, in particular male family members, would support those deemed destitute but fifteen-year-old George, who would usually provide support for his parents, was unable to do so as he had recently been imprisoned for supplying a bottle of rum to Tommy, an Aboriginal man, at Fremantle Park.[100] Mary died eight months later from uterine cancer and was buried in the Skinner Street Cemetery in Fremantle.[101] Mowbray was taken in to the Mt Eliza Poor House for men where his comments to a commission of inquiry in 1898 indicate that his life may have been improved by the change.[102] Poverty and destitution were very real possibilities for convict men and immigrant women who had become too old or infirm to work, unless their children were in a position to support them.

In many ways, Mary's lived experience was typical of the women of Perth and Fremantle's criminal underclass. Like many other underclass

[99] "Police Intelligence," *West Australian*, 14 October 1893, 2.

[100] *Destitute Persons Relief Ordinance 1845* (WA); Resident Magistrate Fremantle to Colonial Secretary, 1895, S675 cons527 1895/2227, SROWA; "Fremantle Police Court," *West Australian*, 10 August 1895, 3.

[101] Death certificate, Mary Ann Wood, no. 611, 1896, Fremantle; "Alma and Skinner Street Burial Records," City of Fremantle, accessed 6 May 2022, https://www.fremantle.wa.gov.au/sites/default/files/Alma%20and%20Skinner%20Street%20Burial%20Records%201831%20-%201899.pdf.

[102] "The Mt. Eliza Depot," *West Australian*, 10 August 1898, 7.

women she was a recidivist, appearing time and again in the magistrates' courts for petty crimes and occasionally in the Supreme Court for more serious crimes. Her life, and her ability to care for her family, was impacted not only by the times she spent in prison for these crimes, but also by the times her husbands, or partners, were imprisoned, absent, or out of work. The fact that Mary Jane Hayes stepped in to care for Mary Woods's children, when both Mary and James were imprisoned, is typical of the support networks operating between underclass women. Less typical is that, despite Mowbray being charged with owning a brothel in 1893, Mary does not appear to have been charged for offences related to sex work, such as being idle and disorderly, and she is not referred to as a prostitute in news texts. Neither are there records for disorderly conduct and only rarely for drunkenness, or obscene language.[103] Mary's statements, that she pawned stolen clothing because there was "nothing in their house" and that she took items in repayment of a debt, suggest that her offending was linked to poverty.[104] If she was not earning money through sex work, as many other underclass women did, then these crimes, like the support networks women developed, may well have been a necessary survival strategy to combat the precarity of existence for women on the margins of society.

Single Women Assisted Immigrants

Although male convicts were sent to Western Australia from 1850, the colony refused to accept female convicts, complaining that these "most vile and degraded of human beings" would exert a corrupting moral influence in the colony.[105] The majority of convicts were unmarried and only a few married convicts took advantage of an available scheme to

---

103 For example, see "September 15," *ICN*, 22 September 1893, 22; "Police Intelligence," *West Australian*, 15 June 1893, 2.

104 "Law Intelligence," *ICN*, 12 July 1876; "Police Intelligence," *West Australian*, 14 October 1893; *R v Mary Woods*.

105 Joanne Hyland, "'The Vilest and Most Degraded of Human Beings': An Investigation into Why Female Convicts Were Not Transported to Western Australia," *Studies in Western Australian History* 34 (2020): 154, 162.

send for their families once they had achieved freedom.[106] In an attempt to balance the number of the sexes, and provide domestic labour for the colonisers, the British Government sent 2,072 single female immigrants to Western Australia between 1850 and 1872.[107] British officials selected women who were single, usually between eighteen and thirty-five years old and deemed to be capable of domestic service. Women selected to emigrate had their costs paid by the imperial government as part of the scheme.[108]

With the increase in the number of women came an increase in women's crime. Many of the women came from a background of poverty and had been selected from Irish and English workhouses. Their decision to emigrate was often influenced by a desire to find better lives for themselves, either through situations in domestic service or through marriage.[109] While some women did find employment and a lasting marriage in Western Australia, usually marrying convicts who had achieved their ticket-of-leave, others found themselves joining the underclass communities in the Old Establishment Yard or Fiddler's Cottages. For some, the cycle of poverty and institutionalisation continued in the colony when their husbands died, deserted their wives, or were imprisoned for continued reoffending. Like other immigrant women who had left family support networks behind, these women were also at risk of poverty if they left their husbands to escape abuse. Some became recidivists, imprisoned for crimes such as vagrancy, theft, or crimes related to prostitution. Many requested admission to the Poor House and some also found themselves incarcerated in the Fremantle Lunatic Asylum.

106 R.T. Appleyard, "Western Australia: Economic and Demographic Growth, 1850–1914" in *A New History of Western Australia*, ed. C. T. Stannage (Nedlands: University of Western Australia Press, 1981), 213.

107 Jan Gothard, *Blue China: Single Female Migration to Colonial Australia* (Carlton South, Victoria: Melbourne University Press, 2001), 10, 233.

108 Gothard, *Blue China*, 22, 10; Emily Jayne Chambers, "The Immigration of Domestic Servants to Western Australia in the 1850s and 1890s" (honours thesis, Murdoch University, 2017), 32.

109 Chambers, "The Immigration of Domestic Servants," 7.

Case Study: Mary Goodall

Behind the old police court in Barrack Street, Perth, now part of the complex known as the State Buildings, once stood the holding cells for the Barrack Street Police Court, which were demolished to make way for a restaurant and the new Supreme Court of Western Australia. Public heritage interpretation, consisting of the names of men and women incarcerated in those cells, includes the name of Mary Goodall (Fig. 2.4). It reads "MRS. GOODALL, —8 FEBRUARY 1875—, WIDOW, DESTITUTE, OF VERY WEAK INTELLECT, FORMERLY AN INMATE OF THE LUNATIC ASYLUM." While these words may encapsulate the way in which Mary was perceived by Western Australian society in her later years, it tells us nothing of the young woman who left Ireland, in 1859, for a better life in Western Australia. The case of Mary Goodall exemplifies the way underclass women could find themselves trapped in a cycle of poverty and institutionalisation. While some of Mary's story has been examined by Rica Erickson and Alexandra Wallis, a close examination of Mary's life, from the time of her arrival in Western Australia, until her death, reveals patterns of poverty, institutionalisation, and alcohol abuse common to underclass women at that time.[110]

Mary Murphy, a twenty-year-old domestic servant from County Tyrone in Ireland, arrived in the port of Fremantle, Western Australia, on 20 October 1859, travelling on the *West Australian* as an assisted immigrant.[111] In less than four months, she had met and married ex-convict William Goodall. William was a skilled farm labourer who found work on various farms south of Perth.[112] By 1865, William had found work with Benjamin Piggott of Australind and was living with Mary and their

[110] Erickson, *The Bride Ships*; Alexandra Wallis, "Hysterical Women: Moral Treatment of Female Patients in the Fremantle Lunatic Asylum, 1858–1908" (PhD diss., University of Notre Dame, 2020).

[111] "General Intelligence," *Perth Gazette and Independent Journal of Politics and News (PGIJPN)*, 23 September 1859, 2; Passenger list of assisted emigrants, 1859, AN 371 acc 115, SROWA.

[112] "Quarter Sessions," *PGIJPN*, 11 January 1861, 2; Benjamin Piggott, Accounts and farm journals, 1845–1887, MN 729 Acc 2247A, SLWA.

Fig. 2.4 Interpretation for the police court's holding cells in Barrack Street, now demolished, showing Mary Goodall's name. Photograph—Caroline Ingram

three children, William, Elizabeth, and James, at Warren River, 280 kilometres south of Perth.[113] In March that year, a man named Hope came to their hut, while William was working. Mary said he shared his bottle of gin with her after which he "outraged" (raped) her. When she told William, three months later, he ordered her to leave the house but Mary did not do this. Instead, the next day, while William was at work, she stabbed nine-month-old James multiple times before running to where William was working "in a most excited state," to confess to him that she had killed their child.[114] This tragedy marked the beginning of many cycles of institutionalisation and alcohol abuse which were to characterise the remainder of Mary's life.

[113] Piggott, Accounts and farm journals, 1845–1887, MN 729 Acc 2247A, SLWA; Birth, William Goodhall no. 6094, 1861, Crendon, "Online Index Search Tool," Department of Justice, accessed 16 January 2023, https://www.wa.gov.au/organisation/department-of-justice/online-index-search-tool; Birth, Elizabeth Goodall no. 7054, 1863, Crendon, "Online Index Search Tool," Department of Justice, accessed 16 January 2023, https://www.wa.gov.au/organisation/department-of-justice/online-index-search-tool; Birth, James Goodall no. 8170, 1864, Blackwood, "Online Index Search Tool," Department of Justice, accessed 16 January 2023, https://www.wa.gov.au/organisation/department-of-justice/online-index-search-tool; Erickson, *The Bride Ships*, 172.

[114] No title, *PGWAT*, 21 July 1865, 2.

On 3 August, William and Mary travelled to Perth for her trial.[115] Although initially remanded in the Perth Lockup, Mary was transferred to the Fremantle Lunatic Asylum on 13 September on the recommendation of the Medical Board.[116] She appeared in the Supreme Court on 4 October charged with the murder of her son, but on returning a "confused answer," rather than a plea, the jury was ordered to instead decide on Mary's sanity.[117] Wallis argues that women like Mary would have been considered to have been suffering from puerperal insanity. A form of insanity supposed to occur shortly after childbirth, this illness was often ascribed to married women who attempted to harm their own children, as society had no other way of explaining a crime considered so shocking.[118]

In court Dr George Attfield gave evidence that Mary had been under his care at the Lunatic Asylum and testified that she was "perfectly insane," spoke incoherently, and "seemed to labor under delusion."[119] Mary stayed in the Asylum for over a year and was released on 25 August 1866.[120] She returned to live with William and, in 1867, gave birth to her fourth child, who was also named Mary.[121] The next year, Mary was again sent to the Asylum and it appears that her daughter, Mary, may have been sent to an orphanage or the Perth Poor House because, in a second tragedy, young Mary, now one year old, died in Perth from dysentery just three weeks later.[122] Once more, Mary was kept at the Asylum for over a year, being discharged and "given over to her husband" in

115 "Shipping Intelligence," *PGWAT*, 4 August 1865, 2.

116 Colonial Secretary to the Sheriff, 12 September 1865, S2755 cons49 46 35, SROWA; Register of Female Patients, 13 September 1865, S507 cons1120 04 84, SROWA.

117 Calendar of criminal trials, October 1865, S2941 cons36 558 89, SROWA; "Supreme Court—Criminal Side," *ICN*, 11 October 1865, 2.

118 Wallis, "Hysterical Women," 213, 198, 208–209.

119 "Supreme Court—Criminal Side," *ICN*, 11 October 1865, 2.

120 Register of Female Patients, 25 August 1866, S507 cons1120 04 84, SROWA.

121 Baptismal Register St Mary's Perth, Mary Goodall, 27 June 1868, vol. 2 no. 112, digital image, accessed 16 January 2023, https://www.familysearch.org/ark:/61903/3:1:3Q9M-CSKG-R9NW-L?i=159&cat=989263; Birth, Mary Goodall no. 10057, 1867, Brunswick, "Online Index Search Tool," Department of Justice accessed 16 January 2023, https://www.wa.gov.au/organisation/department-of-justice/online-index-search-tool.

122 Register of Female Patients, 15 June 1868, S507 cons1120 04 101, SROWA; Death certificate, Mary Goodall, no. 1112, 3 July 1868, Perth.

August 1869.[123] Marriage laws meant that women had no separate legal existence from their husbands at this time, and most married women who were admitted to the Asylum entered on the information of their husbands and, when discharged, often at their husband's request, were released into their care.[124]

In June 1871, William wrote to the Colonial Secretary. He complained that, on 5 June, expiree Charles Tomlinson had been invited to stay with the family and that, while William was at work, Mary and Tomlinson had "unlawful connection," although William did not say if this was consensual. Mary contracted a sexually transmitted infection, which she then passed on to her husband. William asked if he could obtain a legal separation from his wife or have her committed to the Asylum again. He claimed that Mary was not in a sound state of mind, and was incapable of taking care of herself, but that he could not afford to pay her expenses at the Poor House or the Lunatic Asylum, as he had two children to support.[125] Regardless of William's concerns, the couple were still together at the end of October when William requested Resident Magistrate William Clifton to have Mary admitted to the Perth Poor House. Mary's husband paid for her passage to Perth and promised to pay for her maintenance while in the Poor House. It is clear that both William and Clifton were concerned about Mary's state of mind, Clifton stating that she had been "in that state of mind that it is hardly fit for her to be at large," but there is no indication that either sought medical treatment for her or that William sought a medical certificate to have Mary admitted to the Lunatic Asylum.[126] There is also no indication that Mary's wishes were consulted before she was sent to the Poor House. As a married woman in the nineteenth century, it was expected that Mary's husband would make decisions for her. Mary would apply to enter the Poor House several more times during her lifetime, seemingly considering it as a place of refuge when her life was particularly difficult or seemed out of control.

---

[123] Register of Female Patients, 9 August 1869, S507 cons1120 04 101, SROWA.

[124] Hetherington, *The Marriage Knot*, 5; Wallis, "Hysterical Women," 90–91.

[125] William Goodall to Colonial Secretary, 17 July 1871, S2941 cons36 695 162, SROWA.

[126] Resident Magistrate Bunbury to Colonial Secretary, 28 October 1871, S2941 cons36 698 169, SROWA.

On 3 September 1872, a third tragedy occurred. William was badly injured when the horse he was riding ran into a tree. He was driven the thirty kilometres into Bunbury Hospital in a cart where he died five days later. It must have been an agonising journey. This tragedy affected not only Mary but also her children. Mary's oldest child, William, now eleven years old, was taken into the Piggott household to be indentured as a farm worker, while Elizabeth was to be cared for by the Rose family of Parkfield, who intended to train her for domestic duties.[127] Another daughter, Theresa, who may have been born while Mary was in the Poor House is not mentioned but probably remained with her mother as Mary is listed travelling from Bunbury to Perth with a child on 8 October.[128] Young William did not have a pleasant time with the Piggotts. Nearly a year later he is reported to be nearly blind, "scarcely able to find his way from room to room." Clifton was scathing in his assessment of Piggott's treatment of William, writing that the boy had been suffering from bad eyes for months. "From Piggott's own statement I consider there has been great neglect on his part, in not having provided proper medical treatment in a case of so serious a nature."[129] William was admitted to the Colonial Hospital and, although there is no record of the outcome of his time there, government records show that he was taken in by the Roman Catholic orphanage and in January 1875, was admitted to the Colonial Hospital again, spending at least two months there for an ulcerated throat.[130] Although Piggott states in 1873 that Mary was an inmate of the Lunatic Asylum, the archival records don't support this and it is more likely that she was either living independently in Perth or was still a resident of the Poor House.[131]

By 1875, Mary was destitute and was tried summarily with having no visible means of support. Having heard from Police Sergeant McLarty

---

127 Piggott, 4–11 January 1872, MN 729 acc. 2247A, SLWA.

128 "Shipping Intelligence," *PGWAT*, 11 October 1872, 2; St Joseph's Orphanage register- Girls from Poorhouse, 1868–1885, Institute of the Sisters of Mercy and Papua New Guinea Archives (ISMAPNG), Sydney.

129 Resident Magistrate Bunbury to Colonial Secretary, 25 October 1873, S2941 cons36 746 198, SROWA.

130 Officer in Charge Poor House to Colonial Secretary, 15 March 1875, S2941 cons36 805 92, SROWA.

131 Benjamin Piggott to Colonial Secretary, 25 October 1873, S2941 cons36 746 200, SROWA.

that Mary was a "person of very weak intellect" Magistrate Edward Landor sentenced her to fourteen days imprisonment as "an act of charity," and to allow the medical officer to give an opinion as to her sanity.[132] Other poverty-stricken women also suffered from periods of incarceration as "acts of charity"; in one case a woman suffering from measles was imprisoned when the hospital refused to admit her.[133] The view that incarceration was a suitable solution to poverty, as well as a form of punishment for deviant behaviour, was voiced by judges and given added authority by newspaper reporting of trials.[134]

For the rest of her life Mary continued to be charged with offences such as being idle and disorderly, drunkenness, vagrancy, and destitution. Over the next twenty-two years she was charged at least twenty-three times and sentenced to periods of imprisonment ranging from one week to three months.[135] By 1875, Mary had begun to be referred to as a prostitute and it is possible that sex work may have been her only means of support.[136] In 1878, she was readmitted to the Lunatic Asylum on the advice of Dr Alfred Waylen who stated that she was "continually roaming about," not taking care of her child, and "indulging in lewd talk."[137] She was carrying her ten-month-old baby, John Martin Goodall, when admitted and her case file notes that she had three other children who had been admitted to the orphanage.[138] Mary's baby was

---

[132] "Perth Police Court," *Western Australian Times*, 16 February 1875, 3.

[133] "City Police Court," *DN*, 5 March 1885, 3; "Saturday, January 12, 1884," *DN*, 12 January 1884, 3.

[134] For examples see "City Police Court," *DN*, 5 March 1885, 3; "Perth Police Court," *Western Australian Times*, 13 November 1874; "The Daily News," *DN*, 9 February 1884, 3.

[135] "Newspapers & Gazettes," Trove, accessed 7 May 2022, https://trove.nla.gov.au/newspaper/; *PGWA*, SLWA, accessed 7 May 2022, https://slwa.wa.gov.au/collections/collections/police-gazettes.

[136] Officer in Charge Poor House to Colonial Secretary, 15 March 1875, S2941 cons36 805 92, SROWA.

[137] Mary Goodall, 14 August 1878, S4397 cons7543 0340X, SROWA.

[138] Case book - Female Patients, 15 August 1878, S2219 cons5759 1 291, SROWA; Baptism, Joseph [sic] Goodall, Baptismal Register St Mary's Perth, 3 December 1877, digital image, accessed 16 June 2023, https://www.familysearch.org/ark:/61903/3:1:3Q9M-CSKG-R9FP-J?i=242&cat=989263. William, Theresa and Mary, who was born in 1875, were all sent to the Roman Catholic orphanages; St Joseph's Orphanage register- Girls from Poorhouse, 1868–1885, ISMAPNG; Officer in charge Perth Poor House to Colonial secretary, 15 March 1875, S2941 cons36 805 93, SROWA.

also removed and taken to the Poor House, as the Asylum's doctor, Dr Henry Calvert Barnett, considered that the child was "in the most imminent risk amongst a number of lunatic women who strive to nurse and caress the little one."[139] It was suggested that an inmate of the Poor House could care for John but it seems that the Poor House was no safer for him than the Asylum or his mother's care. A year later, while Mary was still in the Asylum, John died in Perth and was buried in East Perth Cemetery.[140] The cause of death was given as "debility."[141] Mary's continued periods of institutionalisation meant that her children were also institutionalised, and their lives thereby endangered.

Mary also spent several periods of time as an inmate of the Poor House. In 1877 she applied to enter the Poor House with her two-year-old daughter, Mary, but was refused entry by Dale who wrote that she was "a woman of bad character."[142] Penelope Hetherington's research shows that, from 1873, destitute women applying to enter the Poor House were subject to increased surveillance of their moral lives. Women who were not considered "respectable" were often denied entry, making it harder for those who were in a relationship outside of their marriage, who had been convicted of crime, or who earned a living from sex work to gain access to the Poor House. This was in contrast to destitute men whose admission was seldom denied.[143] Mary was instead granted outdoor relief, Dale writing that "she has on many occasions been an inmate of the Poor House but for many reasons she is best out of it."[144] In December 1882, Mary again applied to enter the Poor House. Dale once again referred to her character, labelling her as a prostitute, and again refused her entry. In a memorandum to the Colonial Secretary, he stated that Mary had recently been released from gaol "and I have

[139] Barnett to Colonial Secretary, 15 August 1878, S675 cons527 169, SROWA.

[140] "Goodall, John," East Perth cemeteries, accessed 14 January 2023, https://www.eastperthcemeteries.com.au/explore/burial-search/burialsite/129795.html.

[141] Register of Deaths - Colonial Surgeon, S4015 cons2799 1, SROWA.

[142] Officer of Poor Houses to Colonial Secretary, 13 June 1877, S2941 cons36 871 83, SROWA.

[143] Hetherington, *Paupers Poor Relief and Poorhouses*, 128, 116–117.

[144] Officer of Poor Houses to Colonial Secretary, 13 June 1877, S2941 cons36 871 83, SROWA.

no doubt she will soon find her way back again." She was again recommended to receive outdoor relief.[145] In 1883, Mary did gain entry to the Poor House, and remained there until the end of 1885, leaving shortly before Christmas.[146] During this time her offending appears to have ceased. Life was strictly controlled for inmates; visitors were forbidden and they were not allowed to leave the premises without permission. Female inmates were engaged in domestic chores such as laundry work, commissioned needlework, or sewing bags for the postal service.[147] Under these conditions there would have been little opportunity for Mary to indulge in behaviour that would lead to arrest, such as drinking, sex work, or sleeping outdoors. Mary died at the age of fifty-six and was buried in East Perth cemetery. Her last days were spent at the Poor House, known at that time as the Perth Female Home (Fig. 2.5).[148]

Mary's case illustrates the recidivism of many underclass women charged with public order offences due to the choice, or necessity, of earning their living through sex work, and by the demonstration of behaviour which, fuelled by alcohol, deviated from the discourse of respectable femininity. Institutionalisation in Western Australia had begun for Mary with the tragedy of her son's death and continued following the death of two further children and the accidental death of her husband. Institutionalisation affected not only women but also their children who often accompanied their mothers into the Poor House or, like Mary's children, were sent to an orphanage. Mary's life revolved around the prison, the Lunatic Asylum and the Poor House. For many underclass women, institutionalisation in prisons and the poor house was part of their lived experience. For a few, like Mary Goodall, Mary Jane Hayes, Lola Wright, and Mary Kirtley, it also included the Fremantle Lunatic Asylum (Fig. 2.6).[149]

---

[145] Superintendent Poor House to Colonial Secretary, 1 December 1882, S675 cons527 1882/1491 189, SROWA.

[146] "Perth Police Court," *West Australian*, 10 February 1885, 3.

[147] Hetherington, *Paupers, Poor Relief and Poorhouses*, 115.

[148] "Goodall Mary," East Perth Cemeteries, accessed 7 May 2022, https://www.eastperthcemeteries.com.au/explore/burial-search/burialsite/129796.html.

[149] Case Book Female Patients, 1878–1897, S2219 cons2724 03, SLWA; Case Book Female Patients, 1873–1878, S2219 cons5759 1, SLWA; Register of Female Patients, 1858–1873, S507 cons1120 04, SLWA.

Fig. 2.5 Perth Female Home, previously known as the Perth Poor House, Goderich Street, 1899. SLWA, W.A. Parliament Votes and Proceedings vol. 1 part 2, 1901, paper 7

Infanticide

> Poor Edie Adams. Oh, I am so grieved to write about her. I never, never thought it possible of her. She had a little baby last Wednesday night and took it away out into the cold night. I am afraid she killed it. Oh dear, I am so sorry for her and her poor old mother. Perhaps it was born dead. Oh I trust it was. ... It was such a pretty little baby. Oh how I wish this troubled time was over.[150]

Although legal records, when read "against the grain" can tell us a little about the lives of the working-class women who appeared in court, they are unlikely to reveal details of the very real emotions these women must

[150] Frances Louisa Brockman, *Pioneer Daughter: The Diary of Frances Louisa (Fanny) Brockman (nee Bussell)*, ed. Gillian Lilleyman (Claremont: Gillian Lilleyman, 2018), 196.

Fig. 2.6 Women patients and staff at the Fremantle Lunatic Asylum, mid-1890s. Women admitted to the Asylum would have their hair cropped when entering the institution. Courtesy City of Fremantle History Centre, E001017

have felt, and we are left to guess at the fear women may have experienced in the courtroom, or the despair that may have led them to commit an illegal act. Occasionally letters, or diary entries, give us a glimpse into these emotions, as in these comments written in 1886 by Edith Adams's employer, Fanny Brockman.

Although the case of Mary Goodall illustrates the cycle of institutionalisation and poverty that could affect underclass women, it is not representative of the majority of cases where the State sought to hold a woman accountable for the death of an infant. Infanticide, used here to mean the killing of an infant by his or her mother, was a not uncommon solution for young, unmarried women in nineteenth-century Britain and Australia, for whom the birth of an unwanted child could mean social and economic disaster. In 1887, when Lucy Paterson suspected that her domestic servant, Theresa Arnold, might be pregnant, she was advised by Dr Edward Scott to "give the girl a small bonus and send her away."[151] Women with children would be unlikely to find a position as a domestic

[151] "Police News," *ICN*, 23 February 1887, 5.

servant and the shame of an illegitimate child was immense, as a constant reminder of a woman's "fall" from the feminine attributes of modesty and chastity.[152]

Numerous works have shown that in Australia, as in Britain, women who committed infanticide were usually treated sympathetically in the criminal justice system.[153] Research by historians and criminologists has shown that, as in Britain, most defendants in Australian infanticide cases were young domestic servants or unmarried daughters living at home.[154] As models of masculinity changed during the nineteenth century, with men seen to be more dangerous and more in need of self-discipline, so too did the ideology of femininity change to one where women were seen to be more moral and pious, but also more vulnerable. Women were seen as requiring protection from "bad" men and this led to men increasingly being blamed when mothers killed their illegitimate newborn babies.[155] Most infanticidal mothers were considered to be "respectable" and virtuous women who had been seduced and abandoned by an unscrupulous male and who had killed their child in an act of desperation and despair.[156] Unless demonstrable violence was obvious, women suspected of neonaticide, that is, the killing of a child less than one day old, were usually tried for the crime of concealment of birth, which carried a lesser sentence, rather than for the capital crime of murder.[157]

---

152 Judith A. Allen, *Sex and Secrets: Crimes Involving Australian Women since 1880* (Melbourne: Oxford University Press Australia, 1990), 27.

153 Jan Kociumbas, "Azaria's Antecedents: Stereotyping Infanticide in Late Nineteenth-Century Australia," *Gender & History* 13, no. 1 (2001): 142; Kathy Laster, "Infanticide: A Litmus Test for Feminist Criminological Theory," *Australian and New Zealand Journal of Criminology* 22, no. 3 (1989): 161; David Plater and Sue Milne, "'All That's Good and Virtuous or Depraved and Abandoned in the Extreme'? Capital Punishment and Mercy for Female Offenders in Colonial Australia, 1824 to 1865," *University of Tasmania Law Review* 33, no. 1 (2014): 91.

154 Allen, *Sex and Secrets*, 30; Laster, "Infanticide," 158; D'Cruze and Jackson, *Women, Crime and Justice*, 77.

155 Wiener, *Men of Blood*, 3, 29, 123.

156 For example, see Daniel J.R. Grey, "'The Agony of Despair': Pain and the Cultural Script of Infanticide in England and Wales, 1860–1960," in *Pain and Emotion in Modern History*, ed. Rob Boddice (London: Palgrave Macmillan, 2014); Kociumbas, "Azaria's Antecedents," 146.

157 *Malicious Shooting and Stabbing Act*, 43 Geo III, c 58 1803 (UK).

The fathers of newborn children suspected to have been killed by their mothers were often not mentioned in the resulting court case. Referring to ex-nuptial births in nineteenth-century New South Wales, Allen has argued that the long hours worked by domestic servants, and the little time "off" allowed to them, limited paternity of their child to members of the household or visitors.[158] Shirlee Swain, however, used quantitative data to show that in nineteenth-century Victoria, paternity of the children of domestic servants was most likely to be by a boyfriend or fiancé, with only 9% of children being fathered by a woman's employer.[159] Of the women charged with the suspected killing of a newborn child in this study, the paternity of only one of the children was known to be the woman's employer. Two children were fathered by men who had since left Western Australia and one woman was pregnant before she embarked for Australia.[160] The paternity of the other children is unknown. It is clear, however, that some domestic servants working in urban areas had enough leisure time to visit friends, and meet men, up to several times a week.[161]

Not all infanticides terminated with a trial. In the nineteenth century the bodies of tiny babies were found in rivers and on beaches, secreted in the hulls of ships, hidden in privies, and dropped down wells, and often the mothers of these babies could not be traced.[162] Young women would attempt to hide their pregnancies from friends and family beneath

158 Allen, "*Sex and Secrets*," 26.

159 Shurlee Swain "Maids and Mothers: Domestic Servants and Illegitimacy in 19th-century Australia," *The History of the Family* 10, no. 4 (2005): 465.

160 *R v Jane Green*, October 1840, S122 cons3472 case 226, SROWA; *R v Catherine Kelly*, 7 January 1863, S122 cons3473 10 case 76, SROWA; Police Magistrate Perth to the Colonial Secretary, S675 cons 527 1887 0545, SROWA; *R v Sarah Benny*, 2 October 1889, S122 cons3473 27 case 2210, SROWA.

161 *R v Eliza Hamilton*, 7 November 1863, S122 cons3472 10 case 389, SROWA.

162 Margaret Grellier, "Women and the Family," in *Westralian Voices: Documents in Western Australian Social History*, ed. Marion Aveling (Nedlands: University of Western Australia Press, 1979), 316; Lyn Stephenson and Tom Stannage, "Law and Order," in *Westralian Voices: Documents in Western Australian Social History*, ed. Marion Aveling (Nedlands: University of Western Australia Press, 1979), 79; Allen, *Sex and Secrets*, 32; Judith Allen, "Octavius Beale Reconsidered: Infanticide, Babyfarming and Abortion in NSW 1880–1939," in *What Rough Beast?: The State and Social Order in Australian History* ed. Sydney Labour History Group (Sydney: Allen & Unwin, 1982), 115.

wide skirts and tight corsets.[163] Changes in their bodies were explained by references to dropsy, cancer, tumours or abscesses.[164]

Public sympathy was often at odds with the law in these cases, and most infanticidal mothers were treated as passive victims. Between 1830 and 1890 in Western Australia, thirteen cases involving the death of an infant under one year of age were tried in the upper courts. Eleven of these were suspected neonaticides. The defendants in all cases were the infants' mothers and, in the cases of suspected neonaticides, unmarried. Most worked as domestic servants. These women were not recidivists and often were never charged with any other crime. In most cases their lives, after the court case or their release from prison, followed the course expected of "respectable" women and included marriage and children. The case of Edith Adams exemplifies many of these traits.

Case Study: Edith Adams

Edith was born to Henry Adams and his wife Mary Ann (previously Smith) in Busselton, in the south-west of Western Australia, in 1863.[165] Her father was a ship's carpenter who had left the American whaling barque *Eagle*.[166] Edith's mother, Mary Ann, grew up as a foster sister to Fanny Brockman's mother, Ellen Heppingstone, in a working-class family at the Vasse in south-west Western Australia.[167] When Ellen married Alfred Bussell, who came from a wealthy, land-owning family, the Adams family were employed by Ellen at Ellensbrook and in turn they and their children were employed by Fanny at Wallcliffe House, near Margaret River. Edith would have grown up on her father's farm at

---

163 Lionel Rose, *Massacre of the Innocents: Infanticide in Great Britain 1800–1939*, 2nd edn (London: Routledge, 2016), 72.

164 Amanda Gardiner, "Can Historical Infanticide Investigations Help Us Understand Embodied Experiences of the Past?," *Australian Feminist Studies* 36, no. 109 (2021): 353.

165 Birth, Edith Mary Adams no. 7298, 1863, Busselton, "Online index Search Tool," Department of Justice, accessed 5 January 2023, https://www.wa.gov.au/organisation/department-of-justice/online-index-search-tool.

166 Brockman, *Pioneer Daughter*, 18; Erickson ed., *The Bicentennial Dictionary*, 1:8.

167 Brockman, *Pioneer Daughter*, 11; I.D. Heppingstone, "The Story of Alfred and Ellen Bussell: Pioneers of the Margaret River," *Early Days* 6, no. 3 (1964): 36.

nearby Quindalup. By 1884, Edith was working as a domestic servant for Fanny at Wallcliffe House (Fig. 2.7).[168] On the night of Wednesday, 4 August 1886, Edith secretly gave birth to a baby girl in her bedroom. The child died and Edith carried the body of the little girl through a dark night of rain and strong winds to the water closet and, wrapping her baby in paper and lily leaves, hid the body beneath the floor.[169]

It is not known who the father of Edith's baby was. By 1885, Fanny Brockman's husband, John, was no longer living at Wallcliffe.[170] The baby could have been fathered by any of the young men who lived at, or visited, Wallcliffe, including Fanny's brother John Bussell, or the young men from the Moriaty, Maxwell or Keenan families.[171] The father of Edith's baby may also have been Michael Flemming, whom Edith later married.[172] No case files have been found for the resulting trial on the

Fig. 2.7 Wallcliffe House, near Margaret River c. 1900. Courtesy SLWA, 2932B/25

[168] Brockman, *Pioneer Daughter*, 10, 18, 33–36, 177.

[169] "Notes From Bunbury," *DN*, 1 November 1886, 3; Inquest, 7 August 1886, S675 cons527 1886/3401, SROWA.

[170] "Classified Advertising," *West Australian*, 29 July 1881, 2.

[171] Brockman, *Pioneer Daughter*, 65, 181.

[172] Marriage, Michael Flemming and Edith Adams no. 6333, 1886, Busselton, "Online Index Search Tool," Department of Justice, accessed 5 January 2023, https://www.wa.gov.au/organisation/department-of-justice/online-index-search-tool.

charge of concealment of birth, but it is possible to gain an understanding of the events from the newspaper reports, the inquest, and from Fanny's diary.

The next day, Edith admitted to Fanny that she had given birth after "traces," probably blood, were found in her room.[173] John Bussell searched for the child's body and, finding it under the floor of the water closet, brought it back to the house and placed it in a box. It is clear that, although Edith did not publicly acknowledge her pregnancy, her changing body shape had caused others to suspect her condition. Four days before the birth, Police Constable William Carroll had "a conversation with her about her appearance."[174] Edith told him then she was suffering from dropsy, an explanation she had also given to Fanny.[175] The trials of women suspected of neonaticide in Western Australia at this time, show that most had been taxed by an authority figure, or friend, with being pregnant previous to the birth. All denied this and some, like Edith, attributed changes in their appearance to illness.

Edith might have been considered more fortunate than many of the young women who came to the colony as single assisted emigrants and who therefore had no family close by to support them; however, it seems that Edith's mother was not supportive of her daughter in this case. Fanny sent for Mary when the body of Edith's baby was discovered, but Mary "would not come." Fanny then sent for the police and Constable William Carroll arrived to take the child's body away. He noted a bruise on the baby's left temple, but Fanny prevented him from interviewing Edith saying that it would be too dangerous in Edith's weakened condition.[176] On Friday the police sergeant and the doctor visited to question the household and to leave Carroll at Wallcliffe, in charge of Edith.[177]

At the inquest, which was held in Busselton on 14 August, the jury determined that the baby had died as a result of the navel cord not being tied, "but not wilfully on the part of the mother."[178] They also found that

173 "Notes From Bunbury."

174 Inquest, 7 August 1886, S675 cons527 1886/3401, SROWA.

175 Inquest, 7 August 1886, S675 cons527 1886/3401, SROWA; "Notes From Bunbury".

176 Inquest, 7 August 1886, S675 cons527 1886/3401, SROWA.

177 Brockman, *Pioneer Daughter*, 177.

178 *PGWA*, August 1886, 143, SLWA.

Edith did attempt to conceal the birth of her child, and she was consequently indicted for this crime. In only one case of infanticide during this time period, that of Jane Green, was the defendant tried for murder.[179] Edith was allowed to remain out on bail until her trial in Bunbury on 20 November.[180] A medical expert testified that Edith's baby was full term and born alive.[181] Edith's defence lawyer, George Stevens, argued that it was not possible to determine who concealed the child and that Edith was suffering from temporary insanity at the time of her baby's death.[182] The jury returned a verdict of "not guilty" but the newspaper report does not include information on how they reached this decision.

The defence of "temporary insanity," or diminished mental capacity, was common in infanticide trials.[183] Since the late eighteenth century, medical experts had routinely appeared in trials of infanticide in Britain, testifying to the results of autopsies designed to indicate whether the child had been born alive.[184] This was also the case in Western Australia. These experts, although usually called by the prosecution, would often include testimony regarding the defendant's state of mind. Medical experts testified that women who were giving birth might "become unconscious," might show "symptoms of aberration" or sometimes did not know "what she was about."[185] This defence, conforming to gendered understandings of women as frail and prone to mental instability, would have been understandable to a jury. Historian Georgina Rychner argues that a woman whose appearance and demeanour seemed

---

[179] *R v Jane Green*, October 1840, S122 cons3472 case 226, SROWA; Green was a 17-year-old domestic servant when she was tried for the murder of her new-born son in 1840. She had used scissors to make numerous wounds to the child's body, including cutting the windpipe, and it was likely that this obvious violence engendered the murder indictment.

[180] Brockman, *Pioneer Daughter*, 196.

[181] "Notes From Bunbury".

[182] "Bunbury Jottings," *Victorian Express*, 13 November 1886, 3.

[183] Gilchrist, *Murder, Misadventure and Miserable Ends*, 283; Georgina Rychner, "'The Pendulum of the Public Mind': Insanity and Activism in Capital Trials, 1880–1939" (PhD diss., Monash University, 2020), 55–56.

[184] Katherine D. Watson, "Medical and Chemical Expertise in English Trials for Criminal Poisoning, 1750–1914," *Medical History* 50 (2006): 376–77.

[185] For example see, "Supreme Court—Criminal Sittings," *West Australian*, 8 April 1881, 3; "Quarter Sessions," *PGWAJ*, 3 October 1840, 2; "Supreme Court—Criminal Sittings," *Western Mail*, 5 October 1889, 28.

to meet gendered understandings of respectable femininity, but who had nonetheless committed the unmaternal, and therefore unfeminine, crime of killing her own child, presented a paradox to the jury, which could be reconciled by a narrative of "temporary insanity."[186] The concept of insanity was therefore significant to the way in which infanticide cases were understood and to the outcome of these cases.

Research has shown how news discourse was used to understand women who killed their newly born children. News reports could disempower women when they portrayed deviant women as a danger to society but could also be used to empower women when they sought to position or explain her actions.[187] Following the magistrate's hearing for Edith's crime, the *Western Mail* offered a sympathetic view of the case writing that Edith was "respectably connected" and stating that the case appeared to be "extremely weak."[188] A report appearing in the *Victorian Express* after the trial was more conflicted. The reporter referred to the "horrible case" and bemoaned the fact that local juries were reluctant to "convict criminals." The reporter followed this statement by asserting that he nonetheless did not dispute the verdict as "there seems little doubt of her temporary insanity."[189] The *Victorian Express* was giving voice to the conflicting discourses to infanticide appearing in the press at that time. While newspapers had become increasingly strident in their condemnation of this crime, individual cases were still treated with a sympathetic understanding.[190]

There is no evidence that Edith was ever charged with committing another crime. Within a few weeks of her trial, she had married Michael Flemming and over the years the couple had six children, although only

186 Rychner, "'The Pendulum of the Public Mind," 87, 65.

187 Nicola Goc, *Women, Infanticide, and the Press, 1822–1922: News Narratives in England and Australia* (London: Routledge, 2016), 1, 15.

188 "Busselton News," *West Australian*, 9 September 1886, 3.

189 "Bunbury Jottings," *Victorian Express*, 13 November 1886, 3.

190 Daniel J.R. Grey, "'No Crime to Kill a Bastard-Child': Stereotypes of Infanticide in Nineteenth-Century England and Wales," in *Intersections of Gender, Class and Race in the Long Nineteenth Century and Beyond*, ed. Barbara Leonardi (Cham, Switzerland: Palgrave MacMillan, 2018), 42; Kay Saunders, *Deadly Australian Women* (Sydney: ABC Books, 2013), 84–85; "Miscellaneous," *PGWAT*, 29 June 1866, 3.

four survived to adulthood.[191] The infant mortality rate at this time was high: one fifth of infants registered as born in Perth in the last decade of the nineteenth century died before their first birthday.[192] The family moved around the south-west of Western Australia, with Edith running boarding houses in Karridale and Margaret River, and Michael working in the timber industry.[193] They eventually settled in Margaret River and, when Edith died there in 1952, her obituary referred to her as "a hard worker" who was "esteemed by all who knew her," reinforcing her position as a "respectable" woman."[194]

Edith's story is typical of most of the women in this time period who were suspected of neonaticide. She was charged with the lesser crime of concealment of birth and, similarly to half of those charged with that crime, was acquitted. This result was due to a combination of an able defence lawyer and a sympathetic attitude towards unmarried women who committed infanticide at this time. This was the only time that Edith was known to have appeared in a court of law and she went on to live the life of respectable femininity which society demanded of women at that time.

---

[191] Marriage, Michael Flemming to Edith Adams no. 6333, 1886, Busselton, "Online Index Search Tool," Department of Justice, accessed 5 January 2023, https://www.wa.gov.au/organisation/department-of-justice/online-index-search-tool; Births, Rita Victorian Mcleay Flemming no. 1418, 1888, Quindalup; Grace Adela Fleming no. 1034, 1892, Quindalup; Ruby Mary Mcleay Flemming no. 807, 1895, Quindalup; Melville Adams Mccay Flemming no. 3411, 1897, Quindalup; William Luke Mccay Flemming no. 5046, 1901, Quindalup; Eileen Florence Hemming no. 5925, 1903, Karridale, "Online Index Search Tool," Department of Justice, accessed 5 January 2023, https://www.wa.gov.au/organisation/department-of-justice/online-index-search-tool; Deaths, Grace Adela Flemming no. 814, 5 months, 1892; William Luke Mcleay Flemming no. 2657, one year, 1903, "Online Index Search Tool," Department of Justice, accessed 5 January 2023, https://www.wa.gov.au/organisation/department-of-justice/online-index-search-tool.

[192] Michael Drury, "Infant Mortality in Perth Western Australia, 1870–1914: A Preliminary Analysis," *Studies in Western Australian History* 5 (1982): 66.

[193] "Margaret Notes," *South-Western News (SWN)*, 31 January 1908, 2; "Old Resident Passes," *SWN*, 22 May 1952, 12 "Margaret River," *SWN*, 21 June 1912, 3.

[194] "Old Resident Passes," *SWN*, 22 May 1952, 12.

Conclusion

Although working-class women often left little written trace of their lives, legal records have the ability to increase our understanding of their lived experience. By examining the life courses of women offenders, a greater understanding of the social and economic pressures to which they were subject, can be gained. The case studies of Eliza Cook, Mary Woods, Mary Goodall, and Edith Adams exemplify the precarity of the lives of colonial working-class women. They illustrate the pressures women faced to provide for their families when their husbands were out of work, imprisoned, or abandoned them. They also illustrate the precarity caused by illness, injury, or assault.

Like many other domestic servants in the colony at that time, Eliza Cook came from a difficult background. Her family's beginnings in the new colony were plagued by poverty, and her mother died when Eliza was young. Her crime, the opportunistic theft of clothing, was typical of the larceny charges brought against women at this time. The lives of Mary Woods and Mary Goodall indicate the extent to which women were reliant on income from a male partner. "Respectable" employment for women with children was difficult to obtain and poorly remunerated, and women like Goodall, whose husbands died, or Woods, whose husbands abandoned them, might use sex work or larceny as survival strategies. Their lives were also made precarious by illness and injury, and their life courses were impacted by men in positions of authority who judged their morality and their femininity. For women like Edith Adams, the killing of their children was driven both by the shame of giving birth to a child outside of marriage, and the precarity caused by a lack of employment options for women with children.

For many women, like Eliza and Edith, this was the only time they appeared in a court of law, and their lived experience then followed the path of marriage and children expected of "respectable" women. In contrast, some underclass women, like Mary Goodall and Mary Woods, were unable to escape a cycle of poverty, crime, and institutionalisation. Their lives followed a course of recidivism, appearing time and again for petty crimes in the lower courts and occasionally also appearing in the upper courts for more serious crimes. For these women, and their children, the court, the gaol, and the Poor House were part of their lived experience. For some, institutionalisation also included the Lunatic Asylum. Women could be imprisoned for being drunk, for using "obscene language," for behaving in a "disorderly" fashion, or for vagrancy if they were found sleeping in the open. Some women also found themselves imprisoned as "an act of charity" by judges who considered incarceration as a suitable solution to poverty. Many working-class women were never able to escape the cycle of institutionalisation and poverty and ended their days in a state of destitution.

However, legal records, when supplemented by other sources, can also shed light on the ways working-class women acted to improve their lives and circumstances, and to challenge the authority of the police and the courts. This research shows that underclass women in Perth and Fremantle, many of whom had arrived as single women emigrants, created support networks to care for others' children, look after each other on the streets, and appear as witnesses in court cases. Men and women were able to petition the Governor to effect their release from gaol and many women did this, sometimes successfully. Records also show that women protested verbally against the authority of the courts. The precarity experienced by many working-class women means that deviant behaviour, such as theft, sex work, and neonaticide, may have been used as survival strategies for these women. For those who became recidivists, deviant behaviour may also have become a way of life.

3

Representing Women: The Use of Defence Counsel in Women's Trials

> Mary Jane Gallagher and Agnes Arbuckle were charged with stealing from the person of Joshua Pickersgill, the sum of £33, at Fremantle, on the 6th April last. Prisoners defended themselves, with great readiness, and brazen impudence.[1]

In 1871, Agnes Arbuckle and Mary Jane Gallagher (later known as Mary Jane Berry then Mary Jane Hayes) successfully defended themselves in the Supreme Court of Western Australia against a charge of stealing from the person, otherwise known as "pickpocketing." The two women, who had been described previously by the *Herald* as "two notorious prostitutes," were accused of stealing £33 and a pocketbook from the pockets of Joshua Pickersgill of Bunbury.[2] In his evidence Pickersgill, who was visiting Fremantle, described walking back to his lodgings,

---

[1] "Supreme Court—Criminal Sittings," *Herald*, 8 July 1871, 4.

[2] Alexandra Wallis, "The Disorderly Female: Alcohol, Prostitution and Moral Insanity in 19th-Century Fremantle," *Journal of Australian Studies* 43, no. 3 (2019): 334; "Police News," *Herald*, 18 February 1871, 3; *R v Mary Jane Gallagher and Agnes Arbuckle*, 5 July 1871, S122 cons3473 56 case 451, State Record Office of Western Australia (SROWA); "Advertising," *Herald*, 25 November 1871, 3.

C. Ingram, *Women on Trial*, Palgrave Histories of Policing, Punishment and Justice,
https://doi.org/10.1007/978-3-031-98072-5_3

after an evening of heavy drinking at the Victoria Hotel, in High Street, Fremantle. As he paused on the corner of the street to his lodgings, Mary Jane Gallagher accosted him and, linking arms, asked him to accompany her to the beach. He said he resisted until Agnes Arbuckle came up on his other side and persuaded him to walk further down the street. At the end of the street the two women left him and Pickersgill returned to his lodgings. It was not until the next day that he discovered that his money and pocketbook had disappeared.[3]

During the trial, Gallagher and Arbuckle cross-examined prosecution witnesses and called witnesses to back up their claims that the "new boots" found by police during a search of their premises had been bought several months earlier and not with money taken from Pickersgill's pocket. They also brought in witnesses to give them alibis for the time of the offence. Among the witnesses was Hannah Holmes, also known as Sophia Paviour, who testified that Arbuckle was at her house during the time in question, "but was in and out."[4] Despite a prosecution witness who confirmed that he had seen Gallagher put her hand in Pickersgill's coat and "take something," and testimony from witnesses who stated that the two women had been spending money freely that night, the jury found both Gallagher and Arbuckle not guilty.[5] This was likely due to a combination of the police being unable to find the stolen money during a search of the women's house and the witnesses called by Gallagher and Arbuckle to provide them with alibis. The result may also have been due to the jury's perception of Pickersgill's actions as foolish. The trope of men who visited the metropolis and were robbed by "women of the street" while drunk was familiar at the time, and research shows that juries would often attribute blame to the victim in these cases.[6] Newspaper reports of this case not only mocked the victim but also made fun of Gallagher and Arbuckle. The *Inquirer* called them

[3] *R v Mary Jane Gallagher and Agnes Arbuckle*; "Supreme Court," *Perth Gazette and West Australian Times (PGWAT)*, 21 July 1871, 4; "Advertising," *Herald*, 9 November 1872, 2.

[4] "Supreme Court," *PGWAT*, 21 July 1871.

[5] *R v Mary Jane Gallagher and Agnes Arbuckle.*

[6] Alana Jayne Piper, "Victimization Narratives and Courtroom Sexual Politics: Prosecuting Male Burglars and Female Pickpockets in Melbourne, 1860–1921," *Journal of Social History* 51, no. 4 (2018): 769.

"two notorious nymphs of the pave," referred to Arbuckle as Gallagher's "frail companion," and concluded that their acquittal was "apparently as much to their surprise as their satisfaction."[7] Regardless of the verdict, the charge still affected the women's lives and that of their families. The women were remanded in gaol for three months while awaiting their trial, meaning that their children were left destitute and without anyone to care for them (Arbuckle's husband had left the colony and the father of Gallagher's daughter was unknown). All four children were admitted to the Perth Poor House during their mothers' time in gaol.[8]

This trial raises questions around the subject of defence in trials heard in the upper courts. How typical was this outcome in the cases of women who conducted their own defence? How many women were represented at trial? What effect did the presence of defence counsel have on the outcome of a trial and did this vary from that of the general population? What methods did defence counsel use in order to effect an acquittal in these cases? What access did women have to defence lawyers? The use of defence counsel in criminal trials has long been considered to be advantageous for defendants and its historical use has been studied in both Britain and Australia. However, until recently there has been little quantitative examination of the impact of representation in Australia and that which has occurred has focused mainly on the general population of offenders rather than specific groups.

In this chapter, I examine the impact of defence counsel on the outcome of women's trials and the methods counsel used in an attempt to achieve an advantageous outcome for their clients. Additionally, I examine factors which may have limited women's access to representation including class, ethnicity, and economic status. I argue that, in line with other studies of the use of defence counsel in the general population of offenders, the use of counsel was markedly advantageous overall for nineteenth-century women accused of serious crime in Western Australia, but that representation may have been less effective for women accused of interpersonal crimes. Where possible, counsel emphasised

---

[7] "Supreme Court," *Inquirer and Commercial News (ICN)*, 12 July 1871, 3.

[8] Resident Magistrate Fremantle to Colonial Secretary, 11 April 1871, S2941 cons36 698 69, SROWA; Colonial Secretary to Resident Magistrate Fremantle, 12 April 1871, S2755 cons49 51 1209, SROWA.

those characteristics of their clients which aligned with gendered understandings of feminine behaviour to make them appear less threatening to the jury. However, access to counsel was uneven during this time, with some women unable to access the advantages afforded by representation, raising issues of equity to justice.

I begin the chapter with an overview of the sources, and the methodology, I have used to examine the impact of defence counsel in women's trials and to piece together the case studies. I then examine the rise of defence counsel in the adversarial trial in Western Australia, including conditions peculiar to Western Australia, such as the size of the body of legal practitioners and the assignment of counsel in capital cases. This is followed by an examination of the impact of defence counsel on the verdict generally, and then more specifically according to the type of crime, and the effect of representation on recommendations of mercy and sentencing. I finish with a discussion of the circumstances of access to legal counsel by female defendants.

Sources and Methodology

To explore the use of defence counsel and to determine the impact of legal representation on the trials of female defendants, only prosecutions that proceeded to trial are examined here. Trials of female defendants in the upper courts were identified from the Prosecution Project data base, convict records, and the Colonial Secretary's Office correspondence records.[9] Only those trials in which the defendant did not plead guilty and which were not pronounced *nolle prosequi*, "no case" or "not fit to stand" were analysed.[10] Additionally, as information on defence counsel

---

[9] Mark Finnane, "Western Australia Criminal Trials 1830–1861" (ADA Dataverse, V1, 2019), https://doi.org/10.26193/OW6SR6; Mark Finnane, "Western Australia Supreme Court 1862–1899" (ADA Dataverse, V2, 2020), https://doi.org/10.26193/ESI64N; Colonial Secretary's Office, S2941 cons36, SROWA; Record of court convictions, 1861–1914, S5072 cons1156 v23, SROWA.

[10] *Nolle prosequi* is a decision by the Attorney-General to abandon a case after a true bill has been found. A trial can also be discontinued if the defendant is found not fit to stand trial due to mental incapacity and a defendant can be discharged if the court finds that there is

was gained from newspaper reports of trials which, in the outlying townships of Albany, Geraldton, Roebourne, and Bunbury were often brief, or occasionally non-existent, analysis has been limited to those trials carried out in Perth and Fremantle. Using this method forty-six of eighty-seven cases were identified as being defended at trial.

Cases were analysed to determine the percentage of defendants represented by counsel who received an acquittal compared to those found guilty, or those convicted of a lesser charge. This was compared with similar percentages for defendants who appeared unrepresented or whose defence status was unknown. Where possible, these figures were compared to Alana Piper and Mark Finnane's research into the impact of defence status on the general population of offenders in Victoria between 1861 and 1961.[11] The statistics were also interrogated to determine if retaining counsel was more effective for particular types of crime. I have used case studies to historically contextualise the data, and to gain an insight into the tactics used by defence counsel and the way in which the defence was gendered. These were constructed using information sourced from criminal indictment files and newspaper reports.[12]

Western Australian court registers did not record the names of defence counsel; however, they were often mentioned in newspaper reports of trials. It becomes obvious when examining these reports that the names of defence counsel start to appear more frequently towards the second half of the nineteenth century, which is in line with patterns of representation occurring in other colonies of Australia and in Britain.[13] Although the *Perth Gazette* stated the names of defence counsel in its reports from 1836, early reports did not specifically state whether a defendant appeared unrepresented. From 1861, defence status is noted in newspaper reports for most trials taking place in Perth and these can be

no case due to insufficient or inadequate evidence against the defendant; Damien MacRae, *Encyclopaedic Australian Legal Dictionary* (Sydney: Butterworths, 2002).

[11] Alana Jayne Piper and Mark Finnane, "Defending the Accused: The Impact of Legal Representation on Criminal Trial Outcomes in Victoria, Australia 1861–1961," *The Journal of Legal History* 38, no. 1 (2017): 27–53.

[12] Criminal indictment files, S122 cons3472, S122 cons3473, SROWA.

[13] Alana Jayne Piper and Mark Finnane, "Access to Legal Representation by Criminal Defendants in Victoria, 1861–1961," *University of New South Wales Law Journal* 40, no. 2 (2017): 656.

verified from the bench books of Chief Justice Archibald Paull Burt, where the names of the prosecuting and defending counsels are routinely noted. A comparison between newspaper reports of women's trials and the bench books shows that, over an eighteen year period, there was only one instance where the defence counsel's name did not appear in at least one news report.[14] Bench books do not exist for the period before 1861; however, during the early years of colonisation, only the few cases where the defendant could be considered as middle class are reported as being defended by counsel. Few lawyers were available in the early years of the colony and would, in any case, not have been used until after the passing of the *Prisoners' Counsel Act 1836,* 6 & 7 Wm IV (UK).[15] It is likely that many defendants in this period appeared unrepresented, especially those women from the working classes.

This is further supported by comparative research: for example, Piper and Finnane found that approximately 14% of trials which resulted in a verdict (that is, excluding *nolle prosequi* cases or those where the defendant was pronounced not fit to stand) had an unknown representation status. They note that it seems likely that a greater proportion of these were actually undefended, not only because the results mirror those of unrepresented defendants who were less likely to be acquitted and more likely to receive longer sentences, but also because newspapers were more likely to note the presence of defence counsel rather than their absence.[16] Legal scholar Peter Handford agrees, arguing that nineteenth-century newspaper reports in Western Australia almost always gave the names of the defence counsel, meaning that in cases where defence counsel are not mentioned it is unlikely that the accused used legal representation.[17] Comparison of the statistics for Western Australia for the trials before 1861 where defence status is unknown, with those after this time where defence status is reported as undefended, show that these have

[14] Archibald Paull Burt, notebooks Supreme Court criminal sittings, MN 736, 2850A 1–20, SLWA.

[15] Peter Handford, "Criminal Prosecutions in Western Australia: A View from the Nineteenth Century," *University of Western Australia Law Review* 43, no. 1 (2018): 154; Piper and Finnane, "Access to Legal Representation," 640; 6 & 7 Wm IV *Prisoners' Counsel Act 1836* (UK).

[16] Piper and Finnane, "Defending the Accused," 32, 34, 43.

[17] Handford, "Criminal Prosecutions in Western Australia," 165.

similar rates of acquittal. For these reasons, where the names of defence counsel do not appear in newspaper reports of the trial, or other sources where available, it has been assumed that the defendant appeared unrepresented. Figures for those reported as unrepresented have been conflated with those whose defence status was unknown.

The Role of Defence Counsel

When defending their clients, lawyers worked within a system of exclusionary rules, which dictated which evidence could be heard in the court. These rules of evidence included who was competent (that is, could be heard) to give evidence, which evidence was considered to be "hearsay," the conditions under which testimony from accomplices could be heard, and under what circumstances confessions could be considered to be voluntary.[18] Defendants could not give sworn evidence in court but were able to give an unsworn statement. Because these statements could not be cross-examined, they are usually quite short and were considered to be a lesser quality of evidence.[19] By 1844, in Western Australia, a defendant's previous convictions could not be used in evidence unless the defendant themself brought in evidence of good character.[20]

In cases where no defence counsel was retained, defendants had to conduct their own defence and cross-examine prosecution witnesses. Witnesses were also often questioned by the judge and sometimes even by members of the jury.[21] Although English law allowed defence counsel to address the jury from 1836, such Acts did not apply in the colonies until accepted into local legislation, and this law was not formally

[18] John M. Beattie, *Crime and the Courts in England, 1660–1800* (Princeton: Princeton University Press, 1986), 364, 365, 374; John H. Langbein, "Historical Foundations of the Law of Evidence: A View from the Ryder Sources," *Columbia Law Review* 96, no. 5 (1996): 1169; John H. Langbein, "Shaping the Eighteenth-Century Criminal Trial: A View from the Ryder Sources," *The University of Chicago Law Review* 50, no. 1 (1983): 103.

[19] Enid Russell, *A History of the Law in Western Australia and its Development from 1829 to 1879* (Nedlands: The University of Western Australia Press, 1980), 140.

[20] *Imperial Acts Adopting Act* 1844 (WA).

[21] Handford, "Criminal Prosecutions in Western Australia".

adopted in Western Australia until 1844.[22] Nevertheless, it appears that from 1836 this practice was generally adopted in Western Australia.[23]

Lawyers were present in Western Australia from its inception and were practising from the beginning of Western Australia's colonisation. In the early days, the number of men practising in the legal profession was very small, and women were not admitted to practise until the early years of the twentieth century. Most legal practitioners appeared in the civil courts but not all appeared with any regularity in the criminal courts and very few of the early criminal trials used a defence counsel.[24] The cost of hiring a defence counsel was usually covered by the defendant, albeit with some exceptions which are covered later in the chapter.

Case Study: Sarah Theodosia Hall

The first case of a female defendant to appear represented in a criminal trial in the Western Australian Court of Quarter Sessions was Sarah Theodosia Hall. Sarah, the wife of Henry Hall, was not typical of the working-class women who often appeared on criminal charges. Her husband's occupation was listed as "gentleman" on the indictment and the family belonged to the land-owning classes of the Swan River colony.[25] When the family emigrated on the *Protector* in 1830, they brought with them ten servants, livestock, farm machinery, garden and agricultural seeds, and equipment for a blacksmith's and a wheelwright's shop.[26] However, by 1834, the Halls found themselves in financial difficulties with Henry forced to request rations from the government to feed his family and servants, and, a year later, they were forced to sell many

---

22 Piper and Finnane, "Defending the Accused," 30.

23 Enid Russell, *A History of the Law in Western Australia*, 136; Handford, "Criminal Prosecutions in Western Australia," 158; see also *R v Sarah Theodosia Hall*, 3 June 1836, S122 cons3472 26 case 146, SROWA.

24 Russell, *A History of the Law in Western Australia*, 67; Handford, "Criminal Prosecutions in Western Australia," 165.

25 *R v Sarah Theodosia Hall*.

26 "A Bridgetown Pioneer," *Western Mail*, 24 October 1929, 36; H. Margaret Wilson, *Sarah Theodosia and the Hall Family* (Perth, W.A.: Margaret Wilson, 1994), 4.

of their possessions.[27] On 31 May 1836, Sarah was accused of stealing ten nightcaps and four yards of calico from the shop of Elizabeth Pace in High Street, Fremantle.[28] Sarah testified that she had visited this store with her seventeen-year-old daughter, Sarah Louisa, in order to pay a bill. Elizabeth Pace's servant, Sarah Scott, testified that Sarah Hall had asked to see some collars. Scott was absent from the room a short time while retrieving the collars but said, when she returned, she thought there was something under Sarah Hall's shawl. Emma Mould, also in service to the Pace family, related at the trial how she had seen Sarah Hall put something under her daughter's shawl and push her out the door. Scott ran after the seventeen-year-old and returned with the caps and calico.[29]

At the trial, Sarah Hall was defended by William Owen, who had arrived in the colony in 1829 and belonged to the same land-owning class as the Hall family. There is no mention in the newspapers of Owen being admitted to practise, and it is likely that he had no legal training or qualifications. In this trial, it was not only Sarah's sex that was anomalous but also her class. The trial excited considerable attention in the colony, and Owen was at pains to call attention to Sarah's class during his defence, arguing that Elizabeth Pace, her daughter and servants had conspired together, against Sarah Hall: "It was ... a conspiracy to reduce this respectable family to affliction—it was all an invention founded on falsehood and malice."[30] The Chairman of the Quarter Sessions, Henry Mackie, made reference in his address, not only to Sarah Hall's sex, but also to her class, telling the jury that "they had a painful duty to perform, from the respectability and sex of the accused."[31] Owen's defence was not successful, and Sarah Hall was convicted of larceny. The *Perth Gazette* then relates that "a flaw" was found in the indictment, although it does

---

[27] Wilson, *Sarah Theodosia*, 14; "Classified Advertising," *Perth Gazette and Western Australian Journal (PGWAJ)*, 8 August 1835, 541.

[28] *R v Sarah Theodosia Hall*; "The Western Australian Journal," *PGWAJ*, 23 January 1836, 638 "Classified Advertising," *PGWAJ*, 12 July 1845, 3; Bob Reece, "Glimpses of Fremantle," in *Voices From the West End: Stories, People and Events that Shaped Fremantle*, eds Paul Longley Arthur and Geoffrey Bolton (Welshpool: Western Australian Museum, 2012), 26.

[29] "Quarter Sessions," *PGWAJ*, 2 July 1836, 719.

[30] "Quarter Sessions," *PGWAJ*, 2 July 1836, 719; "The Western Australian Journal," *PGWAJ*, 11 June 1836, 708.

[31] "Quarter Sessions," *PGWAJ*, 2 July 1836, 719.

not state who discovered this. The indictment had recorded Elizabeth Pace's name incorrectly as "Jane." Sarah Hall was therefore discharged without being sentenced and, although she was bound to appear at the next sessions, the case was not brought up again. Owen's name does not appear in the newspapers again in relation to a criminal trial, and this case appears to be the only one he defended.

The legal profession in Western Australia remained small for many decades. In 1836 three men were formally admitted to the profession, but only William Nairn Clark, a solicitor from Scotland, and William Temple Graham, who had no legal qualifications, appeared regularly in the criminal court.[32] In 1838, Irish barrister John Schoales came out to Western Australia, followed the next year by his brother-in-law, Richard West Nash, also a solicitor. In 1841 Edward Wilson Landor was also admitted to the legal profession.[33] By 1850, although nine men had practised in the legal profession, only four remained, the others having died or left the colony, and only two practitioners, Graham and Irish solicitor Bartholomew Vigors, were known to appear in the Court of Quarter Sessions.[34] Although George Walpole Leake and Nathaniel Howell were admitted in the 1850s, Enid Russell wrote in her history of the law in Western Australia that, at this time, "There were so few legal practitioners in Perth that it was difficult to find counsel and attorneys for each side of an action."[35] By 1860, the legal profession in Western Australia was again reduced to only four practitioners, prompting the *Inquirer* to write:

> Our bar is small, without power and without influence. It is composed of four members. Of these, two hold official appointments and a third is in partnership with the Advocate-General.[36]

---

[32] Russell, *A History of the Law in Western Australia*, 100; Handford, "Criminal Prosecutions in Western Australia," 165.

[33] Russell, *A History of the Law in Western Australia*, 68; Handford, "Criminal Prosecutions in Western Australia," 165.

[34] Handford, "Criminal Prosecutions in Western Australia," 165.

[35] Russell, *A History of the Law in Western Australia*, 68.

[36] "The Inquirer & Commercial News," *ICN*, 14 November 1860, 2.

Over the next thirty years, the names appearing most frequently as defence counsel in women's trials were those of Nathaniel Howell, Stephen Henry Parker, and Septimus Burt (the son of the Chief Justice). Between 1836 and 1880, only twenty-four men had been admitted to practise.[37] In 1855, a correspondent writing to the *Perth Gazette* under the pseudonym "Vigilans" was incensed that twenty-three-year-old Nathaniel Howell, who was in practice with the Advocate-General, George Frederick Stone, defended Bridget Hurford and Enoch Dodds, in a case of murder. Vigilans maintained that it was improper for Howell to appear for the defence when his partner would be prosecuting the case.[38] The *Perth Gazette* was forced to apologise when lawyer George Walpole Leake pointed out that Howell was the only defence counsel available.[39] As late as 1877, Leake, now the Crown Solicitor, had to appear for the defence because all other members of the Bar were involved in prosecution before the magistrate.[40] There were also few lawyers practising in the outlying towns of Albany, Bunbury, Roebourne, and Geraldton although during the 1880s Alfred Farrelly defended some cases in Geraldton, and Augustus Roe and Julian Harper practised in Roebourne.[41] Such a small legal profession would have affected access to legal counsel for defendants.

[37] Handford, "Criminal Prosecutions in Western Australia," 166.

[38] "To the Editor of the Independent Journal," *Perth Gazette and Independent Journal of Politics and News (PGIJPN)*, 28 September 1855, 3.

[39] George Walpole Leake, "Correspondence," *ICN*, 3 October 1855, 3; "The Independent Journal," *PGIJPN*, 5 October 1855, 2.

[40] Handford, "Criminal Prosecutions in Western Australia," 165.

[41] For example see "Geraldton Quarter Sessions," *Victorian Express*, 4 September 1886, 5; "District News," *Victorian Express*, 28 January 1888, 3; "Supreme Court—Criminal Sittings," *West Australian*, 2 July 1885, 3.

The Impact of Defence Counsel

Verdicts

An analysis of the verdicts in women's trials indicates that representation was highly advantageous for female defendants. Just over one half of the defendants whose trials proceeded to a verdict were acquitted.[42] The acquittal rate was much higher for women who utilised defence counsel with two-thirds of represented defendants being acquitted compared to one-third of defendants who appeared unrepresented, or whose representation status was not stated (Table 3.1).[43] These figures are higher than those found by Piper and Finnane for the general population of defendants in Victoria where under one half of defendants were acquitted overall, a little over one half of defendants who were represented by counsel were acquitted and only one quarter of defendants without representation were acquitted.[44] This suggests that, although defence status was an important predictor of the likelihood of acquittal among both men and women, women overall may have had a greater chance of acquittal than men and is similar to Piper and Finnane's research which found that 58% of women in their sample were acquitted: a figure 14% higher than that of the male defendants.[45]

It is possible that, for women, part of the success of being represented in court lay in the ability to have a man speak on their behalf. The quiet and passive demeanour expected from respectable women at that time meant that the agency required to speak in their own defence could be seen as deviant behaviour and might prejudice their chances of receiving a favourable outcome at trial. Women who deviated from gendered assumptions of "respectable" femininity were seen as a dangerous to the moral order of society. As was seen in the case of Agnes Arbuckle and Mary Jane Gallagher, female defendants who exhibited agency could be mocked in newspaper reports. Women who defended themselves in

---

[42] 54 percent (n = 87) of defendants were acquitted.

[43] 70% (n = 46) of represented defendants were acquitted. 37% (n = 41) of unrepresented defendants were acquitted.

[44] Piper and Finnane, "Defending the Accused," 33.

[45] Piper and Finnane, "Defending the Accused," 37.

Table 3.1 Verdicts of female defendants by representation status

	Defended	Undefended	Unknown	Total
Guilty	13	10	12	35
Partial verdict	1	3	1	5
Not guilty	32	7	8	47
Total	46	20	21	87

Compiled from data in Mark Finnane, "Western Australia Criminal Trials 1830–1861"; Mark Finnane, "Western Australia Supreme Court 1862–1899"; "Newspapers & Gazettes," Trove, accessed 7 May 2022, https://trove.nla.gov.au/newspaper/

court were sometimes reported to have made "rambling" statements or might be denigrated by adjectives such as "vituperative" or "brazen," implying that they were unsuitably outspoken, aggressive, or unashamed, and therefore transgressed accepted feminine behaviour.[46]

Defence Counsel and Their Tactics

While some defence counsel were undoubtedly more successful than others, many defended only one or two women in the upper courts during their careers. The two who defended the greatest number of women were Nathaniel Howell, who defended seventeen women, and Henry Stephen Parker, who defended ten. Of the two, Howell was decidedly the more successful, gaining acquittals in ten cases. Howell was only twenty-one when he arrived in the colony in 1853. He entered into partnership initially with George Stone and was formally admitted in 1856.[47] He appeared in the criminal court more regularly than any other lawyer during the late fifties and early sixties, prompting the *Perth Gazette* in 1861 to write "the Quarter Sessions are a kind of saturnalia to Mr Howell, who has all the fun to himself."[48] Although Howell was not able to secure an acquittal for Bridget Hurford in 1855, he was

46 "Quarter Sessions," *PGIJPN*, 5 April 1861, 3; "Supreme Court," *PGWAT*, 7 July 1871, 3 "Insolvency Court," *Freeman's Journal*, 2 May 1874.

47 Geoffrey Bolton and Geraldine Byrne, *May It Please Your Honour: A History of the Supreme Court of Western Australia 1861–2005* (Perth: Supreme Court of Western Australia, 2005), 27.

48 Russell, *A History of the Law in Western Australia.*

more successful with those of his female clients charged with less serious offences. In 1859, he defended twelve-year-old Maria Norrish who was accused of stealing two pieces of ribbon from Thomas Dickson's store in Howick Street (later Hay Street), Perth (Fig. 3.1). Maria said that she took the ribbon "for a lark." At the committal hearing in the Perth Police Court, Howell brought in a witness, Mrs Robinson, to testify that Maria had recently moved from Kojonup to be educated at the Sisters of Mercy school in Perth and that her father was "a very respectable settler." Howell argued for leniency, not only on account of Norrish's youth, but also her "utter ignorance on the usages of society and the customs of shops."[49] While these arguments were not sufficient to have the case dismissed at the committal hearing, it is highly likely that Howell used the same arguments of youth, respectability, and ignorance when he was able to gain Norrish's acquittal later at her trial in the Court of Quarter Sessions.[50]

Unlike Howell, Stephen Henry Parker was born in the colony. Born in 1846 to Stephen Parker, a farmer and member of the Legislative Council, Stephen Henry Parker was a dashing young man, known for his sporting prowess and horse racing, in his youth. Early in his career, he gained a reputation as "the people's Harry" for his support of the underdog when he publicly criticised Chief Justice Burt's ruling against one of his clients.[51] His record of acquittal in women's trials was not so high as that of Howell, achieving five acquittals out of the ten women he defended. In 1878, Parker was called upon to defend Louisa Hearne who was charged with assault occasioning actual bodily harm. Hearne was the intimate partner of Joseph Bolitho Johns, also known as Moondyne Joe, a convict known for his numerous escapes from prison. Johns lived in Suffolk Street, Fremantle, near the notorious Old Establishment Yard. Hearne was accused of assaulting Lydia Dysart, the estranged wife of a pensioner guard, who also lived in Suffolk Street and earned her living as a washerwoman. Dysart accused Hearne of cutting her clothesline into pieces while she was attempting to hang out her washing, and of breaking

49 "Perth Police Court," *PGIJPN*, 5 August 1859, 3.

50 Finnane, "Western Australia Criminal Trials 1830–1861".

51 Wendy Birman and Geoffrey Bolton, "Parker, Sir Stephen Henry (1846–1927)," *Australian Dictionary of Biography*, accessed 7 November 2021, https://adb.anu.edu.au/biography/parker-sir-stephen-henry-7957/text13853.

Fig. 3.1 Thomas Dickson's store, from where twelve-year-old Maria Norrish stole ribbon, on the corner of Howick and Pier Streets, 1860s. None of the three women are named, but as the woman and child on the left are not wearing hats (and therefore not dressed for outdoors) they may well be Thomas's wife Bidelia Dickson and one of her daughters. The more fashionably dressed woman on the right is likely to be a customer. The photograph was taken by Alfred Hawes Stone. SLWA, 6923B/4

her window. She claimed that Hearne later hit her on the head with a bottle. This statement was supported by Dysart's next-door neighbour, Samuel Carmichael, who said he saw Hearne pass his door, heard her say to Dysart "Take that you b—" and heard Dysart groan. Dysart, who was by then crying and bleeding profusely, went to her friend, Annie Green, at the Old Establishment Yard, who helped her to the doctor. Green testified at the hearing that, after she had returned home, Johns came to her house and "offered to pay me if I would not go against Louisa Hearne at the Court."[52] Hearne's anger with Dysart might be explained by her comment to arresting officer Sergeant O'Connell: "No one can believe that old bitch. She lagged Docherty," a reference to the trial of

[52] *R v Louise Frances Hearn*, 3 July 1878, S122 cons3473 93 case 843, SROWA.

Peter Docherty three months earlier in which Dysart had appeared as a witness for the prosecution.[53]

Parker's defence strategy in this case centred around discrediting the victim. He argued that Dysart had fallen off a well and that she did so while drunk: "He considered the case was at best a drunken squabble which ought never to have come to the Court."[54] To support this argument, Johns was brought in as a defence witness.[55] His testimony does not appear in the judge's bench book but in his deposition given at the hearing he testified that both women were drunk and that he did not see Hearne hit Dysart, although he said both women were using bad language and had thrown bottles at each other on previous occasions. The defence strategy was successful, and the jury brought in a decision of "not guilty." Asserting that the victim of a crime was at fault was a common defence strategy used by barristers and was used as a defence in both property and interpersonal offences.[56] A frustrated Burt added a notation in his bench book: "Very wrong and improper verdict. Case admitting of no doubt. Note. My experience is that it is difficult to obtain verdicts against loose women."[57] Although Burt's attitude towards disorderly women is interesting, his perception of their conviction rate may be incorrect. During his time as Chief Justice, the majority of women tried in the Supreme Court who were known to be recidivists, engaged in sex work, or had received a "bad character," were convicted.

In cases of larceny, defence counsel might attempt to discredit a plaintiff's claim to ownership of stolen goods, knowing that juries were reluctant to convict when ownership of stolen articles could not be proven.[58] In 1841, Maria Smith was charged with the theft of a shirt from her employer, Robert Viveash of Yangedine near York, 90 kilometres east of Perth. Viveash's shirt had the initials "SV" embroidered into it. He claimed that these had been partly picked out and also that Maria

---

[53] *R v Louise Frances Hearn*; "Supreme Court—Criminal Side," *Herald*, 6 April 1878, 3.

[54] "Supreme Court-Criminal Side," *Herald*, 6 July 1878, 3.

[55] Calendar, 3 July 1876, S122 cons3473 93, SROWA.

[56] Piper and Finnane, "Defending the Accused," 49.

[57] Burt, notebooks, MN 736, 2850A 19, SLWA.

[58] Alana Jayne Piper, "In Bad Company: Female Criminal Subcultures in Brisbane and Melbourne, 1860–1920" (PhD diss., University of Queensland, 2013), 79.

had access to his bedroom where his shirts were kept because part of her duties included making his bed. Maria argued that the shirt had been given to her by Dr William Sholl who, like Maria and her family, had travelled to the colony from England in 1840 aboard the *Shepherd*.[59] At her trial, Maria was defended by Schoales whose defence "dwelt chiefly on the ground of defective evidence as to the identity of the shirt" and also the fact that Maria had sold the shirt to Elizabeth Quartermaine, another of Viveash's servants, indicating that Maria was not attempting to hide her possession of it. This tactic proved successful, and Maria was acquitted at her trial in 1841.[60]

Researchers have referred to a "blurred line" between servants' expectations of being able to "borrow" objects belonging to their employers and employers' expectations regarding their ownership of these objects.[61] This was echoed in the Sarah King case in 1848 when shopkeeper Lionel Samson of Perth accused his shopman, George Wood, and domestic servant, Sarah King, of stealing tea, sugar, soap, pepper, vinegar, wine, and spirits from his shop. Wood was charged with stealing and King with receiving. During the trial Samson's nursemaid, Eliza Flaherty, gave evidence for the defence. She said that she and King were given an allowance of soap from Samson's wife, Fanny, for household use but considered it allowable to keep any leftover soap for themselves. She also stated that the tea allowance given to them by Samson was "undrinkable" and that she and King would pool their money to buy their tea from the store. The prosecution brought in a witness, Chinese servant Ah Fat, to testify that he had seen Wood take parcels from the store to give to King. This evidence had to be translated for the court by another of Samson's servants, Ah Ping.[62]

---

59 *R v Maria Smith*, 4 December 1841, S122 cons3472 50 case 255, SROWA; "Shipping Intelligence," *Inquirer*, 25 November 1840, 66; Rica Erickson, *The Bicentennial Dictionary of Western Australians*, vol. 4 (Nedlands: University of Western Australia Press, 1988), 2109.

60 "Quarter Sessions," *PGWAJ*, 8 January 1842, 2.

61 Shani D'Cruze and Louise A. Jackson, *Women, Crime and Justice in England since 1660* (Basingstoke, U.K.: Palgrave Macmillan, 2009), 36.

62 *R v George Wood and Sarah King*, 4 October 1848, S122 cons3472 78 case 424, SROWA; Jan Ryan, *Ancestors: Chinese in Colonial Australia* (Fremantle: Fremantle Arts Centre Press, 1995), 109.

King and Wood were defended by Richard Nash. Although the *Gazette* did not elaborate on Nash's defence strategy, Samson took the unusual step of publicly voicing his dissatisfaction in the newspapers. Shortly after the trial, Samson sent an angry letter to the *Inquirer* complaining that Nash's defence meant that domestic servants could keep for themselves any surplus supplies given to them for household use.[63] Samson clearly considered this as theft. Nash's reply called Samson's claims "ludicrous" and stated that his argument was concerned with servants' rights to reimbursement:

> If a servant receives stores for the use of the house whenever required, any surplus is the property of the master—BUT if, as was proved in the present case, the master furnish only rations, too short at one season, obliging the servant, with her own money, to buy more to make up the deficiency for his service, then the servant has a right to the surplus of another season to reimburse herself.[64]

This argument obviously convinced the jury, but not Samson, who sent another letter to the *Inquirer* complaining that his, and not Nash's, version of the trial was correct and stating that he would treat Nash's "invectives with the contempt I entertain for himself."[65]

It can be seen from these examples that defences for women accused of crime were varied. Lawyers would use legal arguments, and the status and "respectability" of defendants, when they could, or, if unable to do this, might instead attempt to discredit the complainant. Charges of theft against domestic servants were common but did not always result in a conviction. If the ownership of the stolen articles could not be proven or employers were seen to be treating their servants unfairly, these charges could end in an acquittal.

---

[63] Lionel Samson, "Correspondence," *Inquirer*, 11 October 1848, 3.

[64] R.W. Nash, "Correspondence," *Inquirer*, 18 October 1848, 4.

[65] Samson, "Correspondence," *Inquirer*, 25 October 1848, 4.

Type of Crime

While the statistics indicate that the use of defence counsel was advantageous for defendants overall, was this advantage consistent over different crime types? Analysis of the evidence shows that while the use of defence counsel was clearly advantageous for women accused of property offences, it may have been less so for the smaller number of women accused of interpersonal crime. Of the twenty-two women indicted for crimes against the person, ten were acquitted. The acquittal rate was the same for both represented and unrepresented defendants, with half of the defendants being acquitted, regardless of their representation status (Table 3.2). These numbers may have been influenced by the high proportion of murder cases. Seven women were tried for murder or attempted murder, and all but one of these were tried with a male co-defendant. The exception was Jane Green, who was indicted for "the murder of her infant child" and was the only defendant tried as a solo accused. Although another six women appeared in court following the death of their newly born children, these cases were indicted for concealment of birth rather than murder. Of the seven murder cases, only two women were acquitted.[66] It is harder to prove self-defence, accident, or provocation, the usual defences to murder, if more than one defendant is involved, and juries may have been more likely to consider killings involving two or more defendants as intentional.[67]

Case Study: Mary Watkins

The second case to be acquitted of murder was that of *R v Hicks and another*, where Mary Watkins was indicted for aiding and abetting Charles Hicks in the murder of Charles Jones at Kojonup in 1882.[68]

---

[66] *R v Mumbleby and Belo*, January 1865, S122 cons3473 28 no. 64, SROWA; *R v Hicks and another*, 4 October 1882, S122 cons3473 114 case 1014, SROWA.

[67] Mark Finnane and Andy Kaladelfos, "Race and Justice in an Australian Court: Prosecuting Homicide in Western Australia, 1830–1954," *Australian Historical Studies* 47, no. 3 (2016): 454.

[68] *R v Hicks and another*.

Table 3.2 Verdicts in criminal trials by representation status—Perth and Fremantle, 1830–1890

	Property			Personal		
	Guilty	Partial	Not guilty	Guilty	Partial	Not guilty
Defended	7	2	24	3	1	5
Undefended	6	1	3	4	2	4
Unknown	10		7	1	1	1
Totals	23	3	34	8	4	10

Compiled from data in Finnane, "Western Australia Criminal Trials 1830–1861"; Finnane, "Western Australia Supreme Court 1862–1899"; Newspapers and Gazettes; Archibald Paull Burt, notebooks Supreme Court criminal sittings, MN 736 acc 2850A, SLWA

The case is significant for the light it throws on the role of gender in the outcome of women's trials. Mary's childhood was not easy. Her father, John Luff, was a convict, sentenced to fifteen years in 1848 for horse theft, and transported from England to Western Australia.[69] Luff, a labourer who lived in Huntington, England, asserted at the time that he had stolen only to relieve his family's poverty.[70] The Luff family was one the few convict families to take advantage of the scheme available for bringing out the wives and families of convicts.[71] In 1852, three-year-old Mary emigrated to the colony with her mother and two siblings on board the *Anne Maclean*.[72] When Mary was eleven years old, her father was killed in a tragic accident. While attempting to help a neighbour who had been buried while digging a well in the loose sand of the Swan River Plain, Luff was himself buried, both men dying in the accident. Mary's mother was left destitute with a family of six children and a debt of £30 owing on the estate, some of which was due to the government for the family's passage to the colony.[73] In a second tragic twist, Mary's mother

69 Character book, convict registers, 1850–1857, S5056 cons1156 R17, SROWA.

70 General register, convict registers, S5056 cons1156 R21A, SROWA.

71 R.T. Appleyard, "Western Australia: Economic and Demographic Growth, 1850–1914," in *A New History of Western Australia*, ed. C. T. Stannage (Nedlands: University of Western Australia Press, 1981), 213.

72 Passenger lists of assisted emigrants, 1851–1867, AN 371 acc 115, SROWA.

73 "Local and Domestic Intelligence," *ICN*, 10 October 1860, 2.

died of tuberculosis several months after her husband.[74] The children were divided among local families, with Mary and her younger sister, Harriett, staying with farmer Richard Davis.[75]

By the time she was sixteen, Mary was working as a domestic servant for the school mistress of Perth Girls School, Ann Veall. Also in the household was Veall's younger brother, twenty-year-old Thomas Flindell. When it became obvious that Mary was pregnant and shortly to give birth she was sent to live with her older sister, Betsy Cook, in Fremantle. When Betsy was unable to support Mary, Henry Symmonds, Resident Magistrate of Fremantle, organised for Mary to be sent to the Poor House in Perth for the birth of her child. In his letter, Symmonds placed the blame for Mary's predicament squarely on Flindell, stating that she had been "seduced by Thomas Flindell," and asking that he be compelled "to provide for the expenses necessarily incurred."[76] Fathers were legally responsible for the support of their wives and children, both legitimate and illegitimate, and the Poor House was anxious to recover costs.[77] Thomas and Mary were married in 1869 and, by 1874, were living in Kojonup, where Thomas worked as a blacksmith.[78] Thomas died five years later after being kicked by a horse while travelling between

[74] "Alma and Skinner Street Burial Records," City of Fremantle, accessed 6 May 2022, https://www.fremantle.wa.gov.au/sites/default/files/Alma%20and%20Skinner%20Street%20Burial%20Records%201831%20-%201899.pdf; Death, Mary Ann Luft [sic] no. 1459, Fremantle, 1860, "Online Index Search Tool," Department of Justice, accessed 28 February 2023, https://www.wa.gov.au/organisation/department-of-justice/online-index-search-tool.

[75] "Local and Domestic Intelligence," *ICN*, 10 October 1860, 2; Zachary Barry, "Correspondence," *ICN*, 5 December 1860, 2; Government Resident Fremantle to Colonial Secretary, 5 September 1863, S2941 cons36 524 39, SROWA.

[76] Resident Magistrate Fremantle to Colonial Secretary, 25 June 1868, S2941 cons36 618 198, SROWA.

[77] *Ordinance to Provide for the Relief of Deserted Wives and Children 1845* (WA); Penelope Hetherington, *Paupers, Poor Relief and Poor Houses in Western Australia 1829–1910* (Crawley, W.A.: UWA Publishing, 2009), 62.

[78] Marriage, Thomas Shenstone Flindell to Mary Luff, no. 2980, 1869, Fremantle, "Online Index Search Tool," Department of Justice, accessed 10 June 2023, https://www.wa.gov.au/organisation/department-of-justice/online-index-search-tool; Merle Bignall, *First the Spring: A History of the Shire of Kojonup, Western Australia* (Nedlands: University of Western Australia Press, 1892), 115.

Kojonup and Albany.[79] Horses were the primary mode of transport in nineteenth-century Australia, and horse-related accidents were not uncommon; sometimes, as in Thomas's case, they were fatal.[80] The next year Mary married one of Thomas's employees, a fifty-year-old wheelwright named John Watkins.[81] On 15 September 1882, Mary Watkins was at home in Kojonup with her six children. Also in the house with them was her husband John and two employees: blacksmith Charles Hicks and labourer Charles Jones. Both employees slept in a detached room of the house but ate their meals with the family. Later that evening Jones was found dead in the house, killed by a ball fired from a gun, with a knife lying on the ground nearby. Both Mary and Hicks were arrested: Hicks for murder and Mary for aiding and abetting the murder.[82]

Much of the information of the events of that night comes from the testimony of Mary's oldest daughter, 15-year-old Mary Charlotte Flindell, at the trial, which took place in Perth on 5 October. She testified that Jones asked her mother for money, which her mother gave to him. He was later seen drinking in the Kojonup Inn. Later that evening, when Mary's daughter set the table, she said she missed a knife and told John Watkins. While the family was eating supper, Jones again came to the house and this time asked John Watkins for money. When Watkins refused, Mary's daughter said Jones made a threat saying, "This knife, a deed of blood."[83]

After supper, John Watkins left the house to enlist the help of the police. He told his wife to lock the doors and not to let Jones into the house in his absence. At the police station, he reported Jones's threatening behaviour to Police Constable William McCreery and threatened to shoot Jones if he returned to the house that night "as he did not want

---

79 Death, Thomas Flindell, no. 10170, 1879, Department of Justice, "Online Index Search Tool," accessed 7 January 2023, https://www.wa.gov.au/organisation/department-of-justice/online-index-search-tool; "Official Notifications," *Western Australian Times*, 4 October 1878, 2; "Western Australian Bank," *ICN*, 16 July 1879, 3; "Notes from the Port," *ICN*, 23 July 1879, 3.

80 Catie Gilchrist, *Murder, Misadventure and Miserable Ends: Tales from a Colonial Coroner's Court* (Sydney: HarperCollins Publishers, 2019), 231.

81 "Supreme Court—Civil Sittings," *West Australian*, 21 April 1882, 3.

82 *R v Hicks and another*.

83 "Law Intelligence," *Daily News (DN)*, 5 October 1882, 3; *R v Hicks and another*.

a second Newcastle Jack affair."[84] Newcastle Jack was the name given to ex-convict John Fawell, a shearer who, in 1878, assaulted Thomas Phillips, the Kojonup publican, and three other people, with an axe, after a heavy bout of drinking.[85] Mary's daughter said that as soon as Watkins left the house, she pushed the wooden bolts across all three doors. Jones returned saying, "All's well so far, but it won't be in a few minutes."[86] He told Mary to let him in but she refused. He said, "I will have the bloody door open."[87] As Jones broke open the back door, Mary's daughter said she saw her mother go into the bedroom, retrieve her father's gun, and hand it to Hicks. "She told Hicks to fire." Mary's daughter said "I was so frightened I scarcely knew what I was doing."[88] She opened the front door and fled into the night.

McCreery related how he had seen Mary's daughter when on his way up to the house. She shouted "Come quick, for Charles Jones has broken into the house and will kill my mother and sisters."[89] McCreery walked as quickly as he could towards the house but, when close by, he met John Watkins, who told him he was too late; Jones had been shot dead by Hicks. On his arrival at the house, McCreery said he found Jones's body inside the house and a knife, just outside the door and about three feet from the body (Fig. 3.2).[90] Although neither Hicks nor Mary Watkins were defended at the committal hearing, both had defence counsel during the trial. Mary was defended by Septimus Burt and Hicks by Nathaniel Howell.

From the beginning, counsel tried to show that Mary exhibited the characteristics of femininity expected of "respectable" women. Howell was able to elicit from Dr John Rosselloty, Resident Magistrate of Williams, that he considered Mary Watkins to be "anything but a strong-minded woman; she is very thin and nervous" and that Hicks was "rather

84 *R v Hicks and another.*

85 "Summary for the Colonies," *Western Australian Times*, 22 November 1878, 2; "Local Topics," *Eastern Districts Chronicle*, 23 November 1878, 2.

86 "Law Intelligence," *DN*, 5 October 1882, 3.

87 *R v Hicks and another.*

88 "Law Intelligence," *DN*, 5 October 1882, 3.

89 *R v Hicks and another.*

90 *R v Hicks and another.*

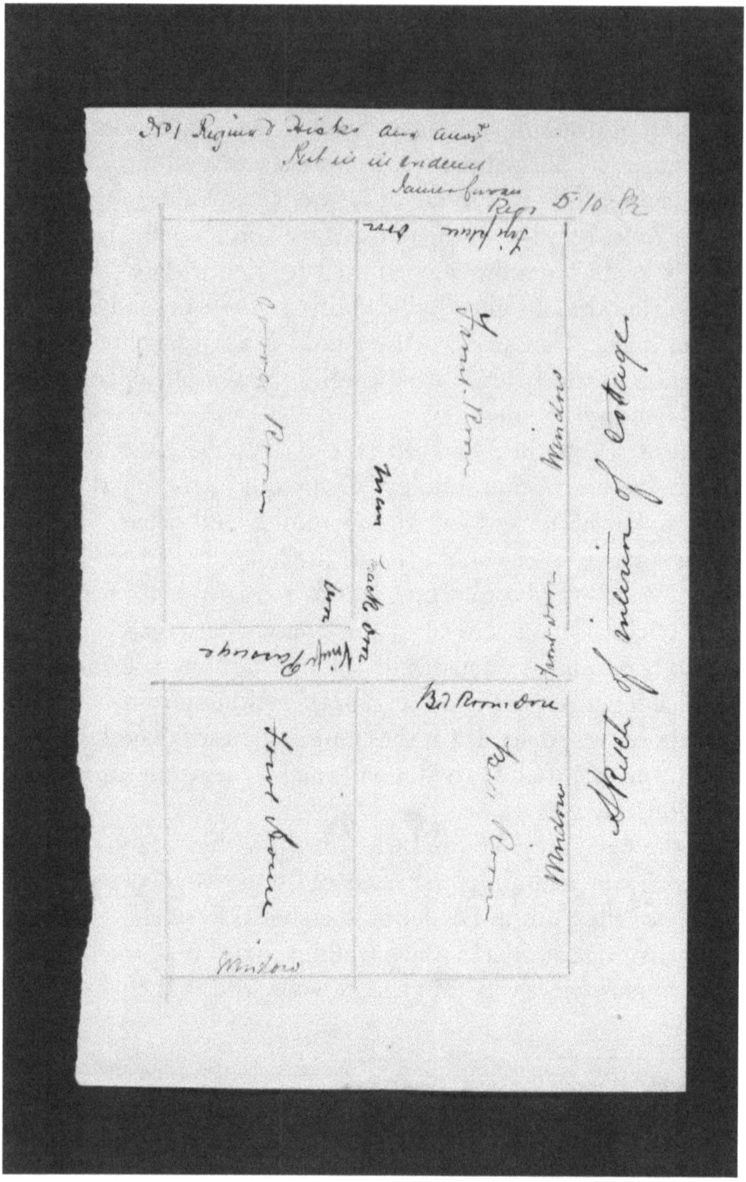

Fig. 3.2 Plan of the Watkins cottage, presented in evidence in 1882, showing the position of the body, the doors, and the knife. Courtesy SROWA, *R v Hicks and another*, 4 October 1882, S122 cons3473 114

a soft simple-minded young man."[91] In his address to the jury, Septimus Burt made a point of noting that Mary's daughter had provided dinner for Jones, even though Jones was "away from time to time, neglecting his work."[92] This testimony not only showed that Mary exhibited the frailty expected of women, but also demonstrated that she had carried out her responsibility as a "good" woman by ensuring that food was provided for Jones, a member of the household.

Much of the defence relied on assessing Jones's character. The court heard testimony from two prosecution witnesses who testified that Jones was a quiet man whom they had never known to act in a violent manner. McCreery said that Jones was "only violent in words."[93] However, the depositions from the committal hearing contain a statement from Thomas Chipper, a farmer of Kojonup, stating that he had heard Jones make uncouth comments behind John Watkins's back, had said that he had been "half-shaved" and that he heard Jones say several times that he would stab any man who robbed him. Chipper testified that he had advised Watkins to "get rid of him or they would be sorry."[94] By including Chipper's evidence, the defence was attempting to demonstrate that Jones could be dangerous; he did not meet gendered assumptions of "respectable" masculinity, where men were expected to eschew violence and instead embrace the concepts of self-control and self-discipline.[95]

Just as deviation from gendered assumptions of femininity could cause a jury to view female defendants as "dangerous," so also might the behaviour of male victims affect the jury's verdict. The performance of respectable masculinity by men *before* they were killed could mediate the juries' response in these cases. Men who ignored social constructions of masculinity prejudiced their right to be considered as victims.[96] In cases where the victim failed to meet gendered assumptions of respectable

[91] "Law Intelligence," *DN*, 5 October 1882, 3.

[92] *R v Hicks and another*.

[93] "Law Intelligence," *DN*, 5 October 1882, 3.

[94] *R v Hicks and another*. Jones appears to have used to term "half shaved" here to mean "cheated".

[95] Anette Ballinger, "Masculinity in the Dock: Legal Responses to Male Violence and Female Retaliation in England and Wales, 1900–1965," *Social & Legal Studies* 16, no. 4 (2007): 463.

[96] Ballinger, "Masculinity in the Dock," 462.

masculinity before their death, women accused of murder were more likely to receive a favourable outcome at trial. However, whereas violence by men towards "respectable" women, who appeared quiet, passive, and vulnerable, was seen as unmanly, violence directed at working-class women who were deemed "bad," might be treated less seriously.[97]

The *Daily News* was effusive in its praise for Howell's address to the jury, stating that he made a "most excellent and able defence, quoting several precedents from *Russell on Crimes*."[98] Both Howell and Burt argued that this was a case of "excusable homicide," citing the threats made by Jones and the fact that he had broken into the house, meaning that Mary and Hicks were in fear of their lives. Despite Chief Justice Henry Wrenfordsley's cross-examination of Rosselloty, which elicited the information that "Hicks could easily have taken up Jones and turned him out," and Wrenfordsley's summing up, in which he stated that Mary Watkins "wantonly took a gun and gave it to Hicks," the jury acquitted both defendants.[99]

Mary found herself in straitened economic circumstances over the next few years and was forced to accept outdoor relief to support herself and her children.[100] Despite this, there is no evidence that she ever appeared as a defendant in court again. Although Mary's childhood was marked by poverty and tragedy, and despite giving birth to a child while unmarried, it seems that, like many other women in this study, this was the one and only time she was charged with a crime. When her second husband died, she remarried, this time choosing a well-to-do farmer, and appeared to live out the rest of her life in relative prosperity.

---

[97] David G. Barrie and Susan Broomhall, *A History of Police and Masculinities, 1700–2010* (London: Routledge, 2012), 96.

[98] "Law Intelligence," *DN*, 5 October 1882, 3. Refers to a well-known law book "*Treatise on Crimes and Misdemeanours*" by William Oldnall Russell.

[99] "Law Intelligence," *DN*, 5 October 1882, 3. William Blackstone defined excusable homicide as a killing which had taken place in self-defence or in the defence of another family member; William Blackstone, *Commentaries on the Laws of England*, vol. 2 (Oxford: Clarendon press, 1765–1769), 184–86.

[100] Rev J. Withers to Colonial Secretary, 27 February 1884, S675 cons527 1884/1266, SROWA; Mary Watkins to Colonial Secretary, 1 August 1887, S675 cons527 1887/2786, SROWA.

Mercy Riders and Partial Verdicts

While it is clear that the use of defence counsel was advantageous for accused in terms of the verdict, retaining counsel might also have advantages for those who were found guilty. Although juries were not responsible for the sentence given to those they convicted, they could exercise a limited degree of control over sentencing by adding a rider recommending mercy to their verdict or by finding the defendant guilty of a lesser crime (sometimes termed a "partial verdict").[101] Recommendations to mercy might be taken into account by judges when deciding on sentencing, or by the Executive Council in capital cases. Convicted female defendants in this dataset, who were represented by counsel, had a higher chance of receiving a recommendation to mercy than those who appeared unrepresented. Over one quarter of the represented cases who were found guilty were recommended to mercy by the jury, compared to a little over one tenth of those who were undefended, or whose defence status was unknown.[102] Piper and Finnane found a similar situation in their study, noting that convicted defendants who were represented by counsel were 1.6 times more likely to be recommended to mercy than those unrepresented.[103] This suggests that defence counsel may have been better able to convince the jury of mitigating factors in the defendant's case, such as illness, youth, or penury, than the defendants could alone.

The case of Margaret Farmer illustrates the types of gendered arguments that might be used by counsel in an effort to persuade the jury to exercise leniency towards a client. In 1844 Margaret Farmer, the wife of shoemaker, Patrick, was charged with shoplifting from the store of Frederick Croft. At Croft's store, situated at 4 St George's Terrace in Perth, residents could purchase anything from "prime Irish pork and butter"

---

[101] Richard G. Fox, "When Justice Sheds a Tear: The Place of Mercy in Sentencing," *Monash University Law Review* 25, no. 1 (1999): 9; John M. Beattie, "Crime and the Courts in Surrey 1736–1753," in *Crime in England: 1550–1800*, ed. J.S. Cockburn (London: Routledge, 2015), 170.

[102] 29 percent (n = 14) of represented cases received mercy recommendations. 12 percent (n = 26) of unrepresented cases received mercy recommendations.

[103] Piper and Finnane, "Defending the Accused," 34.

to gunney bags, or choose from an "assortment of linen drapery."[104] Margaret, who had the stated intention of purchasing some tape, tapped on the store's counter to attract attention. When Croft arrived to serve her, he asked her to take a pair of boots to her husband to mend but was suspicious when Margaret refused to carry the boots in her basket, instead holding out a handkerchief to wrap them in. A search of the basket uncovered a mousseline de laine (light woollen) dress and a piece of soap, both of which he identified as being from his shop. Margaret's statement, that his assistant, Charlotte Stone, had placed the items in her basket as a present, was denied by Stone and not believed by the jury.[105] She was indicted for larceny at the next Quarter Sessions, where she was defended by Schoales who called the Colonial Surgeon, Joseph Harris, to testify that Margaret was soon to give birth and that "confinement in a gaol would add much to the dangers of childbirth."[106] This was to be Margaret's tenth child. While the presence of the dress and soap in Margaret's basket was taken as proof of guilt by the jury, they included a rider recommending her to mercy. The magistrates sentenced her to six months with "labour suited to sex" and Margaret's child, Catherine, was born while she was in Fremantle Gaol.[107] Sadly, the Colonial Surgeon was proved correct, and Catherine died twenty-four hours later from a "malformation of the throat."[108] Newborn life was precarious in the nineteenth century, and the deaths of young children were not uncommon.[109] It is not known whether Catherine's birth in Fremantle Gaol contributed to her death. While, in this case, we don't know the reasons for the jury's mercy rider, it is likely that Margaret's obvious pregnancy, and the Colonial Surgeon's testimony, was instrumental in their decision.

---

104 "Classified Advertising," *PGWAJ*, 20 May 1843, 1.

105 *R v Margaret Farmer*, 3 July 1844, S122 cons3472 62 case 305, SROWA.

106 "Quarter Sessions," *PGWAJ*, 6 July 1844, 3; "From the Government Gazette," *PGWAJ*, 11 February 1843, 4.

107 "Quarter Sessions," *PGWAJ*, 6 July 1844, 3; Birth, Catherine Farmer no. 125, Fremantle Jail [*sic*], 1844, Department of Justice, "Online Index Search Tool," accessed 7 January 2023, https://www.wa.gov.au/organisation/department-of-justice/online-index-search-tool.

108 Death certificate, Catherine Farmer no. 442, Fremantle Jail [sic], 1844.

109 Jan Kociumbas, "Azaria's Antecedents: Stereotyping Infanticide in Late Nineteenth-Century Australia," *Gender & History* 13, no.1 (2001): 140.

Sentencing

Could the use of defence counsel increase a defendant's chance of a shorter sentence? Today, those who plead guilty to a crime are given a sentence reduction by the judiciary, usually as a result of "plea bargaining" between defence and prosecuting counsel. There is insufficient data available to determine whether this also applied for women in nineteenth-century Western Australia, but this type of plea bargaining does not seem to have been present in Australian trials until later in the twentieth century.[110] It is clear that at least some of the women were able to consult with their defence counsel before the trial. Although counsel advised a few women to plead guilty, available evidence does not indicate a relation between a guilty plea and leniency in sentencing.[111]

In the case of the most serious crime of murder, defence status was immaterial to sentence length as this crime attracted a mandatory sentence of death. Analysis of the less serious crimes shows that, overall, female defendants who pleaded not guilty, and were represented by counsel, attracted less custodial time than those who appeared without this benefit. The average sentence length for represented defendants was 7.4 months, whereas the average sentence for those appearing unrepresented was sixteen months. However, this strong association between defence status and sentence length does not hold if a few anomalous sentences are discounted. While the majority of custodial sentences were for periods of less than two years, four stand out as particularly severe. Keziah Lockyer received a sentence of seven years' transportation "over the seas" for perjury, Mary Trubee received a fifteen-year transportation sentence for arson, and Mary Jane Hayes and Jane Dyson both received

[110] Lisa Durnian, "The Rise of the Guilty Plea in Australian Supreme Courts: A History" (PhD diss., Griffith University, 2018), 12.

[111] For example see "Supreme Court-Criminal Sittings," *Western Australian Times*, 9 October 1874, 3; "Monday, April 4," *ICN*, 6 April 1887, 3; "Law Intelligence," *ICN*, 13 October 1875, 1. Once outliers were removed, the average sentence length for women who pleaded guilty (n = 16) was 7.8 months, compared to 7.3 months for those who pleaded not guilty (n = 31). While it would be interesting to look at sentence length against guilty plea while controlling for offence type, the number of guilty pleas for interpersonal crimes (n = 2) does not allow this.

sentences of five years' penal servitude for theft.[112] It is significant that these last two sentences were handed down by Justice Edward Stone, who was appointed as a judge in 1883. Archibald Burt, who was the sole judge of the Supreme Court from 1861 to 1879, never handed down a sentence of greater than twelve months to a woman accused of theft. When these four outliers are removed, the figures show a more similar length of custodial sentence with unrepresented defendants receiving an average sentence of six months and represented defendants receiving a sentence of 7.3 months.

The following two cases of perjury, although receiving similar verdicts, nonetheless indicate a disparity in sentencing between defended and undefended cases. When Bridget Landy was charged with perjury in 1871, she was defended by Stephen Henry Parker. The case was the result of a statement made by Bridget the previous year in the local court. As a result of a claim by Henry Seeligson against blacksmith Edwin Moorhouse, the bailiff had seized various blacksmithing tools from Bridget's house in Wandering, claiming that they belonged to Moorhouse. Bridget, represented by Parker, took out an interpleader summons against the bailiff, claiming that these tools belonged to her, were bought with her own money, and that she did not cohabit with Moorhouse. After further investigation by the police, Bridget was tried for perjury in the Supreme Court where Parker tried to argue that the trial should not proceed because of an informality in the interpleader summons and because a second witness had not been provided to prove the charge of perjury.[113] Nonetheless, Bridget was convicted when witnesses testified that she was living with Moorhouse "as his wife," and she received a sentence of twelve months' imprisonment with hard labour.[114]

---

112 Criminal Indictment Register 1, 1830–1887, S49 cons3422 01, SROWA. When sentencing a defendant to a sentence of transportation, the destination was not usually stated by the judge; this was the responsibility of the sheriff.

113 *R v Bridget Landy*, 4 January 1871, S122 cons3473 54 case 411, SROWA; "Supreme Court," *Express*, 7 January 1871, The *Encyclopaedic Australian Legal Dictionary* defines interpleader as "A proceeding to determine the rights of claimants, by which a person who is sued regarding some property or debt can require competing claimants to that property or debt to resolve their rights"; MacRae, *Encyclopaedic Australian Legal Dictionary*.

114 *R v Bridget Landy*; Criminal indictment files, January 1871, S122 cons3473 54, SROWA.

There was no defence lawyer to argue for Keziah Lockyer when she was charged with perjury in 1839. In a previous case, Keziah had denied saying to her employer, William Temple Graham, "You have had enough of me and now you want to make a whore of my daughter."[115] Indeed, it would have been difficult to find a lawyer to take her case as both Graham and Clark were involved in the case. Although Keziah denied the charge, at trial her two daughters could not, or would not, confirm her testimony.[116] Keziah was sentenced to seven years' transportation but was ultimately granted a pardon by Governor John Hutt, on condition of her "voluntarily transporting herself beyond the seas for the term of her natural life."[117] On 19 April 1839, Keziah departed for Van Diemen's Land on board the *Socrates* where she disappears from the colonial records.[118] While it is impossible to know whether Parker's legal arguments influenced Burt's sentencing of Bridget Landy, it is possible that the use of defence counsel may have resulted in shorter sentences for those convicted of the more serious offences, excepting capital cases. However, the figures indicate that for the less serious charges of theft and larceny the presence of defence counsel did not materially affect the length of a custodial sentence for female defendants.

Unlike in Western Australia, where defence counsel seemed to make little difference to the length of sentence in the majority of cases for women, Piper and Finnane's study found that, for the general population of offenders charged with property crimes in Victoria, representation was generally beneficial with regard to sentencing. The average length of sentence was generally less for those who were represented at trial, although there was little disparity in sentencing for those charged with interpersonal offences.[119] The disparity between this research and that of Piper and Finnane could be due to the greater proportion of women's crime being of a less serious nature than male crime, and further research into men's offending in Western Australia may confirm this.

---

[115] *R v Keziah Lockyer*, April 1839, S122 cons3472 37 case 187, SROWA.

[116] "Quarter Sessions," *PGWAJ*, 6 April 1839, 54.

[117] Warrant, 12 April 1839, S2755 cons49 10 235, SROWA.

[118] "Shipping Intelligence," *PGWAJ*, 20 April 1839, 62.

[119] Piper and Finnane, "Defending the Accused," 43.

Piper and Finnane also found that those cases which were defended had a slightly greater chance of being simply dismissed.[120] While there are insufficient cases which were discharged or dismissed in this study to allow a pattern to be discerned, the case of Alice Hammond is worthy of examination. Alice appeared in the Court of Quarter Sessions in 1875 having been charged with forging Alexander Forrest's signature on a cheque, which she then used to purchase a lamp from George Ingleton's store in Murray Street, Perth. The signature was badly forged, Alice spelling Forrest's name incorrectly, and the cheque was returned when Ingleton presented it at the National Bank.[121] At her trial Alice was described as "a young woman, … very respectably connected" and "a rather nice-looking young woman, and neatly attired."[122] She was represented by Nathaniel Howell who had advised her to plead guilty. Howell made an impassioned appeal to the jury arguing for mercy on account of Alice's youth, inexperience, and her contrition for the "disgrace" she had brought on herself and her family. Arguments for mercy may have been received more favourably by the jury when delivered by the defence counsel, rather than the defendant, as the agency required to deliver the speech may have negated arguments of youth and inexperience. At Chief Justice Burt's request the plea was not entered, and Burt discharged Alice after questioning Henry Hocking, the Attorney-General.[123] Burt stated in his notes that to gain a conviction it was necessary to prove "an intent to defraud," which would not be possible if Alice had acquired the cheque legally.[124] Two years later she found herself in trouble again when she stole a cheque sent to her mother and, in 1907, her name became a household word when, as Alice Mitchell, she was tried for the murder of baby Ethel Booth in a notorious baby farming case.[125] It was shown

120 Piper and Finnane, "Defending the Accused," 43.

121 *R v Alice Hammond*, 6 October 1875, S122 cons3473 79 case 711, SROWA.

122 "Alleged Forgery," *ICN*, 22 September 1875, 2; "Law Intelligence," *ICN*, 13 October 1875, 1.

123 "Law Intelligence," *ICN*, 13 October 1875, 1.

124 Burt, notebooks, MN 736, 2850A 16, SLWA.

125 "The Perth Horrors," *Truth*, 7 April 1907, 9; "The Alleged Defalcations in the Geraldton Post Office," *ICN*, 7 November 1877, 2.

at her trial that thirty-seven of the forty-three children she had cared for had died (Fig. 3.3).[126]

R v Alice Hammond was one of only two cases in the study where a female defendant was discharged at the direction of the judge. It is not possible to know how much Burt's decision was influenced by Alice's perceived respectability or by Howell's plea for mercy on the grounds of youth, inexperience, and contrition. Would Burt have made the same decision had the defendant been older, male, or one of the women recognised as belonging to the criminal underclass? Would he have made the same decision if the crime had taken place a year and a half earlier when Alice was pregnant and unmarried?[127] While it is not possible to answer

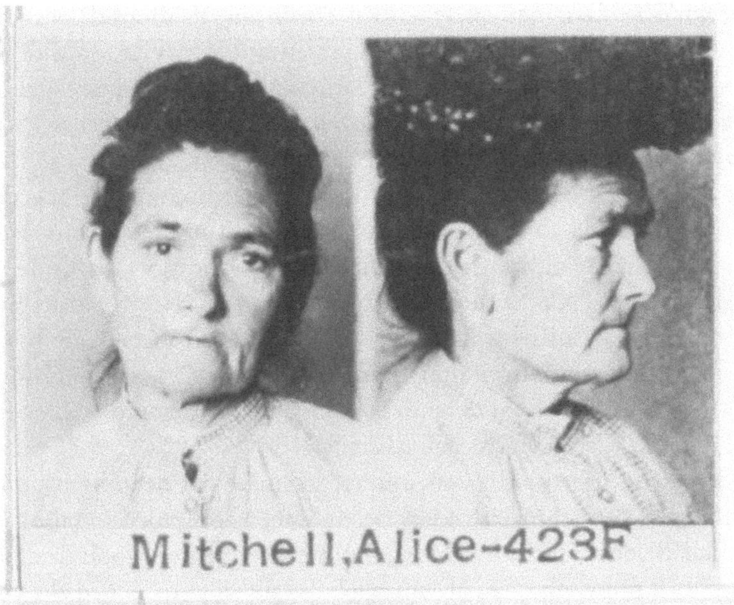

Fig. 3.3 Alice Mitchell (previously Hammond), 1907. Courtesy SROWA, Fremantle Prison Register, 1907, cons4186 2

126 Penelope Hetherington, "Baby-Farming in Western Australia: The Case Against Alice Mitchell," *Studies in Western Australian History* 25 (1907): 89–90.

127 Stella Budrikis, *The Edward Street Baby Farm* (Fremantle: Fremantle Press, 2020), 32; Birth, Eveline May Hammond no. 15500, 1874, Perth, Department of Justice, "Online Index

these questions, it seems probable that Burt may have been influenced by the combination of Howell's address to the jury and Alice's "respectable" appearance.

Access to Counsel

Presumably, defendants who took advantage of defence counsel did so to increase their chances of an advantageous outcome at trial. This brings to the forefront the question of access to counsel. This is significant as it brings into question equity of justice in the upper courts. The cost of hiring defence counsel could be high and, as the majority of defendants were working class, many may not have been able to afford defence. Piper and Finnane's research shows that representation in Victoria was always below 60% during the nineteenth century, although this increased in the twentieth century due partly to the introduction of the *Poor Prisoners Defence Act* 1916 (Vic).[128] It was a defendant's responsibility to pay for their own defence at trial, but, by 1885 it had become the practice in Western Australia to appoint counsel for destitute defendants accused of capital crimes, although only after "proper enquiry" confirmed that the defendants had no means to retain counsel. The fee paid by the government to counsel was £10, a sum considered inadequate by some lawyers.[129] It was not until the passing of the *Poor Persons Legal Assistance Act 1928* (WA) that poor defendants charged with any indictable offence were entitled to apply for legal assistance.[130]

The case of Martha Rendell and her intimate partner Thomas Morris illustrates the difficulties faced by defendants who needed to raise money for their defence. In 1909, Morris sold his carpenter's tools and all his possessions to pay the fees of James Clydsdale, who defended the couple

Search Tool," accessed 7 January 2023, https://www.wa.gov.au/organisation/department-of-justice/online-index-search-tool; Hammond Evalina May, East Perth cemetery records, accessed 11 November 2021, https://www.eastperthcemeteries.com.au/explore/burial-search/burialsite/130130.html.

128 Piper and Finnane, "Defending the Accused," 41, 30; *Poor Prisoners Defence Act* 1916 (Vic).

129 "Local Telegrams," *Victorian Express*, 9 July 1879, 3; Julian Harper to the Governor, 10 July 1885, S675 cons527 1885/2687, SROWA.

130 *Poor Persons Legal Assistance Act 1928* (WA).

on a charge of murder. The loss of his tools meant that Morris, who was acquitted, was thereafter unable to earn his living as a carpenter and was forced to find work away from Perth.[131] These costs put Aboriginal women, poor women, and single women, who were unable to command the higher wages of men, at a disadvantage. However, socioeconomic factors were not the only reason women may not have had access to counsel. As will be seen in this section, lawyers would sometimes refuse to represent their female accused.

While Morris sold his livelihood to raise the required funds for his defence, others stole in order to afford counsel. For example, in 1880, Thomas Casley was arrested for stealing £7 from Jachel (or Jackal) Pyy, a seaman from the *Bonnie Lassie*, at Frederick Caesar's Emerald Isle Hotel in High St, Fremantle (Fig. 3.4).[132] The *Herald* did not portray Pyy as a wronged victim; instead he was represented in a manner common at the time, as reckless and foolish for being too drunk to look after his money. Casley pleaded that he was forced to steal, as he needed the money to send his wife, Julia, back to Champion Bay, where she was to appear in the Court of General Sessions on a charge of making a false registration. Casley was nonetheless found guilty and sentenced to six months' imprisonment.[133] Julia had been charged in October that year with giving the incorrect father's name when registering the birth of her third child, Edith.[134] She was able to retain counsel for the committal hearing, being defended by Arthur Du Boulay, and was released on bail.[135] However, with her husband in gaol, Julia appeared unrepresented at her trial in December. She was found guilty, although sentenced to only forty-eight hours imprisonment.[136] This case, which illustrates how poverty could deleteriously impact the outcome of a woman's case, also exemplifies

131 "Morris Protests her Innocence," *DN*, 30 September 1909, 6; "Sale of Morris's Tools," *DN*, 11 September 1909, 13.

132 "The Herald," *Herald*, 11 December 1880, 2; "Advertising," *ICN*, 4 August 1880, 1.

133 "The Herald," *Herald*, 11 December 1880, 2; "Odds and Ends," *Victorian Express*, 22 December 1880, 3; *Police Gazette Western Australia (PGWA)*, 1880, 195, 200, SLWA; Local prisoners, 1876–1888, S1809 cons1156 F3–F4, SROWA.

134 *PGWA*, September 1880, 153, SLWA.

135 "Geraldton Police Court," *Victorian Express*, 22 September 1880, 3.

136 "Geraldton Quarter Sessions," *Victorian Express*, 8 December 1880, 2.

the manner in which poverty limited equitable justice for working-class women.

Rarely, a defendant who was unable to afford counsel might be represented pro bono (without fee), or they might be the beneficiary of a subscription to cover the costs of defence if local residents felt they were worthy recipients. The case of Jane Green illustrates both of these circumstances. Jane was seventeen years old when she stood in the Court of Quarter Sessions in 1840. Her mother had died when Jane was nine and the name of her father was unknown. She had been sent to the colony in 1837, by the Children's Friend Society, as part of a scheme to increase the labour force by bringing children to the colony.[137] Twenty-eight commissioners, including the Government Resident of Toodyay,

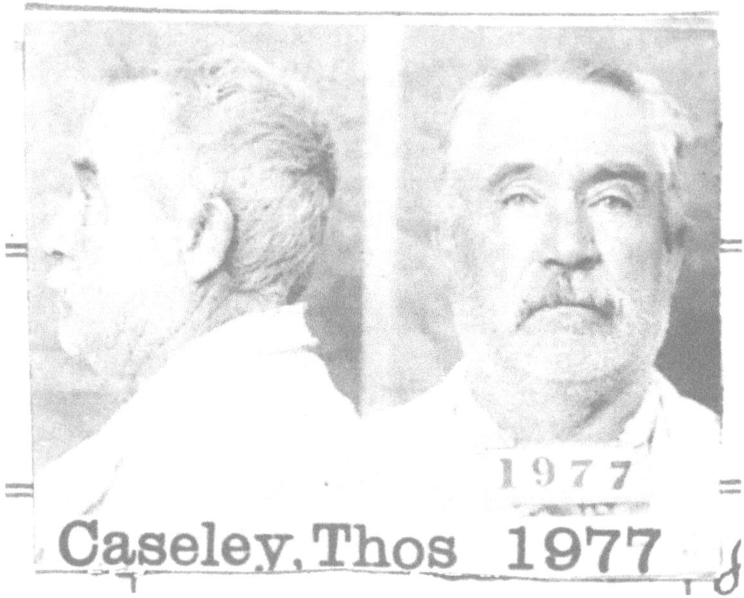

Fig. 3.4 Thomas Casley taken from the Fremantle Prison register c. 1896. Casley was a recidivist imprisoned several times for property offences or crimes against good order. Registers local prisoners,S672 cons 4173 1, SROWA

[137] Geoff Blackburn, *The Children's Friend Society: Juvenile Emigrants to Western Australia, South Africa and Canada, 1834–1842* (Northbridge: Access Press, 1993), 39.

Francis Whitfield, were appointed to be guardians to these children.[138] In July 1839, Jane was apprenticed to Whitfield and his wife Charlotte at Knockdominie, an isolated farm seventy-three kilometres north-east of Perth, where she occupied a room next to the kitchen. On the morning of 15 July 1840, Charlotte was horrified to discover Jane sitting on the floor of her bedroom with her arms covered in blood and the body of a newborn infant hidden under rags at the end of her bed.[139] Francis Whitfield rode thirty miles to fetch Dr Robert Foley and the Resident Magistrate of York, Revett Bland. On arrival Bland took statements from Whitfield, servant William Coates and from Foley, but did not take a statement from Charlotte Whitfield, saying he saw no necessity to do so.[140] Evidence from Foley showed that there were ten cuts and puncture wounds, made with scissors, to the baby's neck and throat including a two-inch transverse wound which severed the child's windpipe.[141] Jane was sent to Fremantle Gaol, and the demonstrable violence used to effect her child's death ensured that she was charged with the crime of murder rather than the lesser crime of concealment of birth.[142]

By August, rumours of the paternity of Jane's child were circulating in the community. Francis Whitfield was no longer admitted to "respectable" households and Charlotte Whitfield had moved out of her home.[143] Jane's case was treated sympathetically in news reports, and a subscription was begun to pay for her defence.[144] However, when Richard West Nash agreed to defend Jane pro bono, the money raised was instead used, in part, to buy Jane new clothing.[145] At the trial, Nash

138 *Guardians to Child Immigrants* 1839 (WA).

139 "Quarter Sessions," *Inquirer*, 7 October 1840, 39.

140 *R v Jane Green*, October 1840, S122 cons3472 43 case 226, SROWA; "Jane Green's Trial continued," *Inquirer*, 14 October 1840, 43.

141 *R v Jane Green.*

142 "Quarter Sessions," *Inquirer*, 7 October 1840, 39; List of prisoners in the jail of Fremantle, August 1840, S2941 cons36 83 13, SROWA.

143 John Wittenoom to Secretary of the Children's Friend Society, 24 August 1841, CO 18/33 208, Australian Joint Copying Project (AJCP); Rica Erickson, "T.N. Yule Esq.: A Gentleman of Misfortune," in *Rica's Stories*, ed. Lenore Layman (Nedlands: The Royal Western Australian Historical Society, 2001), 72.

144 "The Western Australian Journal," *PGWAJ*, 8 August 1840, 2.

145 "Correspondence," *Inquirer*, 24 February 1841, 4.

called two defence witnesses. Dr Joseph Harris testified that, if the umbilical cord was wrapped around the baby's neck, Jane, while in a state of delirium, may have accidentally caused the wounds to the baby's neck while trying to cut the cord.[146] The argument of delirium brought on by childbirth accorded with gendered understandings of women's susceptibility to mental instability and would have been understood by the men who formed the jury.[147] Nash also called Sarah Knott, who had accompanied Jane to Australia, as a character witness. Knott testified that Jane was not cruel or "improper" and that she did not consider her capable of forming "any dark, deliberate design," thereby affirming that Jane met gendered assumptions of "respectable" femininity.[148]

Nash's defence resulted in the partial verdict of "concealment of birth." Consequently, Jane was sentenced to two years' imprisonment, which she served at Rottnest Island Prison, rather than the sentence of death, which she would have received if found guilty of murder.[149] Her place of incarceration was unusual, as only two non-Indigenous women are known to have been sent to Rottnest, and may have reflected the length of the sentence.[150] It is unlikely that Jane was incarcerated in the prison and more likely that she worked for Gaoler Henry Vincent: a man known for his cruelty to both the prisoners and his wife.[151] There is no doubt that the two defence witnesses were instrumental in the verdict, but they incurred an expense, which was met by the Children's Friend Society.[152] The instances of defence counsel working pro bono were not common. For many defendants, who were overwhelmingly working class, the expense of defence counsel and witnesses would not have been possible.

---

[146] "Quarter Sessions," *PGWAJ*, 3 October 1840, 2; "Jane Green's trial continued."

[147] D'Cruze and Jackson, *Women, Crime and Justice*, 49.

[148] "Quarter Sessions," *PGWAJ*, 3 October 1840, 2.

[149] List of prisoners Fremantle Gaol, October 1840, S2941 cons36 83 15, SROWA.

[150] Caroline Ingram, "'There not being any place to keep her': Incarcerating Women in Nineteenth-Century Western Australia," *Australian Historical Studies* 55, no. 1 (2024).

[151] Glen Stasiuk, "Wadjemup: Rottnest Island as Black Prison and White Playground" (PhD exegesis, Murdoch University, 2015), 114; Ann Curthoys, Shino Konishi, and Alexandra Ludewig, *The Lives and Legacies of a Carceral Island: A Biographical History of Wadjemup/ Rottnest Island* (London: Routledge, 2023), 87.

[152] John Wittenoom to Secretary Children's Friend Society, CO 18/33 204 reel 433, AJCP.

Even when defendants could afford representation, working-class women could not always manage to secure it. When Louisa Bridger and Henry Edwards were accused of stealing £7 and a pocketbook from the pocket of Northam farmer John Playle, in 1882, Edwards was defended by Howell, but Louisa appeared unrepresented. When Chief Justice Wrenfordsley asked Edward Scholl to defend Louisa, Scholl declined, stating that "he would rather not undertake the task."[153] Twenty-five-year-old Louisa was described by police at the time as a prostitute.[154] She came from a background of poverty and had been institutionalised in the Poor House with her mother and siblings, in 1867, when her father was sentenced to seven years for forgery.[155] Much of her adult life was spent in and out of prison for petty crimes such as vagrancy, petty theft or being drunk or disorderly.[156] In his deposition, Playle stated that he met Edwards, who he had not previously known, in Perth and the pair spent some time drinking and going about Perth, including a visit to see "the wonders of the Great Exhibition." They were still drinking the next day at Edwards's house when Edwards offered to bring Playle a woman. Playle stated that he refused this but fell asleep and woke to find Louisa leaning over him, his pocket cut, and his money and pocketbook gone.[157] Lance Corporal John Connor of the police testified that he found the money in a clock in Edwards's house and arrested both defendants.

Louisa's story, as told to Connor, was slightly different. She said that she had been released from prison that day to find Edwards waiting for her. He asked her to go straight to his house, offering as an inducement that he had plenty of beer. On arrival, a drunken Playle offered her £1

153 "Supreme Court-Criminal Side," *West Australian*, 17 January 1882, 3.

154 Birth, Louisa Bridger no. 3716, 1857, Picton, "Online Index Search Tool," Department of Justice, accessed 10 June 2023, https://www.wa.gov.au/organisation/department-of-justice/online-index-search-tool.

155 Record of court convictions, 1861–1914, S5072 cons1156 v23, 21 August 1867, SROWA; Alexander Cockburn-Campbell to Colonial Secretary, 7 September 1867, S2941 cons36 597 124, SROWA.

156 Record of court convictions, 1861–1914, S5072 cons1156 v23, SROWA; *PGWA*, SLWA, accessed 5 November 2021, https://slwa.wa.gov.au/collections/collections/police-gazettes.

157 *R v Bridger and Edwards*, 4 January 1882, S122 cons 3473 111 case 991, SROWA; "Thursday, January 12," *ICN*, 18 January 1882.

to have sex, which she later divided with Edwards.[158] Louisa was found guilty of larceny and sentenced to twelve months' imprisonment without hard labour. When addressing the defendants, Wrenfordsley told Louisa that "life had proved a bitterness to her rather than a blessing. He would have given her a lighter sentence but that he wanted to keep her away from the streets of Perth."[159] Edwards was convicted for aiding and abetting Louisa, and Wrenfordsley was resolute in laying the blame for the theft squarely at Edwards's door:

> You are a very bad man; not only are you bad yourself, but you seek to make others so. For many years past you have been a pest to good, honest people. You have been found guilty of inciting a young woman to commit a crime for which I have given her a very light sentence. You waylaid this man, and then procured this woman, whom you pushed into a room, and stood by like a cowardly fellow, to participate in a share of the robbery.[160]

Men and women, like Edwards, who "procured" women for prostitution were considered to be a corrupting influence on young women, leading them into a life of vice.[161]

Sophia Paviour encountered a different problem, arising from the scarcity of available defence counsel, when she appeared in the Supreme Court charged with the unlawful wounding of Mary O'Brien, in 1872. On the morning of 11 September Mary visited the house in Fremantle that Sophia shared with her intimate partner Edward Holmes, requesting the return of some clothes from a visitor to Sophia's house, Elizabeth Barrett. Elizabeth gave evidence that Sophia told Mary "You have got a good cheek to come here after reporting that the child you are pregnant of belongs to my husband." Sophia called Mary a "damned bitch" and ordered her away from the house, following her to the street. The evidence varies from this point onwards. Mary claimed that Sophia was holding three table knives when she came to the door and used one of

---

158 *R v Bridger and Edwards*.

159 "Friday, January 13," *West Australian*, 17 January 1882, 3.

160 "Friday, January 13," *ICN*, 18 January 1882, 4.

161 Piper, "In Bad Company," 39.

these to attack her, wounding her on the face. Three other defendants, including Elizabeth Barrett, testified that they did not see Sophia holding knives or see blood on Mary's face, although one, Susanna Meiklum, was unable to account for spots of blood on her doorstep. Sophia was committed to stand trial at the Supreme Court on 6 November.[162]

Edward Holmes then set about finding a defence lawyer to represent Sophia at trial. He paid Nathaniel Howell £1.2.6 to retain his services and consult with his clerk. On the day before the trial, Holmes and the defence witnesses travelled up to Perth. He was at first unable to find Howell, and when he did finally manage to locate him it was to discover that Howell was drunk and "unable to attend to business." Holmes then said he conducted Howell to a private residence where he was looked after until he left in the morning. At noon Holmes spoke to Howell again and discovered that he did not intend to defend Sophia as "he was not in a fit state to conduct the case." Remarkably, as Holmes explained, Howell then "beg[ged] me to give him a shilling for a pot of beer." Holmes was subsequently able to retain Septimus Burt for a fee of three guineas. Sophia's case came up for trial at 5.30 pm that day but Septimus Burt did not appear, and Chief Justice Burt declined to postpone the case. Holmes rushed off to find Septimus Burt, discovering him half an hour later "walking leisurely along" near the court. Despite pleading from Holmes, Septimus returned the fee and stated that it was too late to attend.[163] These events had several repercussions: Sophia Paviour appeared unrepresented at trial and was sentenced to three months' imprisonment, Septimus Burt was called upon by Chief Justice Burt at the opening of court the next day to show cause why he had neglected to appear in court and Edward Holmes published a letter in the *Herald* detailing his grievances with Howell and Burt. This letter resulted in Howell being suspended from practicing until he had returned Holmes's fees.[164]

Holmes seems already to have gone to considerable trouble to prevent Sophia from being sent to gaol, but there was still one more avenue open

---

[162] *R v Hannah Holmes*, 6 November 1872, S122 cons3473 63 case 542, SROWA.

[163] Edward Holmes, "To the Editor of the Herald," *Herald*, 16 November 1872, 3.

[164] "Supreme Court-Criminal Side," *Herald*, 9 November 1872, 3; Holmes, "To the Editor"; "Supreme Court-Civil Side," *Express*, 12 December 1872, 3.

to him. On 18 December, he sent a petition to Governor Weld, asking that the rest of Sophia's sentence be remitted.[165] In this petition Holmes accused Mary O'Brien of perjury. He began with an attempt to discredit Mary's character, stating that she was a woman of "ill fame," meaning that she earned her money by sex work. He then went on to state that two years earlier, Mary had narrowly escaped a charge of perjury when she falsely stated in the York Court that she had witnessed a stabbing.[166] Holmes claimed that Mary had been drunk when she visited his house on the pretext of collecting clothes and that Sophia, believing Mary intended to seduce Holmes, had "driven her off," but had not wounded her. Holmes stated that Mary had inflicted the cuts to her own face later, having learnt from the case at York. He further stated that if only he had been able to retain counsel, these facts would have been brought out in the courtroom and Sophia would not have been convicted.[167] Chief Justice Burt dismissed these claims out of hand, stating that Sophia was convicted on "clear and unexceptional testimony," and Sophia was forced to serve out the rest of her sentence.[168]

Sophia and Holmes had been intimate partners since 1860 and their daughter, Harriett Maria, was born in 1861, but, in 1891, their lives came to an abrupt and violent end.[169] On 26 February 1891, Detective Constable Robert Connell found the body of Sophia Paviour laid out on boxes in the house that she had shared with Holmes in Kings cottages, Perth, covered with a sheet.[170] King's cottages in Murray Street, was described by the *Inquirer* in 1887 as "that sink of immoral iniquity

---

[165] Edward Holmes to the Governor, 18 December 1872, S2941 cons36 718 171, SROWA.

[166] On 23 January 1871, Jane Grindell filed for alimony from her husband, William Grindell, citing that she had been turned out of her home after her husband had brought Catherine Godfrey, "a common prostitute" back to the house, ostensibly as a servant, but that in actuality her husband had had an "illicit relationship" with Godfrey. Holmes claimed that Mary O'Brien had lied when she stated in court that she witnessed Jane Grindell stab Catherine Godfrey. *Jane Grindell v William Grindell*, 25 January 1871, S35 cons3403, 1871/0010, SROWA.

[167] Holmes to the Governor.

[168] Archibald Paull Burt, letter books, 23 December 1872, MN 736 acc 2829A 7 14, SLWA.

[169] Birth, Harriette Maria Holmes, no. 5961, 1861, Perth, "Online Index Search Tool," Department of Justice, accessed 10 June 2023, https://www.wa.gov.au/organisation/department-of-justice/online-index-search-tool.

[170] Inquest Sophia Holmes, 4 March 1891, S675 cons527 1991/0553, SROWA.

... a portion of the city that is a standing disgrace to Perth."[171] At the resultant inquest it was determined that Sophia had died "through ill treatment inflicted by Edward Holmes." Neighbours testified to seeing and hearing Edward violently assaulting Sophia the previous night and also that they had several times previously seen Holmes physically abuse Sophia "in a very cruel manner."[172] Holmes was arrested and placed in the Waterside Lockup to await trial, where he died shortly afterwards as a result of alcohol withdrawal.[173] Although homicide was not the most common form of death for working-class women, Sophia was not the only woman to die at the hands of her intimate partner. Physical abuse of women by their intimate partners, frequently fuelled by alcohol, was not uncommon.[174]

Sophia Paviour had been institutionalised in English workhouses since she was at least nine years old.[175] In 1858, as a seventeen-year-old, she came to Australia on board the *Emma Eugenia* and, within a few months, was reported by police to be earning her living by prostitution.[176] Unlike some other working-class women, Sophia does not appear to have left Holmes, although she would have been abandoned during his periods of imprisonment.[177] In many ways, the course of her life was controlled by this relationship: the dispute which resulted in her imprisonment was arguably triggered by Holmes's relationship with Mary O'Brien, Sophia was disadvantaged by Holmes's inability to secure defence counsel for her trial, and the physical abuse she suffered at Holmes's hands resulted in her death. Although the events of her life were extreme, they illustrate

---

171 "News of the Week," *ICN*, 8 June 1887, 3.

172 Inquest Sophia Holmes.

173 Inquest Edward Holmes, 14 March 1891, S675 cons527 1891/0554, SROWA.

174 Piper, "In Bad Company," 101; Carolyn Strange, "Masculinities, Intimate Femicide and the Death Penalty in. Australia, 1890–1920, *British Journal of Criminology*, no. 2 (2003): 332; Kay Saunders, "The Study of Domestic Violence in Colonial Queensland: Sources and Problems," *Australian Historical Studies* 21, no. 82 (1984): 68–84.

175 Norwood Schools: Admission and Discharge Register, 1849–1851, WEBG/SM/048/001, London Metropolitan Archives, digital image, *Ancestrylibrary.com.au.*

176 Alfred Durlacher, 25 January 1859, S2941 cons36 408 140–43, SROWA.

177 "Thursday, 3 October 1861," *ICN*, 9 October 1861, 3; Rottnest Island Commitment Book, 1855–1881, cons130, SROWA.

the lack of rights and opportunities experienced by many women at this time.

These examples show that, for some defendants, accessing defence counsel was not always possible. Defence was costly and many defendants were working-class or underclass women whose earning capacity was limited by the employment options open to women at that time and the much lower wages women were able to earn. Sometimes a spouse or intimate partner might pay for the cost of defence but many underclass women lived singly, often due to the imprisonment of their intimate partner or in preference to the physical abuse they had suffered at the hands of their partner. Even when working-class women could afford to pay for a defence, lawyers might refuse to represent them and the small size of the legal profession in Western Australia sometimes made it difficult to obtain representation.

Conclusion

The statistics show that the use of defence counsel was a significant advantage for women tried in the upper courts of Western Australia during the nineteenth century, where defendants who were represented were more likely to receive an acquittal. Two-thirds of represented defendants were acquitted compared to one-third of defendants who appeared unrepresented. These figures are higher than those found for the general population of offenders in Victoria, suggesting that although defence status was an important predictor of acquittal for both men and women, women were more likely to benefit from representation than men. However, it seems that retaining defence counsel may have been less effective for those defendants accused of interpersonal crimes. Outcomes for interpersonal crimes were evenly split with half of the trials receiving an acquittal regardless of defence status. Although the low number of women indicted for interpersonal offences make it difficult to form a definite conclusion, it is possible that this result is due to the high percentage of murder cases; most of which occurred with a co-defendant. These offences had a low chance of acquittal when more than one defendant was involved.

It is also possible that the use of defence counsel may have been associated with beneficial outcomes for defendants who were convicted, including shorter sentences for those accused of more serious crimes. The case studies of Bridget Landy and Keziah Lockyer suggest that the use of defence counsel may have resulted in less severe sentences for serious crimes such as perjury. Similarly, although this dataset only includes seven recommendations to mercy, the figures suggest that retaining defence counsel may have been associated with an increased number of mercy riders by the jury. It was found that over one quarter of defendants with representation received a recommendation to mercy compared to a little over one tenth of defendants without, suggesting that defence counsel may have been better able to convince the jury of mitigating factors such as illness or youth than the women could alone. It may also have been easier for defence counsel to command authoritative figures, such as medical experts, to give opinions on the inadvisability of incarceration for defendants who were due to give birth or were in ill-health.

Defence lawyers used different tactics to obtain an acquittal for their clients depending on the circumstances of the case, but, although using legal arguments where possible, they would also frequently emphasise those feminine characteristics which accorded with the gendered assumptions of femininity prevalent at the time. By doing so, they could emphasise the "respectability" of the defendant and so render her less dangerous in the eyes of the jury. Women who were able to present a respectable persona in the court might achieve a more favourable outcome at the hands of the judge or jury. Thus, Nash argued that Jane Green may have accidentally caused the cuts to her baby's throat while in a state of delirium common to women in labour, and Septimus Burt argued that Mary Watkins possessed the traits of weakness and frailty commonly associated with femininity. Counsel might also use a similar tactic against female victims, as in the case of Lydia Dysart, to imply that a victim whose behaviour deviated from the gendered assumptions of "respectable" femininity was herself to blame for the crime.

However, the research has also shown that the advantage gained from the use of defence counsel was not equitable. Poorer women and Aboriginal women were particularly affected by having less access to counsel, leaving them disadvantaged. Economic opportunities for working-class women were limited and women who were unmarried, whose husband had abandoned them, or whose intimate partner was imprisoned, faced a significant disadvantage gaining access to defence counsel. As some of the case studies in this chapter illustrate, some women were also unable to gain access to counsel when lawyers refused to represent them. Additionally, the low number of legal practitioners available in the colony for much of the nineteenth century made it challenging to find counsel for all defendants in multi-defendant trials, meaning that counsel would have been unable to defend one client at the expense of another. Given the advantages of retaining counsel, this inequity in defence status for female defendants points towards the ways in which justice was not equally available to all women in the colony during the nineteenth century.

4

Jointly Indicted: Women as Co-Accused Defendants

> Bridget Todd and Elizabeth Pickett were jointly indicted for that they, on the 15th of August, feloniously did steal, take and carry away, three hats the property of Mr. John Henry Monger, from his store in Hay Street. The prisoners were also jointly charged with stealing a hat from the store of Messrs. Padbury Loton & Co.[1]

When two or more people are accused of the same crime, or when crimes have arisen from common acts, they are commonly tried together in a "joint trial."[2] Co-defendants may not be called to give evidence against each other in a joint trial and judges are tasked with separating the individual evidence against each defendant in their address to the jury.[3] Although co-defendants may each retain counsel separately, the

[1] *R v Bridgett Todd and Elizabeth Pickett*, 4 September 1872, S122 cons3473 61 case 530, SROWA.

[2] J. A. Andrews, "Joint Trials," *Modern Law Review* 30, no. 6 (1967): 645.

[3] Mark Weinberg, "Joint trials – the Problem of Reciprocal Blame," *Criminal Law Journal* 8, no. 4 (1984): 197; Andrews, "Joint Trials," 645.

C. Ingram, *Women on Trial*, Palgrave Histories of Policing, Punishment and Justice, https://doi.org/10.1007/978-3-031-98072-5_4

more common practice in nineteenth-century Western Australia appears to have been for one lawyer to represent both defendants. Judges may sever trials if they are satisfied that "an accused is likely to be prejudiced in the trial of a prosecution notice or indictment because it also charges one or more other accused," but in practice this rarely happens.[4] Joint trials are usually preferred by the State for reasons of cost and expediency.[5] Legal scholars have long maintained that combining the trials of more than one defendant into one trial is unfair and that defendants who face trials with co-defendants are more likely to be convicted. In 1984, Mark Weinburg wrote, "When two or more persons are tried jointly, the risk that a miscarriage of justice may occur is always present."[6] Reasons given for this have included: guilt by association, where one defendant is tainted in the minds of the jury by their association or proximity to other defendants; "spillover evidence" when evidence from one co-defendant reflects badly on another; an increase in complexity of the trial which decreases the jury's ability to distinguish evidence against accused individuals; and encouraging co-accused defendants to give evidence against each other during cross-examination in return for leniency in sentencing or as part of their defence strategy.[7] This last reason would have been less relevant during the nineteenth century when defendants did not have competence to give sworn testimony and could not be cross-examined.

Until recently there had been little empirical research on this topic, but current technological advances which are now making large digital datasets available, like that of the Prosecution Project, have provided increased opportunities for scholarly research into multi-defendant

4 S.L. Gall, "Effects of Joint Trials on the Proportion of Guilty Verdicts Assigned to Defendants" (master's thesis, Edith Cowan University, 1999), 4; *Criminal Procedure Act 2004* (WA) s 133(3)–(4).

5 Gall, "Effects of joint trials," 4, 8.

6 Weinberg, "Joint trials," 197.

7 Weinberg, "Joint trials"; Andrew D. Leipold and Hossein A. Abbasi, "The Impact of Joinder and Severance on Federal Criminal Cases: An Empirical Study," *Vanderbilt Law Review* 59, no. 2 (2006): 358; Robert R. Calo, "Joint Trials, Spillover Prejudice, and the Ineffectiveness of a Bare Limiting Instruction," *American Journal of Trial Advocacy* 9, no. 1 (1985): 21; Alana Jayne Piper and Lauren Vogel, "Co-Offenders before the Court: The Joinder Effect in Victoria, 1861–1961," *law&history* 5, no. 2 (2018): 112.

trials.[8] Recent scholarship arising from the interrogation of these datasets has found that the presence of a co-accused made only a small difference to the outcome of a trial in twentieth-century Victoria, Australia, and no measurable difference in nineteenth-century Victoria or in twentieth-century USA. However, the research does not focus on subgroups of defendants, such as women, who appear in the upper courts in smaller numbers than men.[9] By contrast, this chapter examines the impact of co-accused status of women tried in multi-defendant trials in Western Australia between 1830 and 1890 and argues that, for these women, co-accused status was not only a significant contributor to the outcome of the trial but was actually advantageous for the majority of female defendants. Women who were tried with co-accused were less likely to be found guilty than those who were tried alone.

There are forty cases of multi-defendant trials in Western Australia before 1891 involving female co-accused. Of these, seven female defendants were Aboriginal and thirty-three were non-Aboriginal. These low numbers reflect the population of the colony at that time, although the small dataset means that, although the impact of co-accused status may be suggested by patterns determined from analysis of the statistics, the data may not be robust enough to provide firm conclusions. However, the qualitative evidence provided through case studies, including the defendant's demeanour and "character," counsel's addresses to the jury, and judge's directions, can be included to support the conclusions indicated by the statistics and suggest reasons for judicial outcomes. Although the jury's reasoning is almost never revealed and addresses to the jury by counsel and judges are only occasionally reported in newspapers, the testimony of witnesses in court cases and the demeanour of the defendants, sometimes revealed in newspaper reports, can suggest reasons for jury verdicts.

In this chapter, I use quantitative evidence to answer questions such as: What crimes were female co-defendants tried for? Were co-defendants

[8] Mark Finnane, "Western Australia Criminal Trials 1830–1861" (ADA Dataverse, V1, 2019), https://doi.org/10.26193/OW6SR6; Mark Finnane, "Western Australia Supreme Court 1862–1899" (ADA Dataverse, V2, 2020), https://doi.org/10.26193/ESI64N.

[9] Leipold and Abbasi, "The Impact of Joinder and Severance," 399; Piper and Vogel, "Co-Offenders before the Court," 116.

male or female? What were the outcomes for women tried with co-defendants? By answering these questions, albeit with a small dataset, it is possible to see patterns which indicate the advantages or disadvantages for women who were tried with a co-defendant. By analysing the qualitative data along the axes of gender, class, and race, I reveal the experiences of these women and the attitudes of the male judges, juries, and police to women accused of committing crime with others.

I begin with a brief discussion of the statistics arising from analysis of this data and an examination of the different patterns discerned between property offences and interpersonal offences. This is followed by an examination of the case of Louisa Garrett, which was the only case of poisoning by a woman to come before the upper courts of Western Australia in this time period, and an investigation into the role of accomplice evidence in multi-defendant trials. I argue that, contrary to recent scholarly research for the general population of offenders, and also to previously held beliefs, the presence of a co-defendant at trial was generally advantageous for women, although this advantage may not have applied to those indicted for interpersonal offences. Additionally, the sentencing of co-accused women was often more lenient than that dispensed to their male co-accused, for all types of crime. Case studies included in this chapter indicate that the reasons for these outcomes might be influenced by a number of legal and cultural factors, however, the experiences of women tried in multi-defendant trials were often different to those of men and were shaped by gendered understandings of women at that time. Women were often perceived as lacking in agency, and this coloured the jury's perspective, especially when the co-defendant was male.

Statistics

Of the 129 cases of female defendants tried in the upper courts in Western Australia between 1830 and 1890, approximately one-third were tried with one or more co-accused. These figures are similar to those found by Alana Piper and Lauren Vogel for the general population of offenders in Victoria. The authors' data showed that the proportion

Table 4.1 Women's trials by crime type, co-accused and solo defendants

	Co-accused		Solo defendants	
Property	27	68%	56	63%
Interpersonal	11	28%	26	29%
Other	2	5%	7	8%
Total	40		89	

Compiled from data found in Mark Finnane, "Western Australia Criminal Trials 1830–1861"; Mark Finnane, "Western Australia Supreme Court 1862–1899"; Record of Court Convictions, 1861–1914, S5072 cons1156 v23, SROWA; Correspondence inwards, S2941 cons36, SROWA; Albany Police Station, occurrence book, S3240 cons364, SROWA

of trials involving co-accused varied over time but overall comprised approximately one-third of all defendants.[10] In Western Australia, the greater proportion of the trials involving female co-defendants were for property crimes with a little over one quarter of the trials being for interpersonal crimes and is similar to that of solo female defendants (Table 4.1).

Analysis of this data shows that, contrary to the long-held assertion that co-accused status is prejudicial to the outcome of a trial, women tried in multi-defendant trials in the upper courts of Western Australia at this time were *less* likely to be found guilty than those who were tried individually (Table 4.2). This finding also differs to those of Leipold and Abbassi and of Piper and Vogel who found that, for the general population of offenders during the nineteenth century, co-accused status made little to no difference to the outcome of a trial. However, a closer examination of the data indicates that category of crime is a significant factor in the verdict. Women tried for interpersonal crimes with a co-accused were more likely to be convicted than those tried in joint trials for property offences. Nearly three quarters of the women tried as co-accused for interpersonal crimes received a guilty verdict, compared nearly one-third of the co-accused women tried for property crimes.[11] Possible reasons for this disparity are explored further in the following sections.

[10] Piper and Vogel, "Co-Offenders before the Court," 115.

[11] Seventy-three percent of the co-accused women tried for interpersonal crimes (n = 11) were found guilty. Thirty percent (n = 27) of the co-accused women tried for property crimes were acquitted.

Table 4.2 Verdicts in multi-defendant trials

	Multi-defendant trials		Single-defendant trials	
Guilty	14	35%	47	53%
Guilty of a lesser crime	2	5%	4	4%
Not guilty	21	53%	33	37%
Jury disagreed	2	5%	1	1%
No case, *nolle prosequi,* or not fit to stand	1	3%	4	4%
Total	40		89	

Compiled from data found in Finnane, "Western Australia Criminal Trials 1830–1861"; Finnane, "Western Australia Supreme Court 1862–1899"; Record of Court Convictions, 1861–1914, S5072 cons1156 v23, SROWA; Correspondence inwards, S2941 cons36, SROWA; Albany Police Station, S3240 occurrence books, cons364, SROWA

Property Offences

Statistics

Women were indicted for a range of property offences including simple larceny, larceny from the person, robbery from the person, breaking and entering a warehouse, receiving stolen goods, and sheep stealing. The items stolen were generally similar to those stolen by solo accused and included clothing, food, and money, although five women were charged with the theft of sheep or cattle. A common form of theft was to invite a victim to enter a house to share a bottle of spirits, such as rum or brandy and, once the victim had fallen asleep, to remove the money from his pockets. While it is probable that most of these scenarios occurred in conjunction with sex work, the only case in which this was admitted to by the victim was that of *R v Christian Geary and Charles Barber* where William Smith, a visiting seaman, was robbed of the money, watch, and jewellery in his pockets after drinking with Geary who, he admitted, he had "met promiscuously."[12]

Like Geary, the majority of women tried in multi-defendant trials for property offences were tried alongside a male co-accused. In only three

[12] "Supreme Court—Criminal Sittings," *Western Australian Times*, 13 October 1874, 3.

Table 4.3 Verdicts in trials for property offences

	Multi-defendant trials		Single-defendant trials	
Guilty	8	30%	33	59%
Guilty of a lesser crime	0	0	1	2%
Not guilty	17	63%	20	36%
Jury disagreed	1	4%	1	2%
Nolle prosequi	1	4%	1	2%
Total	27		56	

Compiled from data found in Finnane, "Western Australia Criminal Trials 1830–1861"; Finnane, "Western Australia Supreme Court 1862–1899"; Record of Court Convictions, 1861–1914, S5072 cons1156 v23, SROWA; Correspondence inwards, S2941 cons36, SROWA; Albany Police Station, occurrence books, S3240 cons364, SROWA

cases were women not indicted with a male co-defendant. The presence of a co-accused was advantageous for women tried for property offences. As mentioned earlier, nearly one-third of the women in multi-defendant trials were convicted, compared to nearly two-thirds of those who were tried singly (Table 4.3). However, being tried with a co-accused for a crime against property did not guarantee that defendants would receive the same verdict as their co-accused. In only a little over half of the trials were verdicts the same for all co-accused.[13] This figure varies from the findings of Piper and Vogel whose research of joint trials for theft offences in Victoria found that 71 per cent of trials resulted in defendants received the same verdict as their co-accused."[14]

Use of Defence Counsel

As detailed in the previous chapter, representation by defence counsel was generally advantageous for defendants tried in the upper courts of Western Australia before 1891, and this also held true for women tried in multi-defendant trials. Uptake of defence counsel for co-accused female defendants accused of property crimes was slightly higher than

[13] 56 percent (n = 27) of trials resulted in homogenous verdicts.

[14] Piper and Vogel, "Co-Offenders Before the Court," 118.

that for solo accused.[15] This slight difference may possibly be accounted for by the economic conditions for women at that time who, if they were employed, were likely to be earning considerably lower wages than men. Although some defendants in multi-defendant trials employed their own defence counsel, for others, one defence lawyer might represent all co-accused, leaving open the possibility that sharing the cost might make defence more affordable for women or that the cost might have been borne by male co-defendants. The advantages of defence counsel were most pronounced for co-accused defendants indicted for property offences where all represented defendants were acquitted. This is in contrast to solo defendants indicted for property offences where only half of the defendants who retained counsel were acquitted.[16] The small number of co-accused women defended in trials for property crimes and the lack of reporting of the defence counsels' addresses to the jury makes it impossible to find a pattern to fully explain the acquittal rate for co-accused defendants. However, on two occasions, women accused of theft who retained counsel were acquitted at the expense of their undefended co-accused, suggesting defence counsel may have been better placed to emphasis feminine characteristics that portrayed their client as lacking in agency and their co-accused as the perpetrator of the crime.[17]

Receiving Stolen Goods

The offence of receiving stolen goods is a crime that has long been associated with female defendants.[18] In three of the cases of property crimes,

[15] 52 percent (n = 27) of co-accused female defendants compared to 46 percent (n = 56) of solo female defendants used defence counsel.

[16] 100 percent (n = 13) of represented defendants were acquitted. 54 percent (n = 26) represented solo defendants were acquitted.

[17] *R v Scully, Wethered and Kierle*, 6 April 1870, S122 cons3473 50 case 363, SROWA; *R v Bridgett Todd and Elizabeth Pickett*.

[18] Kathy Callahan, "On the Receiving End: Women and Stolen Goods in London 1783–1815," *The London Journal* 37, no. 2 (2012): 107; Alana Jayne Piper and Lisa Durnian, "Theft on Trial: Prosecution, Conviction and Sentencing Patterns in Colonial Victoria and Western Australia," *Australian & New Zealand Journal of Criminology* 50, no. 1 (2017): 12. The crime was also associated in Western Australia with Aboriginal men, where the killing of colonists' stock was involved. The dividing of the food according to customary obligations of kinship and seniority

a female defendant was tried for receiving while her co-defendant was tried for the theft of the goods. All three of these women received an acquittal.[19] The crime of receiving is notoriously difficult to prove as, to gain a conviction, the prosecution must not only prove that the defendant knew the goods to be stolen but must also prove that the principal, that is the co-defendant, was guilty of the theft of the goods.[20]

The case of *R v Charles Lovett and Susannah Summerland* illustrates some of the difficulties involved in prosecuting a case of receiving stolen goods. Susannah Summerland stood trial in the Court of Quarter Sessions in Perth on 1 January 1840, charged with receiving goods "then and there well knowing the said last mentioned goods and chattels … to have been feloniously plundered stolen taken and carried away."[21] Charles Lovett appeared with her, charged with the crime of plundering a wreck.[22] Lovett was the second mate of the barque *Elizabeth*, which had sailed into the port of Fremantle on 24 August 1839, under the command of Captain Robert Charles Garrett. It carried an expensive cargo of Chinese porcelain, sugar, coffee, cigars, silks, chocolate, and pepper. Some of this cargo was sold in Fremantle before setting sail for Sydney in the late afternoon of 21 September.[23] The *Elizabeth* had departed the port but had not proceeded far when a sudden storm hit the coast. The ship, with sails shredded, was run aground three miles north of Fremantle near the present-day suburb of Cottesloe. For the rest of that

would attract a charge of receiving, but no Aboriginal women were tried for this type of crime in the upper courts during the time period under examination; Sylvia Hallam and Lois Tilbrook, *Aborigines of the Southwest Region 1829–1840* (Nedlands: University of Western Australia Press, 1990), 144; Kingsley Palmer, *Noongar People, Noongar Land: The Resilience of Aboriginal Culture in the South West of Western Australia* (Canberra, ACT: Aboriginal Studies Press, 2016), 122; for examples see "Report of Conviction of Aboriginal Native Tomkin," S2941 cons36 615 64, SROWA; "General Sessions," *Perth Gazette and Independent Journal of Politics and News (PGIJPN)*, 29 June 1849, 3.

19 *R v Charles Lovett and Susannah Summerland*, 1 January 1840, S122 cons3472 40 case 212, SROWA; *R v George Wood and Sarah King*, 4 October 1848, S122 cons3472 78 case 424, SROWA; *R v Margaret Williams and Bridget Naughton*, 4 July 1855, S122 cons3472 108 case 660, SROWA.

20 Callahan, "On the Receiving End," 108.

21 *R v Charles Lovett and Susannah Summerland*.

22 *R v Charles Lovett and Susannah Summerland*.

23 Graeme Henderson, *The Wreck of the "Elizabeth"* (Sydney: Australian Society for Historical Archaeology, 1973), 2.

day, bags and boxes from the wreck continued to wash up on the beach and a military guard was set to protect the cargo.[24] Lovett was instructed to help gather up the goods that washed ashore and keep them together. On 1 October, Lovett took some shawls, pieces of linen, and silk handkerchiefs to Susannah, the wife of carpenter Abraham Summerland of Fremantle, and asked her if she could wash them for him. Susannah agreed to do so and also bought four pieces of linen and two crepe shawls from him. When word of the sale got back to Lewis Leon, supercargo of the *Elizabeth*, and Captain Garrett, they confronted Susannah. She at first denied buying the goods, but after Garrett and Leon threatened her with a warrant, she reluctantly gave up the goods she had purchased. Leon and Garrett, with Constable Thomas Harwood, also confronted Lovett and searched his chest finding a napkin, a silk shawl, and two silk handkerchiefs. According to Harwood, Lovett was extremely remorseful, repeating that he was very sorry for what he had done, but that he had lost so much of his own possessions in the wreck, and he hoped the theft could be overlooked. As Leon testified that "I never liked the prisoner, and desired the Captain to discharge him," it was never likely that he would excuse the theft.[25] At the trial, Lovett was defended by John Schoales, but Susannah appeared undefended. Susannah's daughter, Susannah Morrell, appeared as a defence witness and gave evidence that her mother had hung the washed articles on a clothesline in view of passers-by. This evidence was enough to demonstrate to a jury that Susannah Summerland had not attempted to hide the articles and therefore must not have known them to be stolen. The jury duly acquitted Susannah but Lovett was found guilty and sentenced to ten years' transportation.[26] Although the prosecution was able to prove that Lovett had stolen the goods, Susannah's daughter's evidence meant that the prosecution was unable to prove that Susannah Summerland knew the goods to be stolen and they were therefore unable to secure a conviction against her. Thus, Susannah

---

[24] "Equinoctial Gale," *Perth Gazette and Western Australian Journal (PGWAJ)*, 28 September 1839, 155.

[25] "Quarter Sessions," *Perth Gazette and Western Australian Times (PGWAT)*, 4 January 1840, 3.

[26] "Quarter Sessions," *PGWAT*, 4 January 1840, 3.

was acquitted according to a legal principle which, nonetheless, resulted from the gendered occupation of washing clothes.

Women's Agency

Cultural assumptions of women's agency also led to juries' willingness to believe that women's crime might have been prompted by a male co-accused. Analysis of the data in some of the cases where a woman was tried with a male co-accused indicates leniency by juries, prosecutors, and judges. In these cases, where evidence could have been applied equally to both accused, the male co-accused only was convicted, suggesting that juries perceived these women to lack agency. In 1861, after a heavy drinking session with his neighbours, Benjamin Froggat of King William Street (now known as William Street), Perth, found that £400 was missing from the cash box in his bedroom and blamed his housekeeper and intimate partner, Catherine Ives, as well as his neighbours, James and Ellen Miller and Edward Holmes. Froggat claimed that he accused Holmes of the theft when he saw him coming out of his bedroom but was then attacked by James and Ellen Miller.[27] Holmes denied stealing the money from Froggat but instead stated that he stole £126 from Catherine Ives when she fell asleep after drinking in his house. It seems that the police, not knowing who to blame, arrested anybody who may have had a connection with the theft, including Catherine Ives; James Kinnead, who lived in a part of Froggat's house; Froggatt's neighbours James and Ellen Miller; Edward Holmes; Holmes's intimate partner, Sophia Paviour; Margaret Kelsey; Mary Flood and Susan Bowers. All were charged with robbery, but Kelsey, Flood, and Bowers were released at the initial hearing.[28] Despite Ives's testimony that she was given frequent access to the key to Froggatt's cash box, that she often appropriated money given to her by Froggat for housekeeping, and Holmes's testimony stating that he had taken money from Ives's person, her case did not proceed to the Quarter Sessions. Police Constable Thomas Harrison reported finding a bag of money outside

---

27 *R v Holmes and others*, 2 October 1861, S122 cons3473 2 case 19, SROWA.

28 "Perth Police Court," *PGIJPN*, 19 July 1861, 2.

a window in the house shared by Holmes and Paviour after searching houses belonging to the various defendants. The *Inquirer* reported that at the conclusion of the trial, which was for larceny, the Attorney-General announced that he "should only press the case against Holmes" and the jury duly turned in a verdict of guilty against Holmes and not guilty against the other defendants.[29] In determining a culprit for the crime, the State had ignored a statement from Holmes that Ives was in possession of the money and had disregarded the fact that the house where the money was found was shared by both Holmes and Paviour.

Similarly to *R v Holmes and others*, police evidence appears to have been accepted uncritically in most of the trials in this dataset. However, there are a few striking examples in the trials of male defendants where this was not the case. In the trial of Yungala for murder in 1881, the police witness was questioned by the Attorney-General when a so called "voluntary" statement was found to have occurred while the prisoner was being questioned and in chains. The judge was highly critical of both the police and the magistrates, who accepted the statement in depositions. The statement was withdrawn from evidence and Yungala, who was defended by George Parker, was acquitted.[30] Despite rare examples like the case of Yungala, it seems that police authority was rarely challenged in the nineteenth-century court, increasing the vulnerability of Aboriginal and working-class defendants.

In 1870, in a case similar to *R v Holmes and others*, Julia Wethered, her intimate partner John Scully, and Isaac Keirle were charged with the theft of large amounts of sugar, duck (canvas), twine, and some sacks from the warehouse of John and Walter Bateman in Fremantle. Police Constable Regan had searched the room that Scully shared with Wethered in Keirle's house in Fremantle and found the stolen items, including the length of duck, which was already in the process of being made into trousers. John Bateman identified these articles as the ones that had been stolen from his warehouse. Keirle testified that he had

---

[29] "Thursday, 3 October 1861," *Inquirer and Commercial News (ICN)*, 9 October 1861, 3.

[30] "Supreme Court—Criminal Sittings," *West Australian*, 28 October 1881, 3; Mark Finnane, "Indigenous Peoples and Settler Criminal Law," in *The Cambridge Legal History of Australia*, eds. Peter Cane, Lisa Ford and Mark David McMillan (Cambridge: Cambridge University Press, 2022), 639.

received a bag of sugar from Wethered in part payment for her rent but maintained that he did not know that it was stolen. Wethered's defence to the police was simply that "she knew nothing about it but that Scully brought it there."[31] Although Scully had stated at his hearing that he would reserve his defence until the trial, when the case was heard he pleaded guilty. Keirle and Wethered were represented by Rowley Loftie and Stephen Parker, respectively. According to the *Perth Gazette*, Parker's defence strategy for Wethered was to contend that "there was no evidence to affect her."[32] Despite the stolen goods being found in possession of both Scully and Wethered, Scully was the only defendant found guilty. He received a six-year sentence and Wethered and Keirle were acquitted of both charges.

These cases suggest that when stolen goods were found in the possession of both male and female co-accused, juries were willing to believe that the male co-accused had perpetrated the crime and to overlook the contribution of the female defendant. In doing so, these gendered constructions not only increased women's chances of acquittal but would also have worked against male defendants whose chances of conviction would have been correspondingly increased. This accords with the dominant discourse of femininity where women were considered to be weak, passive, and lacking in agency and may have been more pronounced when the defendants were intimate partners. This pattern of leniency for women accused of property crime with male co-accused, combined with that for women committed for receiving, account for over one-third of the acquittals among female co-accused charged with property crimes. These two factors account for much of the difference in conviction rates between multi-defendant trials and those of solo defendants.

[31] *R v Scully, Wethered and Kierle.*

[32] "Supreme Court," *PGWAT*, 8 April 1870, 3.

Interpersonal crimes

Women were indicted as co-defendants for a range of interpersonal crimes including murder, aiding and abetting murder, manslaughter, administering poison with intent to kill, assault, and wounding with intent to do grievous bodily harm. By contrast, no women were tried as sole defendants for the charge of murder of an adult, although thirteen were indicted for crimes relating to the death of a child. Invariably, women's co-accused in interpersonal crimes were male.

Patterns of conviction and acquittal for this category of crime varied between multi-defendant trials and those of solo defendants. Women tried as co-defendants for crimes against the person had a greater chance of receiving a guilty verdict than solo defendants accused of similar crimes. Of the eleven women tried as co-defendants for crimes against the person, six received a guilty verdict, two were convicted of a lesser crime, and two were acquitted. In one case of assault, the jury was unable to agree. These figures contrast with those for solo defendants where only eight of the twenty-six cases of interpersonal crime were found guilty of the crime for which they were tried, and a much greater percentage of solo defendants were acquitted (Table 4.4).

In contrast to the cases of property crime, those tried for interpersonal crime in multi-defendant trials were much more likely to receive

Table 4.4 Verdicts of women tried as solo and co-defendants for interpersonal crimes

	Co-defendants		Solo defendants	
Guilty	6	55%	8	31%
Guilty of a lesser crime	2	18%	3	12%
Not guilty	2	18%	12	46%
Jury disagreed	1	9%	1	4%
Nolle prosequi	0		1	4%
Not fit to plead	0		1	4%
Total	11		26	

Compiled from data in Finnane, "Western Australia Criminal Trials 1830–1861"; Finnane, "Western Australia Supreme Court 1862–1899"; Record of Court Convictions, 1861–1914, S5072 cons1156 v23, SROWA; Correspondence inwards, S2941 cons36, SROWA; Albany Police Station, occurrence books, S3240 cons364, SROWA

the same verdict as their co-accused. This is partly as a result of the high percentage of indictments for murder, or intent to kill, in the dataset. Just over half of the women indicted for interpersonal crimes were charged with murder, aiding and abetting murder, or intent to kill.[33] As discussed in the previous chapter, juries were more likely to view multi-defendant killings as intentional, or unlawful, because the standard defences of provocation, accident, or self-defence were harder to prove when more than one defendant was involved.[34] The only case of interpersonal crime where a defendant received a different verdict to their co-defendant was that of *R v Mumbleby and Belo* in which Yamatji man Mumbleby and Yamatji woman Belo were accused of the murder of colonist James Rudd (see Chapter 5).[35] This homogeneity of verdicts indicates that for the most serious crimes, such as homicide, juries were willing to treat evidence as applying equally to all defendants rather than weighing evidence against individuals separately. It is worth noting that this attitude did not always extend to sentencing. In one case of manslaughter and another of wounding with intent to cause grievous bodily harm, judges sentenced Aboriginal female defendants to considerably less custodial time than their Aboriginal male co-accused.[36] For Aboriginal women like Belo, whose cases account for five of the eleven multi-defendant cases of interpersonal crime, the issue of race affected their trials in ways which did not apply to the trials of non-Indigenous women, and these cases are examined in greater detail in Chapter 5, where I consider the experience of Aboriginal women defendants more generally.

---

[33] Six of the eleven women were charged with these crimes.

[34] Mark Finnane and Andy Kaladelfos, "Race and Justice in an Australian Court: Prosecuting Homicide in Western Australia, 1830–1954," *Australian Historical Studies* 47, no. 3 (2016): 443–61.

[35] *R v Mumbleby and Belo,* January 1865, S122 cons3473 28 no. 64, SROWA. Fourteen year old Beegabega testified at the trial that she, Mumbleby, and Belo were from the "interior," and it is likely that they belonged to the Wajarri language group, which is part of the Yamatji people; "Butterabby Graves," Inherit, accessed 6 February 2023, http://inherit.stateheritage.wa.gov.au/Admin/api/file/9d5ab835-f51a-4276-81bc-9fd8017477bb; "Supreme Court—Criminal Side," *PGWAT,* 13 January 1865, 3.

[36] *R v Herbert Johnson and Cooray,* 5 April 1854, S122 cons3472 103 case 592, SROWA; Frederick Pearse, *R v Cunnerbiddy alias Jacky and Narney alias Polly,* 6 January 1886, S675 cons527 1886/0644, SROWA.

Five of the eleven co-accused tried for interpersonal crimes retained a defence lawyer but none of the five Aboriginal co-accused defendants appear to have been represented in court. Although the use of defence counsel appears to have been highly advantageous for women accused of property crimes, the ten defendants tried jointly for interpersonal offences whose cases proceeded to a verdict received little advantage from defence counsel, with four out of five defendants being found guilty regardless of defence status.

Murder

Women in the nineteenth century, as now, were indicted for the crime of murder far less often than men were. When women did kill, they were more likely to offend in the private sphere of the home and their victims were more likely to be family members. Women who killed their infants during this period were usually charged with concealing a birth. Violent crimes by women were seen as contrary to gendered assumptions of feminine behaviour, such as gentleness and nurturing, but women who appeared in court charged with murder were seen as particularly deviant. These cases disturbed culturally held beliefs of what a woman should be.[37] Murder, therefore, is a particularly useful area of study in the field of women's crime as it exposes societal understandings of femininity and criminality.

Murder is defined here as the crimes of wilful murder, murder, intent to kill, and aiding and abetting murder. Seven women were tried in joint trials for these crimes in the years before 1891. Significantly, those women who were convicted of murder were women who were found to have deviated from gendered assumptions of femininity. When discussing women accused of murder in nineteenth-century Australia, David Plater and Sue Milne wrote that "Judges and juries focused their

[37] Lizzie Seal, *Women, Murder and Femininity: Gender Representations of Women Who Kill* (Basingstoke: Palgrave MacMillan, 2010), 1; Victoria Nagy, *Nineteenth-Century Female Poisoners: Three English Women Who Used Arsenic to Kill* (Basingstoke: Palgrave Macmillan, 2015), 2.

strictest scrutiny and harshest penalties on women who violated important gender based behavioural expectations."[38] Women who killed their husbands to cohabit with another man were considered to have offended against their gender roles even further.[39] This is exemplified in Western Australia's history by the case of Bridget Hurford, accused of the murder of her husband in 1855. Testimony at the trial depicted Hurford as a drunken woman who was physically and verbally abusive towards her husband.[40] Bridget and her co-accused intimate partner, William Enoch Dodd, were both convicted of the murder. Only three women have been legally executed in Western Australia. Bridget Hurford, Margaret Cody, and Martha Rendell were all hanged after being found guilty of murder, all were tried with a male co-accused, and all exhibited behaviours that deviated from gendered assumptions of femininity. The cases of Hurford and Cody, which occurred during the time period under examination, are explored later in this chapter. That of Martha Rendell, which occurred in 1909, has been documented extensively by Anna Haebich.[41]

Case Study: Louisa Garrett

The case of Charles Woolley and Louisa Garrett, who were brought before the court in 1861 on the charge of attempting to poison Louisa's husband, is one such case. Louisa Cray grew up in the school attached to the parish workhouse of St Giles and St George: a large workhouse in London which housed destitute members of the working class.[42] The 1851 census shows nine-year-old Louisa living in Heston House School for pauper children with two other young girls of the same family name, presumably sisters. Like many of the other children in the school, their

[38] David Plater and Sue Milne, "'Assuredly There Never Was Murder More Foul and More Unnatural': Poisoning, Women and Murder in 19th Century Australia," *Canterbury Law Review* 25 (2019): 58.

[39] Plater and Milne, "'Assuredly There Never Was Murder More Foul'," 59.

[40] "The Alleged Murder and Forgery at the Vasse," *PGIJPN*, 14 September 1855, 3.

[41] Anna Haebich, *Murdering Stepmothers: The Execution of Martha Rendell* (Crawley, W.A.: UWA Publishing, 2009); Anna Haebich, "Murdering Stepmothers: The Trial and Execution of Martha Rendell," *Journal of Australian Studies* 22 (1998): 66–81.

[42] Durlacher to Colonial Secretary, 11 November 1858, S2941 cons36 408 150, SROWA.

place of birth was listed as "unknown."[43] Louisa was seventeen and living in the St Giles and St George Workhouse at Bloomsbury in 1859 when she was selected as one of a number of young, single women to emigrate to Western Australia on board the *Emma Eugenia* under the British Government's assisted immigration scheme.[44]

When the *Emma Eugenia* departed Plymouth, England, on 10 February 1858, bound for Western Australia, it had on board 188 passengers, 117 of whom were assisted single women emigrants destined to provide domestic service for the colonisers.[45] On arrival in Western Australia the young women were sent to the Immigrants Depot to await prospective employers. However, reports of "bad behaviour" by the women on board the ship were circulating in the colony and many colonists were disinclined to offer the women employment. In fact, feeling was so high that the government demanded a board of enquiry.[46] Women on board emigrant ships were subject to strict rules designed to protect them from the "contaminating" influence of men, to protect their reputations, and, in so doing, to protect the government's investment.[47] Some women refused to comply with these constraints, and on the *Emma Eugenia*, this behaviour was particularly marked. John Simpson Howard, the ship's surgeon, reported that some of the women, including Louisa, were "quarrelsome, idle, given to cursing and swearing and disobedient to the rules."[48] In his journal, Howard classified the women as "a disgraceful set" who exchanged "horrid and frightful language" with the sailors and that the conduct of some of the women was "disgusting."[49] In a report sent to Stephen Walcott, secretary of the Government Emigration Board in Westminster, London, Louisa was reported as "a bad girl."[50] From that

[43] "Louisa Cray," 1851 census, Class HO107 1698 116, digital image, *Ancestrylibrary.com.au.*

[44] Durlacher to Colonial Secretary, 11 November 1858, S2941 cons36 408 150, SROWA; "Correspondence," *ICN*, 7 July 1858, 2.

[45] John Simpson Howard, Surgeon's Report of the *Emma Eugenia*, 8 June 1858, S2941 cons36 408 119, SROWA; "The Independent Journal," *PGIJPN*, 30 April 1858, 2.

[46] "Local and Domestic Intelligence," *ICN*, 2 June 1858, 2.

[47] Emily Jayne Chambers, "The Immigration of Domestic Servants to Western Australia in the 1850s and 1890s" (honours thesis, Murdoch University, 2017), 37.

[48] Howard, Surgeon's Report of the *Emma Eugenia*.

[49] Howard, Surgeon's Report of the *Emma Eugenia*.

[50] Durlacher to Colonial Secretary, 11 November 1858, S2941 cons36 408 150, SROWA.

point onward, the colony refused to accept women sourced from English workhouses.[51]

We don't know if Louisa found employment as a domestic servant, but in March 1860, she married twenty-nine-year-old baker Charles Garrett.[52] As a nineteen-year-old, Charles had been sentenced in London's Central Criminal Court to seven years' transportation for the crime of embezzlement. He had found himself in trouble with the law again, in 1856, when he was convicted in York, Western Australia, for stealing £5.[53] During December of 1860, Charles decided to take a partner into his bakery business. He chose thirty-seven-year-old Charles Woolley who had been transported five years earlier for robbery with violence. Woolley moved into the home that Charles and Louisa shared in Perth, near the Roman Catholic Chapel. Charles later complained that, from the beginning, he "observed an improper intimacy and familiarity" between his young wife and Woolley. One Sunday in January, while drinking tea with Woolley and Louisa, he said he noticed that the tea tasted "nasty and disagreeable."[54] He described symptoms of vomiting, purging, stomach pain, loosened teeth, and pale gums which lasted for four weeks, sometimes lessening, but gradually becoming worse. Towards the end of January, Charles went to see the Colonial Surgeon, Dr John Ferguson, at the Perth Hospital who told him that his symptoms were consistent with the taking of mercury and so, on 29 January, Charles admitted himself to the hospital at Fremantle Prison (also known as the Convict Establishment) where he stayed for three weeks, rapidly recovering under Dr Attfield's care. Attfield confirmed Ferguson's diagnosis of mercury poisoning.[55] Mercury was commonly used to treat syphilis, and, although Charles had used mercury for this reason before his marriage, he told Attfield that he had not taken any

[51] Jan Gothard, *Blue China: Single Female Migration to Colonial Australia* (Carlton South: Melbourne University Press, 2001), 44.

[52] "Thursday, April 4, 1861," *ICN*, 10 April 1861, 3; General register, 1853, convict registers, S5056 cons1156 R31, SROWA.

[53] General register, convict registers, 1853, S5056 cons1156 R31, SROWA.

[54] *R v Charles Woolley and Louisa Garrett*, 12 March 1861, S122 cons3472 136 case 880, SROWA.

[55] *R v Charles Woolley and Louisa Garrett*; Receipts and discharges, 1859–1861, S5073 cons1156 R&D3-R&D4, SROWA.

since.[56] While Charles was in hospital, Louisa and Woolley were arrested for stealing firewood from Alfred Hawes Stone and sentenced to one months' and six months' imprisonment, respectively.[57] The two were initially sent to the Waterside Lockup at Perth. Although Woolley was then sent on to the Convict Establishment at Fremantle, there were no facilities for women there so Louisa stayed in the lockup.[58]

Charles visited his wife at the lockup shortly after he was released from hospital. He brought her box, containing her clothes and other possessions, which he handed to the keeper of the lockup, Michael Benson. While Charles was there, he was overheard by Benson arguing with Louisa and accusing her and Woolley of attempting to poison him. Charles informed the police of his suspicions and, on 12 March, Louisa and Woolley appeared before the magistrate, charged with administering poisons to Garrett with intent to kill. The case was referred to the Quarter Sessions to be heard on 4 April.[59]

During the nineteenth century, there was considerable anxiety around the idea of women who poisoned their husbands. Poisoning, considered a deceitful crime, perpetrated with stealth and secrecy, was regarded with significant revulsion and seen as the ultimate betrayal of a woman's role.[60] In 1885, when Sarah Keep and her mother Mary Ann Burton were convicted in New South Wales of murdering Keep's husband, William, with strychnine, *Freeman's Journal* wrote:

> But it is also a horrid thing to be poisoned by a woman, and when women are not women, but cruel merciless murderesses, to claim for them the slightest attribute or privilege of womanhood is to insult the very sex which it is professed so much to revere.[61]

---

[56] Nicholas Patrick Clements, "Frontier Conflict in Van Diemen's Land" (PhD diss., University of Tasmania, 2013), 326; *R v Charles Woolley and Louisa Garrett*.

[57] General register, convict registers, S5056 cons1156 R31, SROWA; "Perth Police Court," *PGIJPN*, 22 February 1861, 3.

[58] General register, convict registers, S5056 cons1156 R31, SROWA; *R v Charles Woolley and Louisa Garrett*.

[59] *R v Charles Woolley and Louisa Garrett*; "General Intelligence," *PGIJPN*, 15 March 1861, 2.

[60] Plater and Milne, "'Assuredly There Never Was Murder More Foul'," 53; Nagy, *Nineteenth-Century Female Poisoners*, 27.

[61] "Last Night's Mail," *Armidale Express and New England General Advertiser*, 1 May 1885, 13.

Women who poisoned their husbands were seen not only to have betrayed their feminine role of feeding and nurturing, but also to have actually used this role to commit murder.[62] Despite these concerns, research shows that most poisonings during the nineteenth century were actually committed by men.[63] This was certainly the case in Western Australia during the time period under investigation, where five men were indicted in the upper courts for poisoning offences, compared to just one woman.[64]

It was surprising then that, although this was the only case of poisoning by a woman that had been heard in courts of Western Australia, the case attracted little interest in the newspapers.[65] The *Perth Gazette* reported briefly on the initial hearing, and both major Western Australian newspapers reported the evidence submitted at the trial in detail, but there were no follow-up articles and no mention of the case in editorials.[66]

The trial itself took place on 4 April, before the newly appointed Chairman of the Quarter Sessions, Archibald Burt, and a bench of magistrates. Although Woolley was defended by Nathaniel Howell, Louisa appeared unrepresented.[67] This lack of representation was a significant factor in Woolley's defence strategy, as I explore further. Ten witnesses were called for the prosecution but none for the defence.[68] At the trial, Charles Garrett described his illness and explained the measures he had taken to effect a cure, including powders and medicines procured by

---

62 Plater and Milne, "'Assuredly There Never Was Murder More Foul'," 58.

63 David Plater, Joanna Duncan and Sue Milne, "'Innocent Victim of Circumstance' or a 'Very Devil Incarnate' - The Trial and Execution of Elizabeth Woolcock in South Australia in 1873," *Flinders Law Journal* 15, no. 2 (2013): 318.

64 Finnane, "Western Australia Criminal Trials 1830–1861"; Finnane, "Western Australia Supreme Court 1862–1899".

65 *R v Louisa Garrett and Charles Woolley* was the only case of poisoning by a woman heard in the upper courts of Western Australia during the time period under examination, however in 1873 Matilda Padbury was charged with the attempted poisoning of her husband in Bunbury. The case never proceeded to the Supreme Court due to lack of evidence.

66 "General Intelligence," *PGIJPN*, 15 March 1861, 2; "Thursday, April 4, 1861"; "Quarter Sessions," *PGIJPN*, 5 April 1861, 2.

67 "Thursday, April 4, 1861".

68 *R v Charles Woolley and Louisa Garrett*.

Woolley at Charles's request.[69] Police Constable Michael Lally testified that he had gone to Charles's house to search Woolley's box after Charles had returned from the hospital. Lally found bottles of powder and medicine, packages of powders, a salve box, and some pills.

The use of apothecaries and medical practitioners as expert witnesses in poisoning trials had already begun in England before the colonisation of Western Australia. By 1861 English defence lawyers and prosecutors in poisoning cases were able to call on professors of chemistry from large teaching hospitals to act as expert witnesses, a few of whom had developed such excellent reputations that they were in high demand by the courts.[70] George Stone, the Advocate-General of Western Australia, was not able to call on such men as expert witnesses, but he did call on Dr Ferguson to conduct a chemical analysis of the contents of bottles and packets found in Woolley's and Louisa's possession. Ferguson was unable to detect any mercury or arsenic, although he qualified his results by stating that the means available to him for testing were "imperfect." He was, however, able to determine that a small package of powder, which Louisa had removed from her box and given to Benson's wife for safe-keeping, contained "sugar of lead" (lead acetate) and testified that this could be poisonous if "improperly administered." In the nineteenth century, sugar of lead was used medicinally or occasionally as a sweetener.[71]

The most damaging evidence to be submitted was letters written by Louisa and Woolley to each other while imprisoned, which point clearly to an intimacy between the two. These letters were produced as evidence and read out in the courtroom and were also published in full in the newspapers. Woolley addresses both his letters to "My dear affectionate little Pet" and protestations of his love are scattered liberally throughout the letters. He ends with lines culled from a popular book of valentine poetry:

---

[69] Information for this case is sourced from the depositions in the criminal records unless otherwise indicated. *R v Charles Woolley and Louisa Garrett.*

[70] Katherine D. Watson, "Medical and Chemical Expertise in English Trials for Criminal Poisoning, 1750–1914," *Medical History* 50 (2006): 382, 386–387.

[71] John Pearn, "Emigrating to Queensland: Medical Advice for Intending Colonists," *Queensland History Journal* 22, no. 10 (2015): 768.

For dear art thou unto my heart,
Oh search that heart and see,
And from my bosom tear that part
That beats not true to thee.[72]

Louisa begins her letters more formally, beginning both missives with the words "Dear Charles, I have taken the please to right [*sic*] to you hoping to find you in good health as it leaves me," but she refers to Woolley frequently in her letters as "my love" and signs both with her maiden name, "Louisa Cray" (Fig. 4.1). All of this correspondence between Louisa and Woolley was intercepted before it reached the intended recipients, but the evidence casts an interesting light on the methods used by prisoners to communicate with each other and shows how prisoners colluded to work around the restrictions placed on them by the penal system. Louisa determined from conversation with Edward Devine, whose cell overlooked the exercise yard, that he would be going to the Convict Establishment at Fremantle and passed Devine a letter to deliver to Woolley at Fremantle. Two days later, she attached a lock of hair and a stone to a second letter and threw this through the window of his cell. Although Devine did not state his reasons for later handing her letters on to the police, he did this only after learning that Louisa was accused of poisoning her husband and it is possible that, in different circumstances, her letters may have reached Woolley.

There is no record of Woolley attempting to communicate with Louisa until he was returned to the Perth Lockup in March in preparation for his trial. In evidence at the trial, Arthur Simpson, the cook at the Perth Lockup, testified that he had received a shilling from Woolley to deliver three letters to Louisa. In one Woolley had written:

> Please to tell the cook to nod his head at me, if you are going to write, as the cook could bring me any news or message from you, if you can only square him, as he put a note in my bread to give to me.

[72] *R v Charles Woolley and Louisa Garrett*; "The Sentimental Valentine Writer, Containing a Selection of the Best and Newest Valentine Poetry. New and Improved Series. No. 13," Scottish Chapbooks, accessed 22 June 2021, https://scottishchapbooks.lib.uoguelph.ca/items/show/729; Leigh Eric Schmidt, "The Fashioning of a Modern Holiday: St. Valentine's Day, 1840–1870," *Winterthur Portfolio* 28, no. 4 (1993): 220.

Fig. 4.1 A page from one of Louisa Garrett's letters to Charles Woolley written in the Waterside Lockup, 1862 and submitted in evidence at her trial. Courtesy SROWA, *R v Charles Woolley and Louisa Garrett*, 12 March 1861, S122 cons3472 136 case 880

In another:

> I was greatly disappointed last night when I saw Polly and Kate come out as there was no message for me, I waited up till 11 o'clock with the signal out, but no one came, I sadly wanted to send a note to you, but I could not.[73]

Disappointingly, there is no indication of the nature of "the signal" or the identity of Polly or Kate but these letters show how prisoners actively resisted the restrictions placed on them by authorities.

---

[73] *R v Charles Woolley and Louisa Garrett.*

The most damning evidence presented in these letters, however, was the implied acknowledgement of the poisoning by Woolley, Louisa's apparent knowledge of the crime, and her willingness to confess to it. In her letters to Woolley, written on or around 26 February, she told him that Charles had visited her in the lockup and that he intended to charge them with poisoning him. Louisa was literate, but spelled phonetically, so the spelling in the following passages has been corrected for ease of comprehension. She wrote:

> Be on your guard for he came to me on the Monday and said that he knew me and you had been together for he knew it by the sheets ... and he said to me mind that he didn't transport us two for he blamed us for his illness.[74]

Later in the same letter she appears to contradict herself, writing that Charles had told her he "would do nothing to me but would do all to you." She warns Woolley that he should deny any knowledge of the poison but instead say that Louisa had purchased the wrong medicine for him from Birch's store (Fig. 4.2) but that he had kept it because "it might come in useful." She also refers to a lotion, telling Woolley "you must say that it was for yourself." Towards the end of the letter she warns Woolley not to mention "the name," because Birch may have forgotten it and Charles may not have found "the stuff." It appears she is referring to the name of the preparation Woolley purchased from chemist Edmund Birch. At the hearing on 14 March, Birch testified that Woolley had indeed bought mercurial preparations from him over the past year, saying that it was for use in venereal disease, and had purchased corrosive sublimate at the end of the last year; Birch denied ever having sold anything to Louisa.[75]

Throughout both letters runs a theme of concern for Woolley's acquittal. Louisa tells him that she is "almost broken hearted about it, for fear of my love," but he should not be "downhearted" for she will "help all that I can." In addition to exhorting Woolley not to

---

[74] *R v Charles Woolley and Louisa Garrett.*

[75] *R v Charles Woolley and Louisa Garrett.*

Fig. 4.2 Edmund Birch's chemist store on the corner of Howick and Barrack Streets, Perth c. 1870. Courtesy SLWA, 007604D

admit to purchasing the poisons, Louisa also details different schemes for his acquittal. These schemes, which seem implausible, may reflect her naivety and youth. They include her proposal to take Charles to court, once she is released, to make him prove the charges of poisoning and another to claim that she had come to Western Australia under a false name to be with Woolley.

Woolley, however, had a different plan for gaining his release. One of the letters which he attempted to pass to Louisa while in the Waterside Lockup, although strewn with protestations of love, asked Louisa to take the blame for the murder attempt saying, "It is the only way to get me of [*sic*]." In short, he asked Louisa to copy out an accompanying letter and send it to the magistrate. In this letter, which was to be signed by Louisa, he had written:

> I confess that I gave my husband some calomel, which I have kept secreted since my husband had the bad disorder. … I can assure you that

> Charles Woolley has had no act, hand, or part in it, but is as innocent as the child unborn.[76]

Woolley assured her that she would receive no more than six months' imprisonment. He painted a rosy picture of a happy life together saying: "if you should get a longer sentence than me, I will provide a comfortable little home against you [*sic*] come out." These letters were all read out before the jury at the trial. They paint a picture of Louisa as a young woman who was manipulated, or coerced, by an older man, but the implication of guilt would have been damning for Woolley.

Louisa gave an unsworn statement at the trial, which was reported in a derisive tone by both the colony's newspapers:

> In defence the prisoner Garrett made a rambling statement, in which she admitted that she had administered, by mistake, both sugar of lead and mercury, that she told her husband she thought she had done so, and that he replied "never mind, it, can't be helped, if I must die I must die," and entirely exculpated the prisoner Woolley.[77]

By defending only Woolley and not Louisa, Howell was able to argue that Louisa's testimony, that she accidently administered the poison to Garrett herself, meant that Woolley was innocent and should be acquitted.[78] The act of shifting blame by defendants who try to save themselves at the expense of their co-accused is still cited by legal scholars today as one of the risks of joint trials. Defendants are often tempted to "point the finger" at co-defendants, adding an additional layer of accusation to the evidence against their co-accused that they would have not faced if tried separately.[79]

The very act of delivering an unsworn statement may also have disadvantaged Louisa. As shown in Chapter 3, women who conducted their own defence, and spoke up in court, could face disapprobation from

---

[76] *R v Charles Woolley and Louisa Garrett*. Calomel was a form of mercury commonly used to cure syphilis; Plater, Duncan and Milne, "'Innocent Victim of Circumstance'," 344.

[77] "Quarter Sessions," *PGIJPN*, 5 April 1861, 2; "Thursday, April 4, 1861".

[78] "Quarter Sessions," *PGIJPN*, 5 April 1861, 2.

[79] Leipold and Abbasi, "The Impact of Joinder and Severance," 358.

society, while scholarship addressing women and the law indicates that a lack of passivity from women in court could lead to harsher sentencing.[80] Later the Advocate-General was to recall that "her conduct in court during the trial was highly reprehensible and more than once elicited the stern rebuke of the judge."[81] Other evidence given in court would also have presented Louisa as a disorderly woman and would certainly have affected her case. This included evidence from Michael Benson who testified that on 7 March, the day after Woolley had returned to the Waterside Lockup, Louisa was shouting loudly enough for Woolley to hear her:

> Woolley is innocent, I am to blame; Woolley must not suffer, I gave Garrett the poison, I gave him the stuff; I am willing to suffer; I will be revenged of Garrett, I will kill him yet, I wish the Sessions was come, I will let them see how I can take punishment, I will be a ticket-of-leave woman.[82]

Devine testified that Louisa was "shouting at the top of her voice." Police Constable Lally gave evidence during the trial that, when he went to Charles's house to arrest Louisa and Woolley for the theft of the firewood, both were sleeping in the same room.[83] This evidence of agency and of extramarital intimacy between Woolley and Louisa would have indicated to a jury that Louisa's behaviour was neither passive, chaste, or modest and deviated from the gendered assumptions of "respectable" behaviour expected from nineteenth-century women.

The jury found both defendants guilty and Burt recorded a sentence of death for both Louisa and Woolley.[84] It is interesting to speculate whether this sentence came as a surprise to either of the defendants. There is no evidence to indicate that the death sentence was seriously considered as an outcome of the trial by either of them, although

---

80 Frances Heidensohn, *Women and Crime* (London: Macmillan Press, 1985), 42; Shani D'Cruze and Louise A. Jackson, *Women, Crime and Justice in England since 1660* (Basingstoke, U.K.: Palgrave McMillan, 2009), 142.

81 George Stone to the Colonial Secretary, 19 May 1862, S2941 cons36 493 294, SROWA.

82 "Quarter Sessions," *PGIJPN*, 5 April 1861, 2.

83 "Thursday, April 4, 1861".

84 Finnane, "Western Australia Criminal Trials 1830–1861".

Woolley's efforts to gain an acquittal may indicate that he considered this as a possibility. Five days later, the Executive Council commuted both sentences to penal servitude for life.[85] Louisa was returned to the Waterside Lockup to serve out her sentence.[86] In 1865, the *West Australian* published a scathing report of the conditions in this lockup stating that the gaol, which consisted of dark cells and narrow passages, was "unhealthy and therefor unfit for the abode for human beings."[87] Woolley was returned to the Convict Establishment at Fremantle.[88]

It is surprising, given the nature of the crime, to discover that Charles Garrett petitioned Governor Hampton twice for the release of his wife. Charles's first petition, written in December of 1861, was rejected because Louisa was "without character and undeserving of any interference with the due course of the law."[89] Five months later Charles petitioned the Governor again to have Louisa released and to "receive her to his home and treat her as his wife."[90] He explained that he considered Woolley solely responsible for the poisoning and that Louisa had no knowledge of Woolley's intentions and, furthermore, he believed that Louisa was "totally in the power of Woolley" and that her actions during the time of the trial were driven by her desire to prevent Woolley from being executed. The Attorney-General was adamant that it was too soon to release Louisa writing that:

> The object of the Law is not to punish the individual, but the crime, and example is more desired than the physical suffering of the delinquent. If such sentences ... are released so soon, 13 months after they are passed, the beneficial deterring influence on society ... may be considerably, if not altogether, weakened.[91]

85 Executive Council minutes, 9 April 1861, S1620 cons1058 6, SROWA.

86 Charles Garrett to the Governor, May 1862, S2941 cons36 493 294, SROWA.

87 "The Jail at Perth," *West Australian Times*, 10 December 1863, 2.

88 Receipts and discharges, 9 April 1861, S5073 cons1156 R&D3, SROWA.

89 Colonial Secretary to Charles Garrett, 20 December 1861, S2755 cons49 37 259, SROWA.

90 Charles Garrett to the Governor, May 1862, S2941 cons36 493 294, SROWA.

91 Charles Garrett to the Governor, May 1862, S2941 cons36 493 294, SROWA.

Significantly, he also cited Louisa's "reprehensible" conduct during the trial. A year later the Executive Council examined Garrett's petition again. They decided that, because "there exists no proper place of confinement for women" and because Louisa was imprisoned in the lockup, "a place quite unfit for such a purpose," she could be released on a ticket-of-leave, "provided her husband was still willing to receive her."[92] Charles still desired Louisa's release but specified that she should not be released until he was able to be present so that "she will not have an opportunity of visiting her ill advisors … as I wish to keep her in future entirely from them if I possibly can."[93] So Louisa became a "ticket-of-leave woman" but was effectively released into the custody of her husband, whose intention was to control her movements and social relationships.

As she was released on a ticket-of-leave, authorities were still able to track and control Louisa's movements. She returned to her husband until, in October 1864, Charles was convicted of the theft of a bag of flour and sentenced to three years' penal servitude.[94] Louisa, pregnant with their first child, was left without support, and in February 1865, was forced to enter the Poor House for the birth of her baby girl.[95] Within weeks of her discharge, she applied for a pass to move to the Champion Bay district stating that she could "get nothing to do in Perth for myself and child and they will not take me into the home [Poor House] nor do anything for me."[96] Her request was granted and the next communications from Louisa are in 1866 when a request from her to change the conditions of her ticket-of-leave and another to leave the colony altogether are refused.[97] From this point onwards, Louisa's name is absent

---

[92] Executive Council minutes, 13 April 1863, S1620 cons1058 6, SROWA.

[93] Charles Garrett to Colonial Secretary, 22 April 1863, S2941 cons36 493 291, SROWA.

[94] "Supreme Court—Criminal Side," *Perth Gazette and West Australian Times (PGWAT)*, 7 October 1864, 3.

[95] Resident Magistrate York to Colonial Secretary, 28 January 1865, S2941 cons36 561 52, 54, SROWA; Birth, Sarah Jane Garratt, no. 8410, 1865, Perth, "Online Index Search Tool," Department of Justice, accessed 4 August 2023, https://www.wa.gov.au/organisation/department-of-justice/online-index-search-tool.

[96] Louisa Garrett to Comptroller General, 22 April 1865, S2941 cons36 493 293, SROWA.

[97] Colonial Secretary to Louisa Garrett, 14 February 1866, S2755 cons49 39 690, SROWA; Colonial Secretary to Louisa Garrett, 10 December 1866, S2755 cons49 39 1112, SROWA.

from the criminal records. Charles Woolley spent the rest of his life in and out of the Convict Establishment for minor offences and died in 1901.[98] I have found no evidence to suggest that Louisa and Woolley were ever reunited.

Although Louisa contradicts herself numerous times in her letters, the picture they present is that of a young woman attempting to shield an older lover. It seems clear that she knew of a poisoning attempt, although the letters do not make clear whether it was herself or Woolley who was responsible for this. Her case illustrates some of the concerns around the use of joint trials, including the opportunity of shifting blame from one defendant to another, and association of guilt, where one defendant is tainted in the minds of the jury by their association with the other. It also illustrates how behaviour that did not meet gender norms could be detrimental to a woman's chances at trial and in sentencing. Louisa's life during this period was shaped by men, many of whom had the legal power to control her. Her actions and decisions were profoundly affected by her relationship with her lover and her husband, and her later movements were controlled by the Comptroller General.

Crimes Against the State

Crimes in which no clear victims were discerned might be treated differently by the press. On 3 July 1861, John and Catherine Childerhouse and their daughter Agnes were tried jointly on the charge of harbouring an escaped convict.[99] This is the only multi-defendant trial which cannot be categorised as a crime against person or property and, from the outset, it was treated by the press as an occasion for levity. The *Perth Gazette* wrote:

[98] Convict registers, Convict Department, S5056 cons1156 R12–13, SROWA; "Charles Woolley," Metropolitan Cemeteries Board, accessed 5 August 2023, https://portal.mcb.wa.gov.au/name-search/ns-detail/?id=cc789308-de1c-ec11-b6e7-00224814cbaf.

[99] *R v Childerhouse and others*, 3 July 1861, S122 cons3473 1 case 9, SROWA.

> On Tuesday evening last one of the most ridiculous occurrences took place in our metropolis that perhaps ever came to the knowledge of even the most patriarchal of our readers, and has afforded to many, no small amount of genuine fun.[100]

John Childerhouse was an enrolled pensioner guard, employed as a guard on the convict ship the *Palmerston* which arrived in Western Australia on 11 February 1861, a few months before the trial. John and his family travelled out to Western Australia on board this ship with 293 convicts, one of whom was Edward James Salter, also known as Edward Holmes.[101] After his arrival in the colony, Holmes worked under police guard as a boatman. On 4 June, he was noticed to be missing from his work.[102]

Evidence presented at the trial showed that three days previous to this John and Catherine had purchased a suit of clothes in Holmes's size. Holmes, wearing this suit after having discarded his prison uniform, arrived with Agnes at the Freemasons Hotel in Perth on the evening of 4 June, where Holmes ordered a bedroom for "him and his wife." They later had tea in the parlour where they were joined by Agnes's parents. Holmes and Agnes spent the night at the hotel and ate breakfast there before Holmes returned to the convict establishment.[103] All three defendants were found not guilty, at which the observers in the courtroom burst into applause.[104] Not only had Agnes's parents gone to extreme lengths to allow Holmes and Agnes to spend a single night together, but the authorities had been made to look both foolish and incompetent. It seems that crimes directed against the State rather than individuals may not have been considered as serious by society and, in this instance, were treated as an occasion for entertainment and amusement. It also appears

---

[100] "General Intelligence," *PGIJPN*, 7 June 1861, 3.

[101] "Shipping Intelligence," *PGIJPN,* 15 February 1861, 2; *R v Childerhouse and others.* Edward James Salter, also known as Edward Holmes, is not the same man mentioned earlier as Sophia Paviour's partner.

[102] *R v Childerhouse and others.*

[103] *R v Childerhouse and others.*

[104] "Supreme Court—Criminal Side," *PGIJPN,* 12 July 1861, 3.

that the jury was willing, in this case, to treat the evidence, or lack of evidence, as applying equally to all defendants.

Accomplice Evidence

Another legal institution that scholars have cited as contributing to the injustice of multi-defendant trials is the opportunity they gave for the use of accomplice evidence. The practice of using accomplice evidence, where cases against offenders were abandoned in return for their testimony against co-accused, was common in the nineteenth century but carried with it a high danger of perjury.[105] The unreliability of evidence given by witnesses keen to escape the death sentence was recognised by judges at the time, but continued to operate as it was frequently considered the only means of securing a conviction.[106]

In 1833, Mary Burgess was tried in the Court of Quarter Sessions for simple larceny. She was accused of stealing a carpet bag, a pair of fustian trousers, a clasp knife, and a riding habit belonging to Nathaniel Shaw.[107] Unlike Mary, Shaw was not working class. His family had bought land on the upper Swan, and he belonged to a class with both power and influence.[108] Mary had separated from her husband Henry, a sawyer, and lived next door to Luke Leake's store in Perth, while her younger son was boarded with a widow, Christiana Robertson, in Fremantle.[109]

Jane Geake appeared as a witness for the prosecution. Geake, a young, unmarried woman who earned her living through sex work, was lodging in Mary's house at the time.[110] Obviously considered an accomplice in the crime, she was, according to the *Perth Gazette*, "admitted King's

105 Piper and Vogel, "Co-Offenders before the Court," 124; John Langbein, *The Origins of Adversary Criminal Trial* (Oxford: Oxford University Press, 2005), 161.

106 Langbein, *The Origins of Adversary Criminal Trial*, 165.

107 *R v Mary Burgess*, 1 October 1833, cons 3472 14 case 74, SROWA.

108 William Tanner et al., *The Tanner Letters: A Pioneer Saga of Swan River & Tasmania, 1831–1845* (Nedlands, W.A: University of Western Australia Press, 1981), 34.

109 *R v Mary Burgess*.

110 *R v Mary Burgess*.

evidence against her companion."[111] Geake testified that when Shaw stopped at the store, he spent some time talking to her at the door of the house. She said he was "much in liquor" and that, after he had left, she noticed the bag had been left outside the door. This point was disputed by Shaw who argued that the bag must have been left on the road when he removed items from his cart. Geake brought the bag inside where it sat for several days in the hallway. Mary removed the bag to under her bed and, when after eight weeks Shaw had still made no mention of it, she used some of the clothes inside it to make trousers for her son and lined her bonnet, and that of Geake's, with the silk lining of a riding habit found in the bag. Geake's evidence, that Mary had known the bag belonged to Nathaniel Shaw and had cut up the clothes believing that "nobody would know," was damning and Mary was convicted and sentenced to three months in prison.[112]

For some accused, testifying might be the only way to save their lives. In 1855, Phillip Dixon, a convict with a ticket-of-leave, gave testimony against Bridget Hurford and William Enoch Dodd for the murder of Bridget's husband, John Hurford, which took place at Fishleigh in the Vasse district, 213 kilometres south of Perth. Although Dixon was originally arrested for the murder, Police Inspector William Hogan requested at the hearing that the charges against Dixon should be dismissed due to "no sufficient evidence" and instead Dixon gave evidence for the prosecution.[113] At the trial, he testified that Dodd had confessed to him while drunk that he had strangled John Hurford at Bridget's direction.[114] Dodd and Hurford were convicted and both were executed for their part in the murder.[115] At the same Sessions Dixon pleaded guilty to a charge of forging the will of John Hurford, also at Bridget's request. He was sentenced to transportation for life, but the sentence was later remitted in

[111] "Magistrates Court.—Wednesday, 24th July 1833," *PGWAJ*, 27 July 1833, 118.

[112] *R v Mary Burgess*.

[113] "The Alleged Murder and Forgery at the Vasse".

[114] *R v William Enoch Dodd and Bridget Hurford*, 3 October 1855, S122 cons3472 109 case 673, SROWA.

[115] "Public Executions," *PGIJPN*, 19 October 1855, 3.

consideration of his testimony in the murder case.[116] The *Perth Gazette* expressed scepticism that the use of Dixon as a prosecution witness would ensure justice, complaining that "he returned to his place of retirement soon to reappear on the stage in the somewhat strange character of a truthful witness."[117]

Although accomplice testimony was often used by the State to gain a conviction, not all accomplices were willing to turn "Queen's evidence." In 1871, Margaret Cody, who came to Western Australia as the wife of a pensioner guard, was tried with her intimate partner William Davis for the murder of James Holditch in Fremantle. The two were accused of killing Holditch by hitting him on the head with a large stick and disposing of the body in the nearby Swan River (Fig. 4.3). The testimony of Police Sergeant William Dale at the trial created a minor sensation in the newspapers, the *Herald* reporting on the "extraordinary evidence of Police Sergeant Dale, that he had under high authority, visited the woman Coady [*sic*] in prison … and offered her a free pardon to tell all she know about the murder."[118] This was Margaret's best chance to escape execution, and yet she told Dale "I know nothing about it."[119] The antipathy of the working classes for the police has been well documented. They were seen as instruments of the State, whose purpose was to monitor and control the working classes by the prevention of activities such as drinking, loitering, and swearing. Margaret's references to the taking of "blood money" indicate that she considered informing to the police as shameful.[120] Both Margaret and Davis were found guilty of the murder of James Holditch and Margaret became the second woman to be executed in Western Australia.[121]

---

116 "Quarter Sessions" *ICN*, 10 October 1855, 3; "Local and Domestic Intelligence," *ICN*, 10 October 1855, 2.

117 "The Alleged Murder and Forgery at the Vasse".

118 "Summary for the Mails," *Herald*, 15 July 1871, 2.

119 Archibald Paull Burt, notebook Supreme Court criminal sessions, *R v William Davis and Margaret Cody*, MN 736 acc. 2850A, SLWA.

120 Chris Owen, *"Every Mother's Son Is Guilty": Policing the Kimberley Frontier of Western Australia 1882–1905* (Crawley, W.A: UWA Publishing, 2016), 45; *R v William Davis and Margaret Cody*, 5 July 1871, S122 cons3473 56 case 447, SROWA.

121 "Advertising," *ICN*, 19 July 1871, 2.

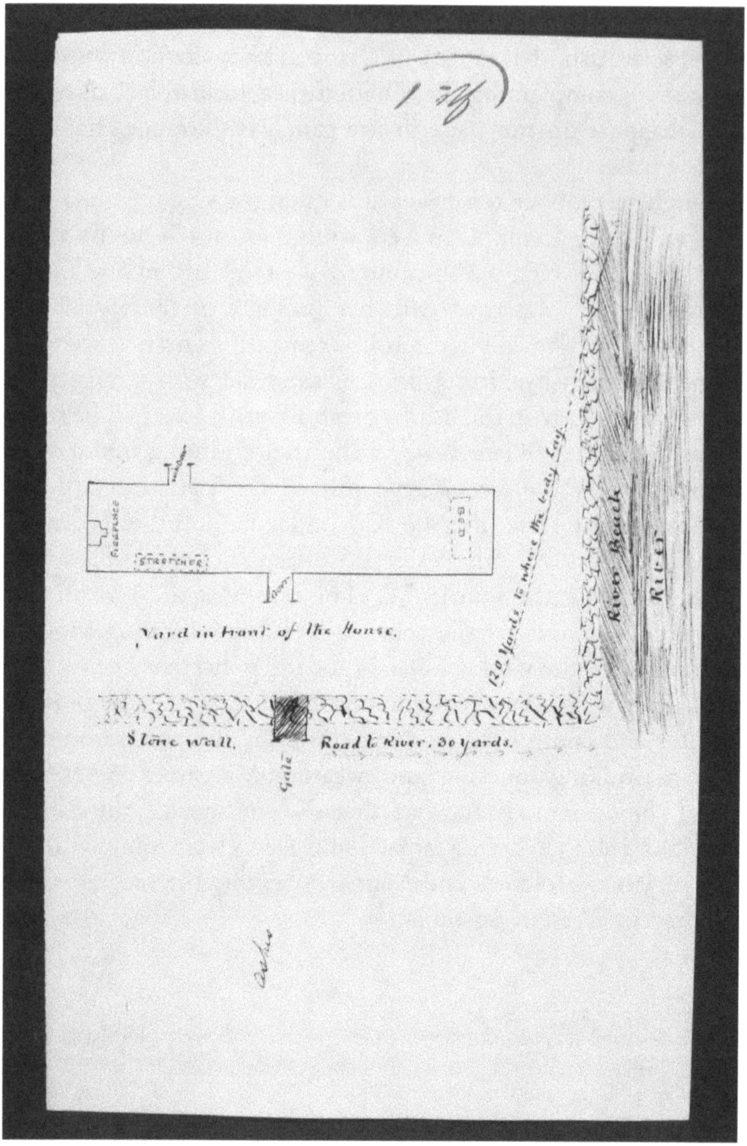

Fig. 4.3 Plan of William Davis's house, presented in evidence in 1871, showing the position of Holditch's body and the Swan River. Courtesy SROWA, *R v William Davis and Margaret Cody*, 5 July 1871, S122 cons3473 56 case 447

Piper and Vogel point to a clear link, based on empirical evidence, between the use of accomplice testimony in theft trials in Victoria, and convictions.[122] Despite the obvious risk of perjury attendant upon the use of accomplice testimony, it is clear that authorities used this means to ensure convictions in trials for both interpersonal crime and property crime in nineteenth-century Western Australia.

Conclusion

This research suggests that for women tried in multi-defendant trials in the upper courts of Western Australia before 1891, patterns of conviction and sentencing vary from those long defined by legal scholars for the general population of offenders. Women who were tried with co-accused were less likely to be found guilty of the crime for which they were tried than those who were tried singly. This is contrary to recent work using "big data" which found that there were no significant differences between the outcomes of multi-defendant trials and those of single defendants.

However, the patterns between interpersonal crimes and property offences varied. Women tried for property offences with a (generally male) co-accused fit the predominant pattern, having a lower chance of conviction than solo accused. One reason for this disparity was the number of women indicted for receiving stolen goods. The case of *R v Charles Lovett and Susannah Summerland* illustrates the difficulty faced by the criminal justice system in securing a conviction against defendants indicted for receiving. In other cases, like those of *R v Scully, Wethered and Keirl* and *R v Holmes and others*, the jury appears to have acquitted female defendants based on societal understandings of women as lacking in agency. Additionally, the use of defence counsel for women tried for property offences was particularly advantageous, with every defended case receiving an acquittal.

In contrast, women who were tried for interpersonal crimes were disadvantaged by the presence of a co-defendant, who were invariably male, and were more likely to be convicted than those who were tried

122 Piper and Vogel, "Co-Offenders before the Court," 124.

as solo defendants. This is partially explained by the high number of charges of murder or intent to kill where the presence of a co-accused makes it more difficult to use the standard defences to murder of self-defence or accident. *R v Charles Woolley and Louisa Garrett* exemplifies this difficulty but is also illustrative of the opportunity joint trials give for one defendant to shift blame to the other, association of guilt, and the manner in which behaviour which did not accord with the ideology of femininity could be detrimental to the outcome of a woman's trial. The homogeneity of verdicts for interpersonal crimes indicates that, for these more serious crimes, juries may have been willing to treat evidence as applying equally to all defendants, rather than weighing evidence against individuals separately. Unlike crimes against property, women indicted for interpersonal crimes did not appear to gain any discernible advantage from representation by defence counsel. Crimes with several co-accused also allowed the State to use accomplice evidence in an attempt to secure a conviction. The case of Bridget Hurford, who was convicted with co-accused William Dodd, after testimony from accomplice turned Queen's evidence, Phillip Dixon, illustrates this point. In only one case, that of *R v Mumbleby and Belo*, was accomplice evidence also the means of gaining acquittal for the female defendant. For Aboriginal women, the issue of race affected the trial in ways which did not apply to non-Aboriginal defendants, and this issue is explored further in Chapter 5.

While overall, women tried in multi-defendant trials were found to have a greater chance of acquittal than solo defendants, this advantage was mediated by the type of crime involved. This contrasts with the findings of previous research for the general population of offenders, but the limited research undertaken on subgroups of offenders, such as women, means that it is yet to be seen whether these findings hold true for other jurisdictions.

5
Aboriginal Women as Defendants

In 1865, Yamatji woman Belo, and her husband, Mumbleby, were tried in Perth for the murder of James Rudd, who died at Butterabby, 360 kilometres north of Perth. At this trial, Mumbleby received a partial verdict of manslaughter but Belo was found not guilty.[1] The *Perth Gazette* considered this to be a weak verdict delivered by men from Perth who had little understanding of conditions on the pastoral frontier. They wrote:

> The Jury found the woman not guilty, and the man guilty of manslaughter only! Is this verdict to be taken as indicative of the view which the settlers dwelling in security, generally take of what is due for the protection of their fellows living exposed to the attacks of savage tribes, to whom the temptation of a few pounds of flour, is at all times sufficient to induce them to take the life of any man in possession of it.[2]

[1] Archibald Paull Burt, *R v Mumbleby and Belo*, notebooks Supreme Court Criminal Sittings, 6 January 1865, MN 736 ACC 2850A/5, State Library of Western Australia (SLWA).

[2] "Quarter Sessions," *Perth Gazette and West Australian Times (PGWAT)*, 13 January 1865, 2.

C. Ingram, *Women on Trial*, Palgrave Histories of Policing, Punishment and Justice,
https://doi.org/10.1007/978-3-031-98072-5_5

The attitude of this newspaper raises several questions around Aboriginal women's experiences of the criminal justice system. Were Aboriginal women treated more leniently in the criminal justice system, or was the *Gazette's* opinion based on a racialised discourse that positioned Indigenous peoples as "savage" and "primitive" and made no allowance for justification or mitigating circumstances? How did the experience of Aboriginal women, tried in the upper courts of colonial Western Australia, differ to that of non-Aboriginal women? How did the intersection of gender and Indigeneity affect the experience of the trial? What types of crime were Aboriginal women indicted for, where did these crimes occur, and how is place significant to their experience in court? Were they tried with a co-defendant and what effect did that have on the outcome of the trial? What can the case studies of women such as Monegan, Cooray, Quanitar, Elim, and Fanny Harris tell us about the experience of Indigenous women in court?

This chapter examines the trials of Aboriginal women tried in the upper courts of Western Australia between 1830 and 1890 and asks how the judicial system treated First Nations women accused of crime. I argue that Aboriginal women's experience of the criminal justice system was influenced by racialised attitudes and unequal laws, although in some instances judges appeared to exhibit an unexpected leniency. Furthermore, the *Courts of General Sessions Act 1845* (WA), where defendants in regional areas were tried in the upper courts before magistrates with little or no legal training, had a disproportionate impact on Aboriginal defendants.[3] This research is based on the eleven trials of Aboriginal women that occurred in the upper courts of Western Australia during the time period under examination. The small amount of quantitative data makes it difficult to point conclusively to a pattern but, when combined with the qualitative data in the case studies, it is possible to suggest trends in the location and categories of crimes. I begin with a short discussion of the English and colonial law used in Western Australia in the nineteenth century, to provide a context for Aboriginal women's trials, followed by a discussion of the numbers and types of crimes for which Aboriginal

[3] See also Amanda Nettelbeck, "'Keep the Magistrates Straight': Magistrates and Aboriginal Management on Australia's North-west frontiers, 1883–1905," *Aboriginal History* 38 (2014): 20.

women were tried, and the outcomes of those trials. Five case studies are included to situate this data within its historical context. They have been selected both for their representativeness and their ability to give insights into the trial process for Aboriginal women and their experience within it.

Aboriginal Women and Western Australia's Legal History

Although Aboriginal people were declared to be British subjects, researchers have detailed the unequal treatment they received at the hands of the law.[4] Aboriginal people were governed by unequal and discriminatory laws, subjected to government sanctioned massacres, and were more likely to receive a harsher punishment in the courtroom.[5]

Despite the fact that at least eleven of the 129 cases of women who appeared in the upper courts of Western Australia before 1891 were Aboriginal, there has been little academic research which examines how these women were understood in the courtroom, nor the pathways that led them there: an important step towards understanding Indigenous women in the criminal justice system today.[6] Today, Indigenous women

[4] For example see Ann Hunter, *A Different Kind of "Subject": Colonial Law in Aboriginal-European Relations in Nineteenth Century Western Australia 1829–61* (North Melbourne: Australian Scholarly Publishing, 2012); Amanda Nettelbeck, "Equals of the White Man: Prosecution of Settlers for Violence Against Aboriginal Subjects of the Crown, Colonial Western Australia," *Law and History Review* 31, no. 2 (2013), 355–90; Chris Owen, *"Every Mother's Son Is Guilty": Policing the Kimberley Frontier of Western Australia 1882–1905* (Crawley, W.A: UWA Publishing, 2017).

[5] Heather Douglas and Mark Finnane, *Indigenous Crime and Settler Law: White Sovereignty After Empire* (Basingstoke: Palgrave McMillan, 2012); Amanda Nettelbeck et al., *Fragile Settlements: Aboriginal Peoples, Law, and Resistance in South-West Australia and Prairie* (Vancouver, Canada: UBC Press, 2016).

[6] Mark Finnane, "Western Australia Criminal Trials 1830–1861" (ADA Dataverse V1, 2019), https://doi.org/10.26193/OW6SR6; Mark Finnane, "Western Australia Supreme Court 1862–1899" (ADA Dataverse, V2, 2020), https://doi.org/10.26193/ESI64N; "Search Trials," The Prosecution Project, accessed 10 January 2023, https://app.prosecutionproject.griffith.edu.au/web/public-search; Record of Court Convictions, 1861–1914, S5072 cons1156 v23, State Records Office of Western Australia (SROWA).

are incarcerated at over sixteen times the rate of the general female population.[7] The gross overrepresentation of Indigenous women in Australian prisons makes the history of First Nations women in the criminal justice system both pressing and significant.

Aboriginal Women in the Criminal Archives

Until 1845, all criminal trials were presided over by the Chairman of the Quarter Sessions, Henry Mackie. Crimes that occurred outside of Perth or Fremantle required either that the court officers travel to the town of the offence to hear the trial, or that prosecutors, defendants, and witnesses be transported to the Supreme Court in Perth. In 1845, the *Courts of General Sessions Act 1845* (WA) was passed. This allowed cases tried in remote districts, including Albany, to be heard before a chairman, appointed by the governor, and a justice of the peace. The Act not only avoided the expense of sending people to or from Perth, but also avoided the problems inherent in having Mackie, as Commissioner of the Civil Court, absent from Perth.[8] Initially, this Act was only used to hold General Sessions in Albany. It was not until the 1860s that the Act began to be used in Geraldton and not until the late 1870s and early 1880s that it was used in Roebourne and Bunbury, respectively.[9]

Trials which took place under the *Courts of General Sessions Act* were not recorded in the criminal records books, and it is possible that the lack of scholarly interest in Indigenous women defendants has been due to an impression that few Indigenous women appeared in the upper courts. In Western Australia, the *Ordinance to provide for the Summary Trial and Punishment of Aboriginal Native Offenders in certain cases* was passed in 1849, meaning that many crimes committed by Aboriginal defendants, which until this time had been heard in the upper courts,

[7] "Corrective Services Australia," Australian Bureau of Statistics, accessed 14 April 2025, https://www.abs.gov.au/statistics/people/crime-and-justice/corrective-services-australia/dec-quarter-2024.

[8] *Courts of General Sessions Act 1845* (WA).

[9] "Government Gazette," *Inquirer and Commercial News (ICN)*, 29 October 1862, 2; "Items of News," *ICN*, 3 July 1878, 1; "Legislative Council," *West Australian*, 13 August 1880, 2.

were tried summarily before magistrates.[10] Additionally, by 1866, the practice of authorities was to avoid committing Aboriginal women whenever possible, possibly due to a perceived lack of suitable, and segregated, gaol accommodation.[11] Nonetheless, nearly one tenth of the female defendants appearing before the upper courts in this period have been identified as Aboriginal.

It is difficult to determine what proportion of the Aboriginal population of Western Australia this constitutes due to the imprecise and conflicting estimates of the number of Aboriginal people during the nineteenth century. The pre-contact population has been estimated to be between 100,000 and 200,000 people.[12] Geoffrey Bolton suggests that by 1870, the Aboriginal population had been reduced to approximately 18,000.[13] If Bolton is correct, the Aboriginal female population may have been as low as 7,200, as contemporary sources estimate the number of Aboriginal women as only 40 per cent of the population.[14] By contrast, the total population of colonists in 1870 was 25,135, including 9,624 women.[15]

---

10 *Ordinance to provide for the Summary Trial and Punishment of Aboriginal Native Offenders in certain cases 1849* (WA).

11 Colonial Secretary to Alfred Durlacher, S2755 cons49 46 906, SROWA.; Caroline Ingram, "'There not being any place to keep her': Incarcerating Women in Nineteenth-Century Western Australia," *Australian Historical Studies* 55, no. 1 (2024): 158–77.

12 Sylvia Hallam, "Aboriginal Population," in *Historical Encyclopedia of Western Australia*, eds Jenny Gregory and Jan Gothard (Crawley: University of Western Australia Press, 2009), 34.

13 Geoffrey Bolton, *Land of Vision and Mirage: Western Australia Since 1826* (Crawley: University of Western Australia Press, 2008), 36.

14 Sylia Hallam, "Aboriginal Demography in Southwestern Australia Census Lists," in *Aborigines of New Norcia, 1845–1914*," eds Neville Green and Lois Tillbrook (Nedlands: University of Western Australia Press, 1989), 186; Gordon Briscoe, "Disease, Health and Healing: Aspects of Indigenous Health in Western Australia and Queensland, 1900–1940" (PhD diss, Australian National University, 1996), 22.

15 R.T. Appleyard, "Western Australia: Economic and Demographic Growth, 1850–1914," in *A New History of Western Australia*, ed. C. T. Stannage (Nedlands: University of Western Australia Press, 1981), 233.

Methodology

I have examined the statistics for cases where Aboriginal women appeared as defendants to determine what types of crime Aboriginal women were tried for, what the outcomes of their trials were, and how this compared to the general population of female defendants in the upper courts. Researchers have noted that reconstructing the lives of Aboriginal people can be challenging as historians may need to rely on often incomplete colonial records, but by reconceiving biographies as "fragments" of a lifetime experience we are allowed glimpses of these lives.[16] Therefore, as in previous chapters, case studies which include the life experience of some women, and the pathways that led to their appearance in court, have been included here to exemplify the data and to place these cases in their historical context.

Historically, a range of factors, including substance abuse, mental illness, and economic deprivation, were particularly associated with women's imprisonment.[17] Case studies of the First Nations women identified in this dataset, however, show that other factors sometimes played a more significant part in their pathway to offending. These factors might include institutionalisation, abuse by non-Aboriginal men, or tensions between the pre-existing system of lore and the introduced colonial legal system.

English Law and Aboriginal Defendants

Although Stirling's 1829 Proclamation of the Colony stated that Aboriginal people would be given the same protection under law as any other British subject, he used a variety of legalistic devices to avoid having to recognise the legal status and rights of Aboriginal people

---

[16] Ann Curthoys, Shino Konishi, and Alexandra Ludewig, *The Lives and Legacies of a Carceral Island: A Biographical History of Wadjemup/Rottnest Island* (London: Routledge, 2023), 110.

[17] Alana Jayne Piper and Victoria Nagy, "Risk Factors and Pathways to Imprisonment among Incarcerated Women in Victoria, 1860–1920," *Journal of Australian Studies* 42, no. 3 (2018): 283.

as the first inhabitants of the land.[18] The prosecution of Aboriginal people in the Court of Quarter Sessions began in 1837 with trials for theft from settlers.[19] Despite protests from Aboriginal inhabitants, and some lawyers, whenever British land, lives, or property were threatened, colonists considered British sovereignty paramount.

As the frontiers pushed further outwards, driven by the colonists' increasing demands for land, new laws applying exclusively to Aboriginal people were created, including legislation designed to regulate the trial and punishment of Aboriginal offenders. These included, the *Act to Constitute the Island of Rottnest a Legal Prison 1841* (WA), which established a prison on Rottnest Island primarily for Aboriginal men, and the *Ordinance to provide for the Summary Trial and Punishment of Aboriginal Native Offenders in certain cases 1849* (WA), which allowed magistrates to prosecute and convict Aboriginal people for non-capital offences and to award up to six months' imprisonment (later increased to two years) and two dozen lashes.[20] Other Acts, such as the *Act to Make Further Provision for the Regulating of Public Houses 1843* (WA), which prohibited the supply of liquor to Aboriginal people, aimed to control the day-to-day activities of the Aboriginal population.[21] This discriminatory system of law provides the context for the trials of Aboriginal female defendants in the upper courts of colonial Western Australia.

Yiman and Bidjara scholar Marcia Langton has written that Aboriginal women are "positioned at the intersection of 'race' and gender (as markers of difference)."[22] Using an intersectional lens to examine women's crime exposes the power relationships operating in the criminal justice system. Goenpul Quandamooka scholar Aileen Moreton-Robinson points out that Indigenous women's experiences resulted

---

18 Hunter, *A Different Kind of "Subject,"* 221.

19 *R v Gear* (1837), Noongar man Gear was prosecuted in January 1837, charged with stealing wheat from George Fletcher Moore; Hunter, *A Different Kind of "Subject,"* xxv.

20 Hunter, *A Different Kind of "Subject,"* 221; Nettelbeck et al., *Fragile settlements*, 135; *An Act to constitute the Island of Rottnest a Legal Prison 1844* (WA); *Ordinance to provide for the Summary Trial and Punishment of Aboriginal Native Offenders in certain cases 1849* (WA).

21 *An Act to make further provision for the regulating of Public Houses 1843* (WA).

22 Marcia Langton, *"Well I Heard It on the Radio and I Saw It on the Television": An Essay for the Australian Film Commission on the Politics and Aesthetics of Filmmaking by and about Aboriginal People and Things* (Sydney: Australian Film commission, 1993), 45.

from differing and overlapping oppressions flowing from differing political, social, and material environments.[23] Gender and racial difference combined meant that Aboriginal women's experience in the criminal justice system was very different, not only to that of non-Indigenous women, but also to that of Aboriginal men. Not only were police, prosecutors, juries, and judges male, but they were also white, and had little understanding of Aboriginal women's customary obligations. Aboriginal women were disadvantaged in the courtroom by their economic situation and by the inability of the court to provide suitable interpreters. However, judges and juries sometimes appeared to judge Aboriginal women to be lacking in agency, and to discount their involvement in crime.

Statistics

Although the number of Aboriginal women appearing in the upper courts at this time was small, an analysis of these cases can still help us to understand their experience. Seven women were found guilty of the charge for which they were tried, two were found not guilty or guilty of a lesser charge, and in two cases the trial appears to have been dropped after the jury failed to agree on a verdict. The most significant difference between the statistics for Aboriginal and non-Aboriginal women is the number of women found "not guilty." Only one Aboriginal woman was acquitted, compared to nearly half of the non-Aboriginal women tried in the upper courts (Table 5.1).

Interpersonal Crimes

The trials of Aboriginal women were relatively evenly divided between interpersonal and property offences. This contrasts with the trials of non-Aboriginal women in which three quarters of the trials were for

[23] Aileen Moreton-Robinson, "Towards an Australian Indigenous Women's Standpoint Theory: A Methodological Tool," *Australian Feminist Studies* 28, no. 78 (2013): 332.

Table 5.1 Verdicts in the trials of Aboriginal and non-Aboriginal women in the upper courts of Western Australia, 1830–1890

Verdict	Non-Aboriginal	Percentage	Aboriginal	Percentage
Not guilty	53	45%	1	9%
Guilty	54	46%	7	64%
Guilty of a lesser crime	5	4%	1	9%
Not fit to stand	1	1%	0	0%
Jury disagreed	2	2%	2	18%
Nolle prosequi or no case	3	3%	0	0%
Total	118		11	

Compiled from data in Mark Finnane, "Western Australia Criminal Trials 1830–1861"; Mark Finnane, "Western Australia Supreme Court 1862–1899"; "Search Trials," The Prosecution Project, accessed 10 January 2023, https://app.prosecutionproject.griffith.edu.au/web/public-search; Record of Court Convictions, 1861–1914, S5072 cons1156 v23, SROWA; Albany Police Station, occurrence book, S3240 cons364, SROWA; Correspondence inwards, S2941 cons36, SROWA

property offences (Table 5.2).[24] The six cases of interpersonal crime for which Aboriginal women were indicted include three cases of homicide, although a fourth case, in which the defendants were originally charged with attempted murder, was downgraded to an indictment of "assault and battery."[25] These four cases have many similarities. Two of the killings, or attempted killings, took place on the frontier and were likely the result of resistance to the encroachment of pastoral stations into Aboriginal lands. A male co-defendant was involved in all four of the

24 Finnane, "Western Australia Criminal Trials 1830–1861"; Finnane, "Western Australia Supreme Court 1862–1899"; "Search Trials"; Record of Court Convictions, 1861–1914, S5072 cons1156 v23, SROWA.

25 *R v Herbert Johnson and Cooray*, 5 April 1854, S122 cons3472 103 case 592, SROWA; *R v Kullinga and Sarah*, 3 July 1878, S122 cons3473 93 case 843, SROWA; *R v Mumbleby and Belo*, January 1865, S122 cons3473 28 no. 64, SROWA; Frederick Pearse, *R v Cunnerbiddy alias Jacky and Narney alias Polly*, 6 January 1886, S675 cons527 1886/0644, SROWA; *Police Gazette Western Australia (PGWA)*, 1886, 8, SLWA. I have used the term "homicide" here to include manslaughter, attempted murder, murder and wilful murder.

Table 5.2 Classification of crimes for Aboriginal and non-Aboriginal female defendants 1830–1890

	Aboriginal defendants		Non-Aboriginal defendants	
Property	5	45%	78	66%
Interpersonal	6	55%	31	26%
Other	0		9	8%
Total	11	100%	118	100%

Compiled from data sourced from: Finnane, "Western Australia Criminal Trials 1830–1861"; Finnane, "Western Australia Supreme Court 1862–1899"; "Search Trials," The Prosecution Project; Record of Court Convictions, 1861–1914, S5072 cons1156 v23, SROWA; Albany Police Station, occurrence book, S3240 cons364, SROWA; Correspondence inwards, S2941 cons36, SROWA

cases and all took place in regional areas. The defendants used Aboriginal cultural implements as weapons including a dowak (throwing stick), a kylie (boomerang), a wanna (digging stick), and a gidgie (spear).[26]

Research into historical homicide cases in Western Australia, by Mark Finnane and Andy Kaladelfos, found that Aboriginal defendants were prosecuted for homicide offences at a much higher rate than others, possibly due to the fact that these offences often included several co-accused. The victims in these cases were not always settlers and were often Aboriginal people. Aboriginal defendants began to be prosecuted for homicide offences in 1838, starting with that of *R v Helia*: an *inter se* murder case, and the first homicide conviction in Western Australia.[27]

The results for Aboriginal women charged with homicide in Western Australia show a similar pattern. Aboriginal women made up one quarter of all homicide trials of women before 1891 but were charged with homicide at a rate four times higher than non-Aboriginal female defendants.[28]

[26] Burt, *R v Mumbleby and Belo*, 6 January 1865, MN 736 acc. 2850A/5, SLWA; *R v Herbert Johnson and Cooray*; Pearse, *R v Cunnerbiddy alias Jacky and Narney alias Polly*; *R v Kullinga and Sarah*.

[27] Mark Finnane and Andy Kaladelfos, "Race and Justice in an Australian Court: Prosecuting Homicide in Western Australia, 1830–1954," *Australian Historical Studies* 47, no. 3 (2016): 449, 445, 453, 454.

[28] Finnane, "Western Australia Criminal Trials 1830–1861"; Finnane, "Western Australia Supreme Court 1862–1899"; "Search trials." Three of the eleven Aboriginal defendants (27 percent) were charged with homicide compared to eight of the 118 non-Aboriginal defendants (7 percent).

All of these cases occurred with a male co-defendant and only one defendant, Belo, received an acquittal.[29] These findings suggest that Aboriginal women may also have been more likely to be charged with homicide offences than non-Aboriginal women due to these offences occurring more often with one or more co-defendants.

In three of the four cases of homicide or assault and battery with intent, the women received a verdict of guilty, or guilty of the lesser crime of manslaughter. Although Finnane and Kaladelfos's study found that half of the Aboriginal defendants charged with homicide offences received a sentence of death, no Aboriginal woman ever received a death sentence.[30] Instead, the four Aboriginal women convicted of homicide or assault and battery received sentences ranging from twelve months' imprisonment to three years' penal servitude. Judges were less lenient with their male co-accused who received sentences ranging from three years' penal servitude to penal servitude for life.[31] When male co-defendant Cunnerbiddy was convicted of assault and battery in Roebourne in 1886, Magistrate John Pearse sentenced him to fifteen years' penal servitude, writing that "In my opinion, no native murderer ever deserved hanging more than did the male prisoner in this case," despite the non-Aboriginal victim recovering from the attack.[32] Attacks upon settlers were held to a different standard to those applied to Aboriginal victims.[33] *R v Cunnerbiddy and Narney* followed directly after a case of murder where Pearse sentenced Aboriginal defendant Wallerabanda,

---

29 *R v Herbert Johnson and Cooray*; Burt, *R v Mumbleby and Belo*, 6 January 1865, MN 736, ACC 2850A/5, SLWA; Pearse, *R v Cunnerbiddy alias Jacky and Narney alias Polly*; *R v Kullinga and Sarah*.

30 Finnane and Kaladelfos, "Race and Justice," 456.

31 Burt, *R v Mumbleby and Belo*, 6 January 1865, MN 736, ACC 2850A/5, SLWA; *R v Herbert Johnson and Cooray*; Pearse, *R v Cunnerbiddy alias Jacky and Narney alias Polly*; *R v Kullinga and Sarah*.

32 Pearse, *R v Cunnerbiddy alias Jacky and Narney alias Polly*. Cunnerbiddy and female co-defendant Narney were most likely from the Thiin or Warriyangka language groups; "Map of Indigenous Australia," AIATSIS, accessed 21 April 2023, https://aiatsis.gov.au/explore/map-indigenous-australia; "News of the Week," *West Australian*, 31 October 1885, 6.

33 Katherine Roscoe and Barry Godfrey, "Postcolonial Churn and the Impact of the Criminal Justice System on Aboriginal People in Western Australia, 1829–2020," *Journal of Criminology* 55, no. 4 (2022): 536; Chris Owen, "'Weather Hot, Flies Troublesome…': Police in the Kimberley District of Western Australia 1882–1901" (PhD diss., University of Western Australia, 2013), 184.

also known as Joe, to five years' penal servitude for killing his Aboriginal wife, Annie, with a tomahawk following her repeated attempts to leave him.[34] Although the small number of Aboriginal women appearing in the upper courts makes it impossible to point to a conclusive pattern, the fact that Aboriginal women accused of murder were either acquitted, or found guilty of a lesser crime, and the shorter terms of imprisonment received by the female defendants, suggests that the judiciary granted a degree of leniency to these women which may not have been afforded to Aboriginal male defendants.

This more lenient sentencing received by Aboriginal women may have been due to a perceived lack of agency by judges and juries. Despite testimony in court showing that Cooray used her wanna (digging stick) to spear Nat Shaw and Narney caused severe injuries when she repeatedly hit Thomas Brown over the head with rocks, both Cooray and Narney received more lenient sentencing than their co-accused.[35] This suggests that judges may have disregarded evidence of Aboriginal women's violent behaviour when in the context of joint trials with a male co-accused.

Research by Badimia Yamatji scholar Robin Barrington gives a view of events in Yamitji Country during the latter half of the nineteenth century from an Indigenous perspective. Barrington refers to the criminalisation of Yamatji men resulting from their resistance to colonial incursions into their Country. By using the judicial process to remove men like Cunnerbiddy from Country, settlers were able to ensure that pastoral expansion could continue. Barrington argues that this was part of a legalised system of dispossession which disrupted cultural practices and obligations and left Yamatji women and children vulnerable.[36]

The manner in which non-Aboriginal defendants indicted for murder were represented in the press could be quite different to the representation of Aboriginal female defendants. Significantly, the three non-Aboriginal women found guilty of murder, who were also indicted

[34] Pearse, *R v Wallerabanda alias Joe and Bulberan alias Toby*, 6 January 1886, S675 cons527 1886/0644, SROWA. Wallerabanda and Annie probably belonged to the Thalanyji people; "Map of Indigenous Australia."

[35] *R v Herbert Johnson and Cooray*; Pearse, *R v Cunnerbiddy alias Jacky and Narney alias Polly*.

[36] Robin Barrington, "A Race War: Tracing Emotions on the Murchison frontier in Western Australia 1880–1915," *Studies in Western Australian History* 32 (2018): 95–117.

with a male co-accused, were represented in the press as women whose behaviour deviated from gendered assumptions of respectable femininity. Reports of the trials of Bridget Hurford, Margaret Cody, and Louisa Garrett all reported on their infidelity. These accounts also related evidence of drunkenness and abusive language in Margaret and Bridget's trials and reported negatively on Margaret's volubility and lack of deference in the courtroom.[37] Newspaper reports used derogatory terms, such as "violent and excitable" and "the agapemone of the colony," to describe the women's behaviour.[38] Although none of these women were likely to have been considered the principal in the crime, they and their co-accused were found guilty of murder. In contrast, Cooray and Belo were represented quite differently in the reports of their trials. The newspaper reports did not comment on their morality, demeanour, or appearance, instead confining their reports to the evidence related in the depositions.[39] The absence of gendered assumptions in the reporting of the trials of Aboriginal women might be seen as an indication that these women were considered as "other," that is, as women from whom the "normal rules" of feminine behaviour were not expected.[40] Despite evidence from two of the Aboriginal women that they had contributed towards the death of the victim, it seems that, as women from whom gendered behaviour was not expected, they were not tainted with guilt by association in the eyes of the jury.[41]

---

37 "The Alleged Murder and Forgery at the Vasse," *Perth Gazette and Independent Journal of Politics and News (PGIJPN)*, 14 September 1855, 3; "Supreme Court," *PGWAT*, 7 July 1871, 3; "Thursday, April 4, 1861," *ICN*, 10 April 1861, 3.

38 "Supreme Court," *ICN*, 12 July 1871, 2; "The Alleged Murder and Forgery at the Vasse".

39 "Supreme Court.—Criminal Sittings," *ICN*, 11 January 1865, 3; "Supreme Court – Criminal Side," *PGWAT*, 13 January 1865, 3; "Quarter Sessions," *PGIJPN*, 7 April 1854, 3; "Quarter Sessions," *Inquirer*, 12 April 1854, 3.

40 Liz Conor, *Skin Deep: Settler Impressions of Aboriginal Women* (Perth, WA: UWA Publishing, 2016), 4.

41 *R v Herbert Johnson and Cooray*; Burt, *R v Mumbleby and Belo*, 6 January 1865, MN 736, ACC 2850A/5, SLWA.

Case Study: Cooray

The case of Cooray, and her co-accused Herbert Johnson, who were indicted for murder in 1853, highlights some of the differences between the trials of Indigenous and non-Indigenous women. It has many similarities to the other three cases of homicide, or extreme violence, by Aboriginal women, although it is the only case which includes a non-Aboriginal co-accused. The case took place in Yued Noongar Country in the Victoria Plains district, 160 kilometres north of Perth. The story begins on 22 November 1853, when Native Policeman Tom visited Herbert Johnson at Waugal sheep station on the Bebano River for the purpose of removing Yued woman Cooray.[42] "Native policemen" were an indispensable part of policing in colonial Western Australia and assisted police in various ways, including tracking escaped convicts and acting as interpreters. They were attached to one police officer but were not paid, although the officer received an allowance with which he paid for his assistants' food and clothing. The assistants did not work within their own Country as this would have limited their ability to apprehend people whom they knew well or to whom they were related.[43] Many had been convicted of crimes and were promised a reduced sentence if they served with the police.[44] Johnson, a ticket-of-leave holder who was cohabiting with Cooray, worked as a shepherd for James Clinch. Later, Constable Joseph Gee related how Tom had told him that Johnson refused to allow him to take Cooray and attacked him with a stick. When Tom told Johnson that he would report him to the resident magistrate, Johnson replied that "he neither cared for Magistrate or Constable, that he would give her up to no one."[45] The next day Tom returned with Gee, and, despite Johnson again refusing to "give her up," Gee handcuffed Cooray and brought her to Anthony Lefroy's station, Walebing, where she was

[42] *R v Herbert Johnson and Cooray*; "Map of Indigenous Australia." As Cooray's father and brother were at "Walebing" in Yued Noongar Country it is most probable that Cooray and her family belonged to the Yued language group which is part of the Noongar Nation.

[43] Owen, "'Weather Hot, Flies Troublesome…', 174–175.

[44] Colonial Secretary, 6 October 1856, S2941 cons36 358 18–34, SROWA.

[45] *R v Herbert Johnson and Cooray.*

released to her father and brother.[46] Although the police handcuffed Cooray, they did not appear to charge either her, or Johnson, with any crime.

The language used by Gee in his deposition is indicative of the way in which Cooray's position as an Aboriginal woman, was perceived by the criminal justice system, society, and the men in her life. Gee said that Tom had been to "get a woman … from [Herbert Johnson]." Johnson "refused to give her up," so Gee ordered Tom to "take her away" before he handcuffed her and "handed her over" to her brother and father at Walebing Station. An annotation to the deposition reads "Nat Shaw had taken the woman from Cullangee and Johnson had taken her from Nat Shaw."[47] Words such as "give" or "take" indicate that these men considered Cooray's body as property that could be owned by the men in her life, and it was this perceived "ownership" that Gee considered gave him the right to handcuff Cooray, to remove her from Johnson's camp and to "hand her over" to her relatives. At no stage is there any indication in Gee's deposition that Cooray was consulted in regard to where, or with whom, she wanted to live.

A short time later, Gee heard that the local Aboriginal people had been searching unsuccessfully for Shaw. In early January, two Aboriginal prisoners, Budebemana and Jettemurre, gave information on Shaw's death, stating that he had been shot by Herbert Johnson.[48] On 14 February, Sergeant Frazer and Constable Gee set out from Toodyay to arrest the accused. Johnson was arrested at the Traveller's Inn on the Gingin Road by Gee, taken to Toodyay, and placed in the lockup pending his trial. Sergeant Frazer arrived at Waugal on 18 February with James Clinch, Cooray (who was hampered by lameness caused by a spear wound), and several other Aboriginal people. Cooray confirmed that Johnson had killed Shaw and showed them where the body was buried. A missing

46 *R v Herbert Johnson and Cooray*; "Walebing," Inherit, accessed 21 April 2023, http://inherit.stateheritage.wa.gov.au/Public/Inventory/PrintSingleRecord/7c4ce972-2a86-4de4-acee-3aba376f28fd.

47 *R v Herbert Johnson and Cooray.*

48 Walkinshaw Cowan, 9 February 1854, S2941 cons36 282 35, SROWA.

front tooth, the result of an accident when Shaw was a child, was used to identify the body.[49]

The hearing was held in Toodyay, during February and March 1854, before Magistrates Joseph Harris, James Drummond, and Walkinshaw Cowan. Johnson gave unsworn testimony that he was going out with the sheep on the day that Nat Shaw was killed when Cooray began to follow him: "The native Cullengee's wife followed me. She stopped behind … She called for me twice."[50] This statement was carefully worded. The detention of Aboriginal women by non-Indigenous men for sexual purposes was a frequent cause of violence and retribution by Aboriginal men and Johnson wanted to show Cooray in the light of a consensual partner. Research shows that not all intimate relationships between Aboriginal women and non-Indigenous men on the pastoral frontier were violent or coerced. Nonetheless, they all occurred in a context of dispossession and violence.[51] When Johnson got back to the station, he found that Shaw had speared Cooray through the thigh, a customary form of punishment for certain types of wrongdoing.[52] Shaw began to follow Johnson, throwing sticks and then stones at him. Johnson said that Shaw threatened to spear both him and Cooray unless Cooray returned.[53]

Gee related that when Cooray first told him of the killing, she said that Johnson had shot Shaw while she was away with the sheep. The account which appears in her deposition, however, is closer to that of Johnson's. In this, Cooray explains how she was asleep with Johnson in his hut when he suggested to her that they should kill Shaw. Johnson went outside and hit Shaw over the head with a stick, killing him. Cooray then speared Shaw in the side with her digging stick. They buried Shaw's body in the riverbed the next morning. Cooray's deposition reads:

---

[49] *R v Herbert Johnson and Cooray.*

[50] *R v Herbert Johnson and Cooray.*

[51] Amanda Nettelbeck, "Intimate Violence in the Pastoral Economy: Aboriginal Women's Labour and Protective Governance," in *Intimacies of Violence in the Settler Colony: Economies of Dispossession Around the Pacific Rim*, eds Penelope Edmonds and Amanda Nettelbeck (Cham, Switzerland: Palgrave Macmillan, 2018), 68.

[52] Lois Tilbrook, *Nyungar Tradition: Glimpses of Aborigines of South-Western Australia 1829–1914* (Nedlands: University of Western Australia Press, 1983), 225.

[53] *R v Herbert Johnson and Cooray.*

> I spear Nat Shaw with my "wanna". White fellow first time killem. Morning time Nat Shaw spear me in leg. He wanted me bush walk. Me walk with Johnson. Sheep walk all day. Dinner time come back. Afternoon mia [hut] get down. Night Johnson come in. Me and Johnson mia get down and sleep. Nat Shaw fire. Get down little way. Sleep. Johnson get up and wonga [say] let you and me killem. Johnson said so because Nat Shaw had thrown sticks and stones at him in the morning. Then Johnson hit him on the side of the head, hit him with big stick. Nat Shaw died (dead I think). I think then me one time gidgied [speared] on the side with wanna. After Johnson struck him he turned round and died. Directly after I struck him with the wanna. Then breakfast time bury him. River bury him. Plenty sleep. Constable come and take me away. Herbert Johnson bury him, me get down fire. Johnson put a rope round his neck and dragged him to the bed of the river. Johnson drive the sheep over him.[54]

Cooray also added further information relating to her husband and intimate partners: "I am the wife of Cullengee. I always live with Nat Shaw. First time I live with Tom Mason, then I live with Johnson."[55]

Johnson's testimony, which may have been designed to transfer blame to his co-accused, is slightly different. He claimed that he feared for his life when he saw Nat Shaw come to the door of the hut with a spear. When Shaw returned outside to sleep, Johnson followed and hit him over the head with a large stick but claimed that he was still alive when Cooray stabbed him:

> I hit him on the side of the head. I hit him as hard as I could. He rose up a little way and fell down again, then the woman speared him with the "wanna". He did not die for an hour afterwards. … The woman's spear I should say went a foot into him. … I killed him because I thought he would kill me. If we had not killed him he would have killed both of us.

Seemingly attempting to downplay his role, he stated, "I deny saying to the woman when in the hut 'let us spear Nat Shaw'."[56]

---

[54] *R v Herbert Johnson and Cooray.*

[55] *R v Herbert Johnson and Cooray.*

[56] *R v Herbert Johnson and Cooray.*

George Leake represented Johnson in court. It is not clear if Leake also represented Cooray, but the wording of the newspaper report, which refers to "the prisoner" in the singular, makes this seem unlikely. James Clinch appeared as a character witness for Johnson, telling the court: "I never knew him guilty of maltreating the natives; he is a quiet well-disposed man."[57] Johnson and Cooray both received a partial verdict of manslaughter. By finding for this lesser charge in murder cases, juries were able, to a limited extent, to control the sentence by eliminating the mandatory death sentence required to be given for murder convictions.

Johnson was sentenced to seven years' transportation: Cooray to twelve months' imprisonment with hard labour.[58] Cooray was imprisoned firstly in Fremantle Gaol and then sent to Rottnest Island Prison.[59] Most scholars writing about the prison on Wadjemup (Rottnest Island) have considered it as a place of imprisonment for Aboriginal men and boys only and have not taken into account that at least six female prisoners were sent to the island.[60] The incarceration of women on Wadjemup is significant and deserves recognition.

Crimes Against Property

Although we don't have information on the reasons why juries reached their verdicts, the higher number of guilty verdicts handed to Aboriginal defendants suggests that juries may have been influenced by racialised understandings of Indigenous peoples. Many colonists at that time supported a belief that Aboriginal people were simple, primitive, and of limited intelligence. Despite Aboriginal people being dispossessed of

---

57 "Quarter Sessions," *Inquirer*, 12 April 1854, 3; "Quarter Sessions," *PGIJPN*, 7 April 1854, 3.

58 *R v Herbert Johnson and Cooray*.

59 Gaol returns Fremantle, 7 May 1854, S2941 cons36 293 23, SROWA.

60 Curthoys, "The Beginnings of Transportation in Western Australia: Banishment, Forced Labour, and Punishment at the Aboriginal Prison on Rottnest Island before 1850," *Studies in Western Australian History* 34 (2020): 59–77; Katherine Roscoe, "'Too Many Kill 'em. Too Many Make 'em Ill': The Commission into Rottnest Prison as the Context for Section 70," *Studies in Western Australian History* 30 (2016): 43–57; Ingram "'There not being any place to keep her'."

their land, water, and food sources, many colonists still believed that Aboriginal people "stole" colonists' food because they were too lazy to work. Lieutenant Colonel James Hansen wrote of the Noongar people in a visit to Western Australia in 1831. Although he acknowledged that the colonists' killing of kangaroos had led to food shortages for the Aboriginal people: "they see their Kangaroos, upon which they chiefly depend for food, destroyed by our people," he still went on to describe them as "sad thieves though and cannot be trusted within arm's length of food ... It is difficult to imagine a race of Savages, more degraded in the scale of humanity than the wretched aborigines of Australia."[61] In 1839, eighteen-year-old James Browne, who had accompanied his parents to Albany at King George's Sound in the south of Western Australia, where his father worked as Commissary General, wrote of the Menang people:

> It is well known that amongst most savages, petty thefts are considered nothing, and where they see a chance of robbing they generally make use of it. But at the start also, it must be remembered that in their savage state they have not the same idea of right and wrong that we have, and what we may consider a great crime, may be considered by them as no crime at all.[62]

The idea of British superiority was firmly ingrained in the colonist population and would certainly have influenced the attitudes of the non-Indigenous men who made up the juries.

There are both similarities and differences between the five cases of Aboriginal women tried for property crimes in the upper courts in this study, four of which took place in and around Albany. In contrast to other areas of the State, relationships between the Menang people and the colonisers in Albany were less strained during the earlier decades of the nineteenth century, due partly to a slower pastoral expansion in the area:

---

[61] James Hanson, *A voyage: from Madras to Swan River, King George's Sound, and Van Diemen's Land in the years 1831 and 1832* (Guildford: G.W. and J. Russell, 1833), 8–9.

[62] James Browne, Holograph statement relating to the natives of King George's Sound, Western Australia, London, for the Aborigines Protection Society, 26 June 1839, Ak 34, Mitchell Library, New South Wales.

although violence did still occur.[63] In 1850 many Menang people were still living on Country within the confines of the township. A report in the *Perth Gazette* complained that "the natives of Albany are frequently insufferable nuisances. They erect their huts in the very town, importune the inhabitants with begging in the streets, and frequently disturb the congregation in church with their fighting and squabling [*sic*]."[64] Contemporary images show some Menang living a customary lifestyle in traditional mias (huts) and wearing the booka (kangaroo skin cloak) (Fig. 5.1). The close proximity of Aboriginal people and colonists in the township allowed greater opportunities for the taking of colonists' possessions.

Fig. 5.1 A group of Menang people wearing bookas (kangaroo skin cloaks), and their mia (hut), at King George's Sound, Western Australia, 1847. Engraving from a sketch by Robert Neill, Assistant Commissary General at Albany. State Library of NSW, "Group of Natives Western Australia," *Quarterly Paper / Society for the Propagation of the Gospel in Foreign Parts* 53 (1850), 1

63 Murray Arnold, *A Journey Travelled: Aboriginal-European Relations at Albany and the Surrounding Region from First Contact to 1926* (Crawley, W.A: UWA Publishing, 2015), 152. Nonetheless, individual acts of violence did occur; for example see "Quarter Sessions, Jan. 5, 1848," *PGIJPN*, 8 January 1848, 2. A particularly violent encounter occurred in 1880, at Kukenarup, 245 km north-east of Albany, when at least thirty Menang Noongar people were killed; "Ravensthorpe," Colonial Frontier Massacres in Australia, 1788–1930, accessed 21 July 2023, https://c21ch.newcastle.edu.au/colonialmassacres/detail.php?r=895.

64 "Bunbury," *PGIJPN*, 10 May 1850, 2.

The victims in all five of the cases of property offences were non-Indigenous men. In two of the trials, the defendants were charged with the theft of blankets, food, or money, another two were charged with the theft of sheep and, in one case, an Aboriginal woman was charged with uttering when she paid for goods with a forged coin.[65] The jury was unable to reach a verdict in the case of uttering but the defendants in all four cases of theft were found guilty. The juries' reluctance to find Aboriginal women "not guilty" suggests that their verdicts may have been influenced by racialised attitudes to Aboriginal people.

Case Study: Monegan

The first case of an Aboriginal woman to be tried in the upper courts of Western Australia was the case of *R v Dilly and Monegan* in 1839. Noongar man Dilly and Noongar woman Monegan were convicted for the killing of a sheep belonging to John Leake in York in Ballardong Noongar Country.[66] Dilly was seen by shepherd Joseph Burges running with a sheep on his back and was later found next to the sheep which had had its throat cut. At the same time, Burges saw Monegan running behind a flock of 150 sheep. At the committal hearing, Dilly and Monegan admitted to both charges but stated that they had done these things at the behest of other (unnamed) Aboriginal people.[67]

According to the *Perth Gazette*, the sessions were tried before Mackie, the Reverend John Wittenoom, Thomas Yule, Richard Brown and, in a possible conflict of interest, John Leake's brother George.[68] In a second possible conflict of interest, John Leake's name appears as part of the

---

[65] *R v Dilly and Monegan*, July 1839, cons 3472 38 case 205, SROWA; *R v Quanita*, 3 December 1840, S122 cons3472 44 case 229, SROWA; *R v Elim*, 8 November 1848, S2941 cons36 177 161, SROWA; Record of Court Convictions, 1861–1914, S5072 cons1156 v23, SROWA.

[66] *R v Dilly and Monegan*; "Map of Indigenous Australia." Dilly was most likely a Ballardong man, but Monegan, who was married to Djubelong, described as a "Guildford native," may have belonged to the Ballardong or Whadjuk language groups.

[67] *R v Dilly and Monegan.*

[68] "Quarter Sessions," *PGWAJ*, 6 July 1839, 107.

grand jury.[69] The *Perth Gazette* makes no mention of a defence lawyer, or an interpreter, although Francis Armstrong interpreted for a previous case in that sessions and may also have been used in Monegan's case. In evidence that appears to conflict with testimony given at the committal hearing, Dilly stated in his defence that the sheep was already dead when he found it and Monegan claimed that, contrary to Burges's assertion that she was attempting to drive away the flock, the sheep merely ran with her when she herself began to run.[70]

Dilly and Monegan were found guilty, with the bench sentencing Dilly to three years' imprisonment with hard labour. In a pattern similar to the trials of Cooray and Narney, Monegan received a lighter sentence of twelve months' imprisonment, also with hard labour.[71] Monegan spent the next year at Fremantle Gaol where she was set to picking oakum, a particularly arduous task where old ropes, frequently covered in tar, were painstakingly pulled apart and unravelled.[72] While newspaper reports did not record the judge's address to the jury, it appears that Mackie may have considered Aboriginal women like Monegan to lack agency, placing the main burden of the blame onto Dilly, who was found in possession of the dead sheep.

Both Aboriginal and non-Aboriginal people appeared in the upper courts of Western Australia charged with the theft or killing of stock. Women formed only a small minority of these, with two Aboriginal and four non-Aboriginal women charged in the upper courts for the theft of sheep, cattle, or horses. All of the women tried for the theft of sheep or cattle were tried with a male co-accused and the only case to be tried as a single defendant was that of sixteen-year-old Naomi Hessell, who took and sold watchmaker Lewis Hasluck's pony when she ran away from home with her younger brother, in 1890.[73]

---

[69] *R v Dilly and Monegan.*

[70] "Quarter Sessions," *PGWAJ*, 6 July 1839, 107.

[71] *R v Dilly and Monegan*; *R v Herbert Johnson and Cooray*; Pearse, *R v Cunnerbiddy alias Jacky and Narney alias Polly.*

[72] Gaol returns Fremantle, 1839, S2941 cons36 71, SROWA; Gaol returns Fremantle, 1840, S2941 cons36 83, SROWA; Lucy Williams and Barry Godfrey, *Criminal Women 1850–1920: Researching the Lives of Britain's Female Offenders* (Havertown: Pen & Sword Books Limited, 2018), 32.

[73] *R v Naomi Hessell*, 2 April 1890, S122 cons3473 154 case 2326, SROWA.

The motivation behind the theft of stock for Aboriginal people, however, was often different to that of colonists. Scholars have detailed how, from the 1830s, Aboriginal people took food and stock from colonists in acts of resistance against pastoral expansion across their land.[74] However, sheep and cattle were also speared for food after the colonists' unsustainable hunting of kangaroos, a major food source for Aboriginal people, severely curtailed their number. In 1848, Henry Camfield, Resident Magistrate of Albany, complained that, although Aboriginal people "see the animal on which they have all depended for food and clothing destroyed and driven beyond their reach they are severely punished if they only kill a stray sheep or calf to satisfy the cravings of hunger."[75] As the "frontier" moved further north, more and more Aboriginal defendants began to be charged with stock theft and were often tried in large numbers on the same charge.[76] Although defendants were usually male, women were detained as witnesses and were also occasionally charged. In 1887, seven women and thirty-five men were tried summarily at Roebourne Magistrates' Court for the theft of 900 sheep from La Grange Station. All were found guilty, most receiving a six-month sentence, although some male defendants were sentenced to eighteen months' imprisonment. The defendants had stated that they had killed and eaten some of the sheep because they were hungry. Magistrate Colonel Edward Angelo was scathing in his report, writing:

> In place of allowing these natives to break the law in sheer necessity of hunger would it not be better to employ them? To punish them is not

[74] Ann Hunter, "The Origin and Debate Surrounding the Development of Aboriginal Evidence Acts in Western Australia in the Early 1840s," *University of Notre Dame Australia Law Review* 9 (2007): 122; Christine Choo and Chris Owen, "Deafening Silences: Understanding Frontier Relations and the Discourse of Police Files Through the Kimberley Police Records," *Studies in Western Australian History* 23 (2003): 144.

[75] Murray, *A Journey Travelled*, 192.

[76] Choo and Owen, "Deafening Silences," 129–56; Mark Finnane, "Indigenous Peoples and Settler Criminal Law," in *The Cambridge Legal History of Australia*, eds Peter Cane, Lisa Ford and Mark David McMillan (Cambridge: Cambridge University Press, 2022), 641; Nettelbeck et al., *Fragile Settlements*, 135.

> possible. These sentences were received by the prisoners with manifest delight when it was explained to them that they would be fed.[77]

Despite his acknowledgement of the precarious conditions in which the defendants lived, Angelo stopped short of acknowledging that the expanding pastoral industry had removed the Aboriginal people's traditional food sources and fouled the water sources they depended on for survival.

Although the non-Aboriginal men and women in this study tried for stock theft and may also have stolen sheep to eat, it was less likely to have been from necessity. In 1872, Ann Munday and her son Henry, charged jointly with the theft of three of her neighbour's sheep at Guildford showed, as part of their defence, that they had purchased a leg of mutton found in their possession.[78] Regardless of whether thefts by Aboriginal people were carried out to resist colonisation, or because of hunger, stock theft impacted the colonisers' aims of pastoral expansion and those found guilty in the courts were removed from Country and imprisoned. Aboriginal men were sent to Rottnest Island Prison and Aboriginal women either to Rottnest or to Fremantle Gaol.

Case Study: Quanitar and Elim

Girls as young as eleven could be tried in the upper courts of Western Australia. Two Aboriginal girls and six non-Aboriginal girls under the age of sixteen appeared in the upper courts in this period.[79] One of these was eleven-year-old Quanitar, a Menang girl indicted for theft and housebreaking in Albany in 1840. Analysis of this case can tell us much about the attitudes of the criminal justice system to Aboriginal defendants at that time and also sheds light on judicial attitudes to Indigenous children. This was Quanitar's sixth offence, although it

---

[77] Edward Angelo to Colonial Secretary, 5 October 1887, S675 cons527 1887/4170, SROWA; *PGWA*, November 1887, 196, SLWA.

[78] *R v Henry Munday and Ann Munday*, 3 January 1872, S122 cons3473 58 case 479, SROWA.

[79] Mark Finnane, "Western Australia Criminal Trials 1830–1861"; Finnane, "Western Australia Supreme Court 1862–1899"; "Search trials".

was her first appearance in an upper court. The authorities had tried and failed to prevent her taking settlers' possessions in the past.[80] The sentence Quanitar received as an eight-year-old in 1837, when she was tried summarily for the theft of a shirt before retired naval lieutenant, Magistrate Peter Belches, seems particularly troubling to the modern reader. Belches sentenced her to:

> thirty lashes over the bare bottom, and to be kept in the house of correction for fourteen days, after which she is to be conveyed beyond the limits of the settlement and to be dismissed from it for twelve months.[81]

Despite the fact that children aged seven and above could receive the same punishment as adults until the *Juvenile Offenders Act 1848* (UK) was adopted in Western Australia, this was not a common form of punishment for girls at this time, although boys were sometimes sentenced to be "birched."[82] Attitudes to the punishment of women were undergoing change and the public whipping of women was discontinued in Britain in 1817.[83] It is likely that racialised attitudes to punishment meant that, for Belches, Quanitar's Aboriginality obviated the need to consider her gender.

When Quanitar faced her first trial in an upper court in December 1840, she appeared before Magistrates William Mackie and John Randall Phillips and a jury of twelve men from the Albany region. She was accused of breaking into the house of a young German naturalist, Johann

---

[80] Criminal record book abstract, December 1840, S2941 cons36 89 36, SROWA.

[81] "Miss Quaniton's case," Plaints – local court, 3 June 1837, S1686 cons348 003, SROWA.

[82] Enid Russell, *A History of the Law in Western Australia and its Development from 1829 to 1979* (Perth: University of Western Australia Press, 1989), 181; Jane Lydon "Racial Punishment from Slavery to Settler Colonialism: John Picton Beete in Demerara and Swan River," *Slavery & Abolition* 44, no. 1 (2023): 1–25; For an example see "Magistrate's Court," *PGWAJ*, 7 February 1835, 438; *Juvenile Offenders Act*, 10 & 11 Vic., c. 82 1848 (UK).

[83] *Whipping of Female Offenders, Abolition Act 1817*, 57 Geo. III, c 75 (UK); Robert Shoemaker, "Streets of Shame? The Crowd and Public Punishments in London, 1700–1820," in *Penal Practice and Culture, 1500–1900: Punishing the English*, eds Paul Griffiths and Simon Devereaux (Basingstoke: Palgrave Macmillan, 2003), 232–57.

Preiss, and stealing gold, money, food, and cigars.[84] The trial records indicate that despite her previous punishments for theft, Quanitar pleaded guilty and received a sentence of two years' imprisonment.[85] She was sent to Fremantle Gaol but was released by the Governor's orders on 29 June 1841.[86] In 1851, Quanitar made use of the criminal justice system for her own advantage when she made a complaint against her husband, Mongubert, stating that he had speared her twice for refusing to "go into the bush" with him. Quanitar was afraid Mongubert would kill her if she did so and wanted to continue working at Kendenup, near Albany. Mongubert was tried summarily and sentenced to three months' imprisonment with hard labour.[87] From that point onwards, Quanitar disappears from the colonial records.

On 9 November 1848, Elim, a twelve-year-old Menang girl from the Albany region, was tried in the General Sessions for stealing two blankets belonging to William Cooper. This was her eighth offence, although her first trial in the upper courts.[88] When detained, Elim agreed that she had taken the blankets and demonstrated how she was able to gain access to the outhouse at storekeeper John Uglow's residence.[89] The fact that Uglow was a member of the grand jury that committed Elim for trial is indicative of the difficulty the courts had in finding sufficient jurors in the small town of Albany but also points to a disregard for the rights of Aboriginal defendants and the disadvantage defendants faced when unable to access representation.

The Chairman of the General Sessions, John Randall Phillips, was clearly troubled by Elim's situation, calling her a "poor unfortunate creature" in his correspondence to the Colonial Secretary. However, this

---

[84] J. H. Calaby, "Preiss, Johann August Ludwig (1811–1883)," *Australian Dictionary of Biography*, National Centre of Biography, accessed 21 April 2021, https://adb.anu.edu.au/biography/preiss-johann-august-ludwig-2561/text3493; *R v Quanita.*

[85] *R v Quanita*; List of prisoners Albany, S2941 cons36 98 4, SROWA.

[86] Quarterly returns of prisoners, July 1841, S270 cons3676 7, SROWA.

[87] Correspondence inwards, 28 January 1851, S2941 cons36 212 47, SROWA.

[88] Phillips to Colonial Secretary, 26 September 1848, S2941 cons36 173 131–32, SROWA; Quarterly return of prisoners, 1848, cons36 179 127, SROWA; Criminal Record Book, S2941 cons36 177 156, SROWA.

[89] Phillips to Colonial Secretary.

letter also suggests a lack of understanding and a disregard of Aboriginal customary obligations. As one of the three wives of Menang man Murnian, Elim had an obligation to contribute a share of the food for the family, but Phillips wrote that he had often punished Murnian for "taking from her the very bread I had given her for her own support." In the same letter Phillips also expressed the opinion that Elim may have committed the offence because she preferred gaol to her present situation, "finding herself better fed and less beaten when in gaol than out."[90] This view seems hardly credible given that, due to insufficient space in the Albany Gaol, Elim was locked in a cell all day, and then "turned out" to sleep in the yard at night, to allow the male prisoners to be locked into the cells.[91] Nonetheless, Phillips and his fellow magistrates, Henry Camfield and John Wright, sentenced Elim to two years' imprisonment and she was sent to Fremantle Gaol in February 1849.[92] On Elim's arrival in Fremantle, Richard Broun, the Government Resident for Fremantle, suggested that she be sent to the "native institution."[93] However, this does not appear to have occurred as she was sent on to the Perth Gaol where she disappears from the colonial records.[94]

Case Study: Fanny Harris

The passing of the *Courts of General Sessions Act* in 1845 meant that quite serious crimes began to be tried in Albany without the benefit of a legally trained judge, but magistrates could be careless and inconsistent when judging cases brought before them and their ignorance of the law could also have negative implications for defendants tried

---

[90] Phillips to Colonial Secretary.

[91] Phillips to Colonial Secretary.

[92] *R v Elim*; Henry Camfield to Colonial Secretary, 8 February 1849, S2941 cons36 189 173, SROWA; Quarterly returns of prisoners, April 1849, 3676 15, SROWA.

[93] Richard Broun to Colonial Secretary, 21 February 1849, S2941 cons36 190 36, SROWA. Broun was probably referring to the Fremantle Native School where he was a patron; Bob Reece, "Richard McBryde Broun: Fremantle's Government Resident, 1834–1858," *Early Days* 101 (2017): 35.

[94] Quarterly returns of prisoners, April 1849, S270 cons3676 15, SROWA.

in their courts.[95] The use of magistrates in the upper courts for more serious crimes impacted more heavily on Aboriginal defendants due to the geographical distribution of their crimes. During the time period under examination, over half of the Aboriginal women were tried under the *Courts of General Sessions Act* compared to just one tenth of the non-Aboriginal women.[96] The use of untrained magistrates presiding over these more serious trials had implications for both the verdict and the sentencing of Aboriginal women.

This is amply demonstrated in the case of Fanny Harris, which took place in Albany in 1866. I have been unable to find any depositions for this trial or any report of the trial in the newspapers. However, correspondence between the Government Resident and Chairman of the Quarter Sessions Sir Alexander Cockburn-Campbell, and the authorities in Perth, gives an understanding of how the magistrates' ignorance of the law, the intersection of gender and Aboriginality, and the differing power relationships at play, influenced the outcome of the case. Fanny was tried before Cockburn-Campbell, Sir Richard Spencer, and Henry Camfield. None of these men had been trained in the law.[97] Cockburn-Campbell's disquiet at the outcome of this trial can be seen in his correspondence to the Colonial Secretary's Office in Perth.

The story of Fanny's childhood provides the background and context to her trial. Her mother was Towser, an Indigenous woman from Portland Bay; her father was a sealer named John Harris.[98] Harris was one of a number of sealers who took up residence at King George's Sound. These sealers were disreputable men with a reputation for violence who

---

95 *Courts of General Sessions Act 1845* (WA); "Legislative Council," *West Australian*, 13 August 1880, 2; Nettelbeck et al., *Fragile Settlements*, 135.

96 Finnane, "Western Australia Criminal Trials 1830–1861"; Finnane, "Western Australia Supreme Court 1862–1899"; "Search Trials." Fifty-five percent of Aboriginal women (n = 11) were tried under the Act compared to 10 percent (n = 118) of non-Aboriginal women.

97 Cockburn-Campbell, Henry Camfield and Richard Spencer to Colonial Secretary, 2 March 1866, S2941 cons36 580 21–22, SROWA.

98 Anne Camfield to Colonial Secretary, 28 October 1859, S2941 cons36 437 49, SROWA; Cockburn-Campbell to Colonial Secretary, 4 January 1866, S2941 cons36 580 4, SROWA. Towser may be the Palawa woman, also known as Tinnermuck, mentioned by Augustus Robinson in 1831 as living on Kangaroo Island with James "Little" West; Brian Plomley and Kristen Anne Henley, "The Sealers of Bass Strait and the Cape Barren Island Community," *Tasmanian Historical Research Association Papers and Proceedings* 37, no. 4 (1990): 105.

began sealing in the islands of Bass Strait and off Kangaroo Island before taking up residence in Albany and the islands off the south-west coast.[99] Many brought one or more Indigenous "wives" with them, who they had obtained either by kidnapping or trade.[100] In addition to gathering food and raising their children, these women helped the men with hunting seals.[101]

It is uncertain when John Harris and Towser arrived at King George's Sound, but we know that Fanny was born at sea near Kangaroo Island around 1845.[102] By 1848, John Harris had left for the eastern states, abandoning Towser and their two young children in Albany.[103] In November 1852, seven-year-old Fanny began attending the Annesfield School for Aboriginal children, which was founded by the Reverend John Wollaston that year.[104] The school was run by Anne Camfield, the wife of the then Government Resident Henry Camfield, who at first housed the children in her own home. The children were indentured to the school for ten years and initially trained to augment the colonial labour force, although by 1871, Anne Camfield, realising that Aboriginal women were liable to sexual exploitation in the homes of colonists, expressed her preference for the girls to marry, rather than to go into service.[105]

The sending of Aboriginal children to "native schools" represents one more way that Aboriginal people were institutionalised by the colonisers.

---

99 Lynette Russell, "'Dirty Domestics and Worse Cooks': Aboriginal Women's Agency and Domestic Frontiers, Southern Australia, 1800–1850," *Frontiers: A Journal of Women Studies* 28, nos 1 and 2 (2007): 20; Arnold, *A Journey Travelled*, 52, 94; William Nairne Clark, "Remarks Respecting the Islands on the Coast of S.W. Australia," *PGWAJ*, 8 October 1842.

100 Russell, "'Dirty Domestics and Worse Cooks'," 20; Sarah Drummond, "Exiles and Island Wives: History, Fiction and the Breaksea Islanders" (PhD diss., Murdoch University, 2015), 79.

101 Kay Merry, "The Cross-Cultural Relationships Between the Sealers and the Tasmanian Aboriginal Women at Bass Strait and Kangaroo Island in the Early Nineteenth Century," *Counterpoints* (2003): 86.

102 Death certificate, Fanny Harris, no. 5400058, Plantagenet, 1932.

103 John Ramsden Wollaston, *Wollaston's Albany Journals, Journals and Diaries (1841–1856)* (Nedlands: University of Western Australia Press, 1975), 199.

104 Green, *Aborigines of the Albany Region*, 115; "Kendenup Notes," *Albany Advertiser*, 29 September 1932, 4; Wollaston, *Wollaston's Albany Journals*, 197.

105 Joan Groves, "The Camfields: 'The Comforts of Civilisation' in Early Colonial Western Australia" (honours thesis, Edith Cowan University, 2006), 42; Wollaston, *Wollaston's Albany Journals*, 196, 199.

In an effort to imbue the Aboriginal population with the same social expectations and values held by the colonisers, a system of schools for Aboriginal children was begun, many of which were funded by the churches. Children were usually separated from the influence of their families and were taught reading, writing, arithmetic, domestic chores, and religious education.[106] For the colonisers, this also meant the creation of a trained workforce able to provide labour for the colony.[107] Although a small number of children were sent to these schools, the system was not generally successful. Aboriginal parents were reluctant to allow their children to live in the schools and many children died from infectious diseases brought into the country by the colonisers.[108]

Although coercion was undoubtedly involved in the admission of many of the children to Annesfield, the reports published by Wollaston and Anne Camfield show real affection for the children. In 1853 Wollaston wrote, “I had them all to the Parsonage, where they enjoyed tea and bread and butter on my verandah and a game of play in my garden, and no children could be more lively and better behaved.” In the same report, Anne Camfield referred to them as “a most interesting and affectionate set of children.”[109] An account published in the *Inquirer* in 1858 gives a glimpse of conditions at the school but also illustrates how the teaching and application of domestic chores was privileged over other forms of education:

> They have iron bedsteads and stretchers, with clean, homely sheets and blankets, and change of dress for the night, together with abundance of water, and soap, and rough towels, which they are made to use freely. The elder girls are taught all useful domestic works. They wash, and iron or mangle, the clothes of the Institute. They bake, and cook, and scrub. At present they have not learnt to milk, but they can make butter, and there is little housework that they are not capable of doing. There are several young children in the school, and there have been some quite young

[106] Lois Tilbrook, “Shadows in the Archives: An Interpretation of European Colonization and Aboriginal Response in the Swan River area” (PhD diss., University of Western Australia, 1987), 334; Arnold, *A Journey Travelled*, 134.

[107] Bob Reece, “The Revd George King,” *Studies in Western Australian History* 20 (2000): 44.

[108] Arnold, *A Journey Travelled*, 134.

[109] Wollaston, *Wollaston's Albany Journals*, 199; Groves, “The Camfields,” 50.

> infants, so that they have a knowledge, too, of nursery duties. The school routine extends not beyond reading and writing, and a little arithmetic. They read well, marking the stops, &c, and they spell very correctly.[110]

In early January 1853, Fanny's mother died from influenza, which was prevalent in the community at the time.[111] Her three-week-old daughter Rebecca was admitted to Annesfield but also died two weeks later.[112] The Aboriginal population had little immunity to the disease and at least two other children at Annesfield were made orphans by influenza that year.[113] Fanny's younger brother, John Edward Harris, was sent to live with fifty-six-year-old retired sealer and whaler, John Williams, whose intimate partner, Fanny Bryan, was an Indigenous woman from the Portland Bay area of Victoria and had been a friend of Towser.[114] Williams had made his wealth in 1850 by salvaging a valuable cargo of copper from the wreck of the *Harlequin.*[115]

In 1859, Anne Camfield sent Fanny, now fourteen years old, to live with Williams and Bryan, who lived at Nunijup, 100 kilometres north of Albany, and were "desirous for Fanny to come to them."[116] Fanny had three years left of her indenture but Anne suggested that Williams sign an agreement to bind him to care for Fanny for the next three years.[117] While there, Fanny worked as Williams's shepherd, despite not receiving the wages promised to her.[118] In May 1865, Fanny gave birth

---

110 "Natives' Institution," *ICN*, 18 August 1858, 3.

111 "Natives' Institution"; Wollaston, *Wollaston's Albany Journals*, 196, 199.

112 St John's baptism register, MN612 Acc. 3540A/1, SLWA; "Natives' Institution"; St John's burial register, Anglican Church Western Australian records, MN612 Acc. 3540A/1, SLWA.

113 Arnold, *A Journey Travelled*, 142, 146; Sandy Toussaint, "Western Australia," in *Contested Ground: Australian Aborigines Under the British Crown*, ed. Ann McGrath (London: Routledge, 2020), 246; Wollaston, *Wollaston's Albany Journals*, 196, 199.

114 Anne Camfield to Colonial Secretary; John Pavey (alias John Williams), files probate, 1883, S34 cons3403 1883/670, SROWA.

115 "King George's Sound," *Inquirer*, 9 October 1850, 3; "Local Intelligence," *PGIJPN*, 1 November 1850, 3.

116 Campbell Beer, *John Bailey Pavey (1797–1882): Mariner, Sealer, Whaler and Plantagenet Pioneer* (Roleystone, W.A.: Campbell Beer, 2009), 44–45; Anne Camfield to Colonial Secretary.

117 Anne Camfield to Colonial Secretary.

118 Cockburn-Campbell to Colonial Secretary, 24 February 1866, S2941 cons36 580 29, SROWA.

to Williams's child. The baby did not live, and Williams, now sixty-eight years old and the only other witness to the birth, was to report later that it was stillborn.[119] This was the first of three children of Williams's that Fanny would give birth to during her time at Nunijup and her later stated dislike of Williams suggests that she was coerced.[120]

On 22 December, Albert Hassell, who ran a nearby property with his brother, complained to the police that Fanny had stolen and killed one of his lambs. On the same day, the police became aware, probably from information given by Hassell, of the birth of Fanny's baby. These two complaints were to set off a chain of events that would have grave consequences for Fanny. Constables O'Keefe and McGuire were sent to Nunijup to arrest her for stock theft.[121] Fearing that the death of Fanny's baby may have been infanticide, they also issued Williams with a summons for failing to register a death.[122] Both constables complained later that while trying to carry out these duties they were threatened and assaulted by Williams, who tried to persuade Fanny to do likewise. However, there was still further hardship for Fanny that day when the horse brought by O'Keefe to convey her to Albany threw her and galloped off, twenty-six miles from the town.[123] The police occurrence book does not state whether Fanny had to walk the remaining distance or whether she rode O'Keefe's horse.

On arrival at Albany, the magistrate committed Fanny for trial at the next Quarter Sessions, and she was sent to Albany Gaol.[124] While there, Fanny was confined in one of the two cells while the other was occupied

---

119 Albany Police Station, occurrence book, 22 December 1865, S2941 cons364 1, SROWA; Cockburn-Campbell to Colonial Secretary, 4 January 1866.

120 Birth, John Williams no. 11046, 1868, Hay District, "Online Index Search Tool, " Department of Justice, accessed 15 January 2023, https://www.wa.gov.au/organisation/department-of-justice/online-index-search-tool; Birth, Edward Williams no. 13110, 1871, Plantagenet District, "Online Index Search Tool, " Department of Justice, accessed 15 January 2023, https://www.wa.gov.au/organisation/department-of-justice/online-index-search-tool; Cockburn-Campbell to Colonial Secretary, 31 March 1866, S2941 cons36 580 34–35, SROWA.

121 Albany Police Station, occurrence book, 22–23 December 1865, cons364 1, SROWA.

122 Cockburn-Campbell to Colonial Secretary, 4 January 1866; Albany Police Station, occurrence book, 23 December 1865, cons364 1, SROWA.

123 Albany Police Station, occurrence book, 26–27 December 1865, cons364 1, SROWA.

124 Albany Police Station, occurrence book, 26 December 1865, cons364 1, SROWA; Cockburn-Campbell to Colonial Secretary, 4 January 1866, S2941 cons36 580 4, SROWA.

by John Bell, also on remand for theft. As a prisoner, Fanny's Aboriginality and gender was a matter of concern for Cockburn-Campbell who wrote to the Colonial Secretary requesting that the gaol should be enlarged so that "males and females and black and white may be kept separate without subjecting the jailer or magistrate to charges of illegal and oppressive conduct towards one class or another."[125] Cockburn-Campbell's concerns are indicative of the wider attitudes of colonial society where Aboriginal people were considered to be a different class to colonists and where prisoners should be separated along racial lines.

Over the next five weeks, Williams was tried for assaulting McGuire and O'Keefe, inciting Fanny to resist arrest, running his sheep on Crown property, and failing to register the birth or death of an infant, for which he received a total of two weeks imprisonment and fines of £17.[126] The charge of trespassing on Crown property appears to have arisen from information given at Fanny's committal hearing.[127] After further enquiry by the magistrates, neither Fanny nor Williams were charged with infanticide.[128] Eventually, on 1 February, following advice from the Attorney-General George Stone, Williams was arrested as an accessory before the fact in the killing of the lamb but escaped custody on the ride to Albany and had to be rearrested in Albany later that night.[129]

Cockburn-Campbell's sympathy for Fanny is evident from very early in the proceedings. Although appointed Chairman of the General Sessions, Cockburn-Campbell's lack of legal knowledge is apparent in his communications with the authorities in Perth.[130] In correspondence to the Colonial Secretary on 4 January, Cockburn-Campbell referred to the "very lamentable case," stating that Williams had admitted to ordering

[125] Cockburn-Campbell to Colonial Secretary, 2 January 1866, S2528 cons346 087, SROWA; Henry Camfield to Colonial Secretary, 17 November 1848, S2941 cons36 179 128, SROWA; Record of Court Convictions, 1861–1914, S5072 cons1156 v23, SROWA.

[126] Albany Police Station, occurrence book, 28 December 1865, cons364 01, SROWA; Albany Police station, occurrence book, 3 January 1866, cons364 01, SROWA.

[127] Albany Police Station, occurrence book, 26 December 1865, cons364 1, SROWA.

[128] Cockburn-Campbell to Colonial Secretary, 4 January 1866.

[129] George Stone, 16 January 1866, S2941 cons36 580 6, SROWA; Albany Police Station, occurrence book, 2 February 1866, cons364 1, SROWA.

[130] "Advertising," *ICN*, 2 January 1861, 2.

Fanny to kill the lamb and asked if Williams could also be held accountable.[131] In reply, Stone explained that an accessory before the fact can be "indicted, tried, convicted and punished as if he were a principal felon" and included an indictment for both Fanny and Williams.[132]

Fanny, Williams, and John Bell were tried at the Albany Quarter Sessions on 21 February before Magistrates Spencer, Camfield, and Cockburn-Campbell. Although Williams was acquitted, the jury found Fanny guilty and the magistrates sentenced her to seven years' penal servitude.[133] On 2 March, the three Albany magistrates wrote to the Colonial Secretary, stating that they felt it was impossible to give a less severe sentence due to the seriousness of the crime but that it was obvious that Fanny was "a mere tool in the hands of her master."[134] They recommended that the sentence be reduced by four years for good conduct. The magistrates would not recommend a further reduction in the sentence, citing Fanny's knowledge of the law concerning the theft of stock. This was the result of information that Fanny gave them regarding a previous theft of 100 sheep by Williams and her knowledge that Williams routinely killed sheep belonging to others, when found in his flocks.[135]

A further three letters written by Cockburn-Campbell after the trial indicate his concern with the outcome of the case and illustrate his lack of legal knowledge. Cockburn-Campbell sent many questions to the Colonial Secretary which he said were "suggested by occurrences during the late Sessions." These included asking what should happen if the jury cannot reach a decision for one of the defendants in a joint trial, what is the correct procedure if a jury member is so sick that he cannot continue, and whether Williams could be fined for the non-attendance at the last

[131] Cockburn-Campbell to Colonial Secretary, 4 January 1866.

[132] George Stone to Cockburn-Campbell, S2941 cons36 580 5, SROWA.

[133] Albany Police Station, occurrence book, 22 February 1866, cons364 01, SROWA; Record of Court Convictions, 1861–1914, S5072 cons1156 v23, SROWA.

[134] Cockburn-Campbell, Spencer and Camfield to Colonial Secretary, 2 March 1866, S2941 cons36 580 21, SROWA.

[135] Cockburn-Campbell, Spencer and Camfield to Colonial Secretary, 2 March 1866, S2941 cons36 580 21, SROWA.

Quarter Sessions of witness Mathew Munday, a young Aboriginal shepherd in his employ. He also stated that he had considered calling Fanny as a witness for the Crown against Williams but did not do so as he "was not certain of the form in which any proposal should be made to her, without throwing discredit on her evidence."[136] This latest request may have been prompted by a private discussion Cockburn-Campbell had with Fanny where she told him details of the case that she had not revealed during the hearing:

> I have very little doubt that Fanny Harris, would, had she known that by so doing she would have avoided punishment herself, have made a plain statement of all the circumstances connected with the killing and eating the lamb, as she did to me afterwards. But I was afraid to propose anything of the kind, lest the jury should have ignored her evidence, and both parties have gone free.[137]

Stone replied to Cockburn-Campbell stating that if a member of the jury was ill then that member must be replaced and a new trial held, that although William's conduct was reprehensible, he could not be held responsible for Munday's non-appearance as all witnesses should be admitted to bail, and that a jury must return a verdict for all defendants in a joint trial.[138] Although Cockburn-Campbell knew that Williams had ordered the lamb to be killed, and despite his clear sympathy for Fanny's predicament, it appears that he was prevented from discharging Fanny in return for her evidence against Williams by a desire to make sure that at least one person paid for the crime.

Cockburn-Campbell also attempted to advocate for Fanny's property, which had been left in the possession of Williams. Seemingly not understanding that, as a convicted felon, Fanny's possessions were forfeited by the Crown, Cockburn-Campbell wished to know whether Fanny had any recourse to prevent Williams from taking and selling her possessions

---

[136] George Stone to Cockburn-Campbell, 2 March 1866, S2941 cons36 580 19, SROWA; Stone to Cockburn-Campbell, 2 March 1866, S2941 cons36 580 27, SROWA.

[137] Cockburn-Campbell to Colonial Secretary, 4 April 1866, S2941 cons36 580 26, SROWA.

[138] Stone to Cockburn-Campbell, 2 March 1866, S2941 cons36 580 19, SROWA; Stone to Cockburn-Campbell, 16 March 1866, S1685 cons346 182 18, SROWA; Colonial Secretary to Cockburn-Campbell, 19 March 1866, S2755 cons49 46, SROWA.

while she was imprisoned as "it seems hard that after many years' service she should lose all her goods."[139] Fanny had listed her possessions as two milch cows, one cow calf, two bull calves, one mare, one foal, one Timor pony, and a box containing clothes and books, which was unable to be locked. Williams had already sold her bull while she was in Albany Gaol. Stone confirmed the forfeiture of Fanny's possessions but stated that legal process must be used to remove them from Williams's possession.[140]

On 4 March Fanny was sent on the passenger cart to Perth to be imprisoned in the Waterside Lockup, but a mistake made by Cockburn-Campbell was to have further consequences for her.[141] On 19 March, Sheriff Alexander Hillman noticed an "irregularity" in the commitment warrant and wrote to the Colonial Secretary pointing out that it had not been signed by Cockburn-Campbell. Upon application, George Stone also noted that the clerk for the General Quarter Sessions at Albany had written his title incorrectly.[142] The warrant was declared void and Fanny was discharged and sent to the Perth Poor House as an interim measure.[143] Cockburn-Campbell was apologetic for using an incorrect form but protested that he had used that same form for every committal from the Court of Quarter Session since he took office in Albany. He remained concerned for Fanny, requesting that employment be found for her in Perth rather than her being returned to Williams, "more of whose nefarious proceedings come to my knowledge from time to time."[144] He noted that Fanny had stated to the gaoler, and to Anne Camfield, that she would rather remain in prison than return to Williams.[145] It seems that, in this instance, Cockburn-Campbell's ignorance of the

[139] Cockburn-Campbell to Colonial Secretary, 3 March 1866, S2941 cons36 580 28–29, SROWA.

[140] Cockburn-Campbell to Colonial Secretary, 3 March 1866.

[141] Albany Police Station, occurrence book, 4 March 1866, S2941 cons364 01, SROWA; Record of Court Convictions, 1861–1914, S5072 cons1156 v23, SROWA.

[142] Sheriff to Colonial Secretary, 19 March 1866, S2941 cons36 576 34, SROWA.

[143] Colonial Secretary to Cockburn-Campbell, 22 March 1866, S2755 cons49 46, SROWA; Record of Court Convictions, 1861–1914, S5072 cons1156 v23, SROWA.

[144] Cockburn-Campbell to Colonial Secretary, 31 March 1866, S2941 cons36 580 34–35, SROWA.

[145] Cockburn-Campbell to Colonial Secretary, 31 March 1866.

correct procedures for the committal of prisoners had acted to Fanny's advantage.

Despite Fanny's wish that she not be returned to Williams, the records show that she bore him another two children. The first, John, was born in October 1868 but lived only a month, and the second, Edward, was born three years later, living for only two months.[146] In 1872, Fanny married William Bonworth Mason, a shepherd for the nearby Hassell family.[147] They had seven children together and lived at Mortigallup, near Nunijup, until Fanny's death in 1932.[148] In 1915, local residents pooled their funds to buy her an invalid chair, suggesting that Fanny was a well-liked and respected member of her community.[149]

We do not have any record of Fanny's demeanour or behaviour during her trial for sheep stealing, but her seven years spent at Annesfield would have made her well aware of the gendered assumptions of behaviour expected from "respectable" women in colonial society. The magistrates' ignorance of the laws concerning bail, accomplice testimony, and the commitment form all contributed to the outcomes of Fanny's case. Although Indigeneity and gender combined to place Fanny in a position where she had no choice but to commit a crime, it was the Albany magistrates' lack of legal knowledge which contributed to her conviction, incarceration and, ultimately, her return to the life she so reviled.

---

146 Birth, John Williams no. 11046, 1868, Hay District, "Online Index Search Tool," Department of Justice, accessed 15 January 2023, https://www.wa.gov.au/organisation/department-of-justice/online-index-search-tool; Death, John Williams no. 4058, 1868, Hay District, "Online Index Search Tool, " Department of Justice, accessed 15 January 2023, https://www.wa.gov.au/organisation/department-of-justice/online-index-search-tool; Beer, *John Bailey Pavey*, 53; Birth, Edward Williams no. 13110, 1871, Plantagenet District, "Online Index Search Tool," Department of Justice, accessed 15 January 2023, https://www.wa.gov.au/organisation/depart ment-of-justice/online-index-search-tool; Death, Edward Williams no. 5085, 1871, Plantagenet district, accessed 15 January 2023, https://www.wa.gov.au/organisation/department-of-justice/online-index-search-tool.

147 Marriage, Fanny Harris and William Mason, no. 3512, 1873, Albany, "Online Index Search Tool," Department of Justice, accessed 4 August 2023, https://www.wa.gov.au/organisation/dep artment-of-justice/online-index-search-tool.

148 "Online Index Search Tool," Department of Justice, accessed 4 August 2023, https://www.wa.gov.au/organisation/department-of-justice/online-index-search-tool; "Kendenup Notes," *Albany Advertiser*, 29 September 1932, 4.

149 "Advertising," *West Australian*, 7 December 1915, 1.

Access to Counsel, Competency to Give Evidence, and Interpreters

Aboriginal defendants appearing in the upper courts had to contend with difficulties not experienced by British colonists, and they were unable to take advantage of many of the rules and procedures designed to protect defendants during a trial. None of the Aboriginal women in this study appears to have been represented at trial, even for the most serious crime of murder. Many were unfamiliar with the criminal justice system and would, in any case, have been unable to communicate with lawyers. Landor represented some Aboriginal male offenders accused of *inter se* murder during the early 1840s, and defence counsel were appointed for capital crimes during the mid-1850s but this ceased in 1858 and was not resumed until 1879.[150] As it is clear that the use of defence counsel was generally advantageous for defendants, this lack of access to counsel represents an inequity for Aboriginal defendants tried in the upper courts of Western Australia.

Another difficulty experienced by Aboriginal defendants was the issue of the competency of a witness to give evidence against their spouse. Although married witnesses were not competent (that is, could not be heard) to give evidence against their spouse, the court would not recognise Aboriginal marriage under customary law.[151] The accomplice testimony of fourteen-year-old Beegabeega in the trial of Mumbleby and Belo in 1865, helped to convict Mumbleby of manslaughter. The depositions refer to her as one of Mumbleby's "two women," and therefore possibly one of Mumbleby's wives.[152] Aboriginal wives were routinely used as witnesses against their husbands in trials for homicide and stock

[150] "Local Telegrams," *Victorian Express*, 9 July 1879, 3; Julian Harper to the Governor, 10 July 1885, S675 cons527 1885/2687, SROWA.

[151] Douglas and Finnane, *Indigenous Crime and Settler Law*, 105; "Supreme Court," *West Australian Times*, 7 April 1864, 3.

[152] R *v Mumbleby and Belo,* criminal indictment files, January 1865, AU WA S122 cons3473 28 no. 64, SROWA.

theft throughout the nineteenth century and this ruling disadvantaged Aboriginal defendants.[153]

The court also frequently had difficulties navigating the translation of languages. For many years Francis Armstrong was designated as the government interpreter, but as the frontiers pushed further outwards, Armstrong found himself unable to translate these more unfamiliar languages.[154] Although interpreters were supposed to be made available for Aboriginal defendants when required, the arrangements for translation were often improvised and dependant on circumstance.[155] Often Aboriginal police assistants, or sometimes the arresting police officer, would be pressed into service when the official court officer was unable to understand the defendant's language.[156] The "fairness" of a trial is, in part, dependant on all participants, particularly the defendant, witnesses, members of the jury, and the judge, understanding the charges and evidence brought into court. It is doubtful whether the level of interpretation in the courts at this time could be said to meet this standard.

Conclusion

This is the first study to show that 9 per cent of women tried in the upper courts of Western Australia in this time period were Aboriginal. Aboriginal female defendants have been previously overlooked due to the low number of Aboriginal women prosecuted in the upper courts and the geographical location of their crimes. This is even more significant given the authorities' reluctance to prosecute Aboriginal women, which has been uncovered by this research. The case studies examined in this chapter illustrate the distinctive experience of Aboriginal women in

153 Douglas and Finnane, *Indigenous Crime and Settler Law*, 105; "Supreme Court-Criminal Sittings," *West Australian*, 27 April 1883, 3. For example see *R v Wallerabanda alias Joe and Bulberan alias Toby*, 6 January 1886, S675 cons527 1886/0644 4, SROWA.

154 Lewis J. Bayly to Colonial Secretary, 17 March 1864, S2941 cons36 546 200, SROWA.

155 Douglas and Finnane, *Indigenous Crime and Settler Law*, 10; Finnane, "Indigenous Peoples and Settler Criminal Law," 637.

156 Nettelbeck, "'Keep the Magistrates Straight'," 25.

the criminal justice system of Western Australia. The case of Monegan, jointly indicted for stock theft with Dilly, illustrates the high value placed on stock by the colonists and exemplifies trials of Aboriginal people held in the upper courts for stock theft before the advent of the *Ordinance to provide for the Summary Trial and Punishment of Aboriginal Native Offenders in certain cases.* Like some other Aboriginal women indicted for homicide offences, Cooray was tried jointly with a co-accused, but received a lesser sentence than her male partner. The cases of Quanitar and Elim illustrate magistrates' disregard of the customary obligations of Aboriginal women and judicial attitudes to the punishment of Indigenous children, but also demonstrate that Aboriginal women could, and did, use the law to gain justice for themselves, in some circumstances.

Aboriginal women's indictable crime invariably occurred outside the settled areas of Perth and Fremantle, meaning that, from 1845, these women were disproportionately impacted by the *Courts of General Sessions Act* where trials were presided over by magistrates rather than a legally trained judge or chairman. Fanny Harris's case shows us that women appearing before magistrates in places such as Albany might expect a very different experience to those who appeared before a legally trained judge. Magistrates could be careless and inconsistent when judging trials and their ignorance of the law could adversely affect the course of the trial and defendants' experience.

Analysing the legal factors involved in these trials alongside issues of gender, class, and race shows that the outcomes of Aboriginal women's trials were affected by racialised understandings of Indigenous peoples, a lack of comprehension of Aboriginal lore, and a lack of adherence to the rules and procedures dictated by the judicial system. Magistrates often did not understand customary lore, as in the cases of Elim and Quanitar, who would have been expected to share food with members of their group, and judges would not recognise customary marriage laws, which disadvantaged Aboriginal defendants. However, there is evidence that a degree of leniency was shown in the sentencing of some Aboriginal women, possibly due to a perception of Aboriginal women as lacking in agency, and that Aboriginal women were sometimes able to use the judicial system to their advantage.

Aboriginal women indicted for crime in Western Australia were subject to unequal laws. In court they were disadvantaged by a lack of access to defence counsel, lack of competent interpreters, and judicial disregard for the rules of evidence. For many, the pathway to crime resulted from their lived experience as Aboriginal women and was dictated by their gender and Indigeneity. These women were members of a colonised people whose lands had been dispossessed with a consequent loss of food sources and destruction of social and cultural ties. Aboriginal women appeared in front of juries composed entirely of non-Indigenous men who did not accept a pre-existing legal system or comprehend the women's cultural obligations. Aboriginal women were less likely to receive an acquittal than non-Indigenous women, had a greater chance of being indicted for violent crime, and a greater likelihood of being convicted for the crimes for which they had been charged.

The English legal system brought to Western Australia with the colonists punished Aboriginal women, and Aboriginal men, for defending their Country from colonial invasion and for seeking justice for the deaths or incarceration of their people. Although this book looks at events of the nineteenth century, scholars have detailed how the trauma of colonial injustices still resonates among Indigenous people today.[157] Today, Indigenous women, as well as Indigenous men, are grossly overrepresented in Australia's carceral system. Perhaps the last words for this chapter should belong to Anangu man Abraham Poulson, quoted by Mark McKenna in his 2022 essay "Yukun's Return." When McKenna asked Poulson about the Australian legal system he replied: "That law is still governing [our communities] like an umbrella, police are still doing the wrong thing. Whitefella law is the wrong law."[158]

[157] Finnane, "Indigenous Peoples and Settler Criminal Law," 631; Glen Stasiuk, "Wadjemup: Rottnest Island as Black Prison and White Playground" (PhD exegesis, Murdoch university, 2015), 70; Eileen Baldry and Chris Cunneen, "Imprisoned Indigenous Women and the Shadow of Colonial Patriarchy," *Australian & New Zealand Journal of Criminology* (2014): 292.

[158] Mark McKenna, "Yukun's return," *The Monthly* (2022), accessed 10 May 2023, https://www.themonthly.com.au/issue/2022/december/mark-mckenna/yukun-s-return.

6

The Quality of Mercy: The Use of Mercy and Leniency in Women's Trials

> On Thursday evening the 3rd of January between the hours of eight and nine PM I was passing William Dixon's house. He called me in and gave me a shilling and a glass of ale. I remained with him about an hour. When I left him he told me not to be such a stranger. ... I deny having stolen any money from William Dixon's house.[1]

In 1861, Elizabeth Shea was indicted for the theft of a purse, with money and a promissory note worth £42.6.9, from the house of William Dixon in Pakenham Street, Fremantle.[2] Elizabeth was the wife of Pensioner Guard, Patrick Shea, and had emigrated with him to Western Australia onboard the *Dudbrook*, in 1853.[3] The couple had six children. The jury found Elizabeth guilty of the theft but added a mercy rider.

[1] *R v Elizabeth Shea*, 3 April 1861, S122 cons3472 case 877, State Records Office of Western Australia (SROWA); While the offer of alcohol and money suggests a sexual encounter, one shilling was well below the usual rate for sex, see Raelene Frances, *Selling Sex: A Hidden History of Prostitution* (Sydney: University of NSW Press, 2017), 67.

[2] *R v Elizabeth Shea*.

[3] M.S. James, *A Superior Body of Men* (Bloomington: Authorhouse, 2014), 1148.

C. Ingram, *Women on Trial*, Palgrave Histories of Policing, Punishment and Justice,
https://doi.org/10.1007/978-3-031-98072-5_6

They recommended her to mercy "on account of her large family."[4] She was sentenced to imprisonment for six months "with labour suited to her sex."[5]

The use and recommendation of mercy or leniency by juries or judges could affect the outcome of a trial. Many scholars have written on the lenient treatment meted out by the courts to women charged with infanticide in Britain and Australia from the beginning of the eighteenth century. In this chapter I analyse the verdicts and sentencing of women's trials to ascertain the manner in which recommendations of mercy and leniency in sentencing were used in Western Australia, and which defendants were considered worthy to receive them. I also consider the form in which leniency was dispensed, whether the character or identity of the victim mediated the response by the jury or judge and who was able to give or recommend mercy. In this chapter, I argue that women in Western Australia who killed their infant children before 1891 were treated leniently in the criminal justice system due to cultural constructions of infanticidal mothers as "virtuous" women and acknowledgement of the pressures these women faced. I also argue that defendants who were unable to present an image of respectable womanhood were less likely to receive the benefit of mercy or leniency. Thus, for example, women convicted for the crime of larceny from the person, also known as pickpocketing, were less likely to receive leniency as these women were usually recidivists and overwhelmingly known to police as "prostitutes."

I begin this chapter by examining the use of mercy and leniency in trials in general. I then set out the methods used to identify and analyse the data. This is followed by an examination of the trials in the dataset, to uncover which defendants benefitted from recommendations of mercy or leniency, who was able to give or recommend this, the reasons given for the recommendations, and what effect this had on the outcome of the trial.

---

[4] "Quarter Sessions," *Inquirer and Commercial News (ICN)*, 10 April 1861, 3.

[5] Criminal record book, 3–9 April 1861, S2941 cons36 490 5, SROWA.

The Use of Mercy and Leniency in Criminal Justice

Research into the use of mercy in women's trials in nineteenth-century Australia indicates that particular factors may have applied to women. Although the consideration of mercy was perceived to be a crucial aspect of the sentencing of capital offenders, women convicted of capital offences who were seen as virtuous might expect mercy from the criminal justice system and a commutation of the death sentence, but those who were seen as "depraved" or "abandoned" would receive little sympathy and were unlikely to receive judicial mercy.[6] These findings appear to be borne out in Western Australia by the cases of Bridget Hurford and Margaret Cody, the only two women to be executed during the period of this research, both of whom exhibited behaviours that deviated from gendered assumptions of femininity, such as drunkenness, infidelity, and volubility.

Juries were also able to add a rider to their verdict. Juries used riders when they wished to comment on issues that they considered needed to be redressed and matters that influenced their verdict, or that they found troubling. Mercy riders may also have been used as a compromise solution when a minority of jurors wished to acquit the defendant. Jury riders were reported in the newspapers indicating that the press considered the views of the ordinary person significant in criminal trials.[7]

Another way mercy was shown in the criminal trial during this period was by the use of leniency in sentencing. Infanticide was one area where both English and Australian law were at odds with society's expectations. There is a large body of research surrounding the crime of infanticide during the nineteenth century, in both Britain and Australia, which shows that mothers who were held to account for the death

[6] David Plater and Sue Milne, "'All That's Good and Virtuous or Depraved and Abandoned in the Extreme'? Capital Punishment and Mercy for Female Offenders in Colonial Australia, 1824 to 1865," *University of Tasmania Law Review* 33, no. 1 (2014): 136.

[7] Mark Coen and Niamh Howlin, "The Jury Speaks: Jury Riders in the Nineteenth and Twentieth Centuries," *American Journal of Legal History* 58 (2018): 533–534, 505.

of their infants were treated leniently in the criminal justice system.[8] The jury considered infanticide as a "special" crime that deserved a different consideration to other crimes and very few resulted in a conviction.[9] As the "civilising offensive" gained traction during the nineteenth century, changing the definition of masculine behaviour to one of chivalry and restraint, so too did women come to be seen as vulnerable innocents requiring protection.[10] An understanding of the social and economic pressures faced by infanticidal mothers meant that sympathy was extended to these women, who were considered to be both respectable and virtuous.[11] The more closely a defendant could fit her story to the generally understood narrative of the virtuous woman who was seduced and abandoned by an unscrupulous man, the more likely it would be that she was viewed sympathetically by the judge and jury.[12]

Methodology

In this chapter, I use qualitative data to analyse the application of leniency and mercy in women's trials. To do this, I examine the charge on which the defendant is indicted, the number of partial verdicts returned, the use of mercy riders, and the severity of sentencing. Recommendations to mercy were found in the criminal indictment files, Colonial Secretary's

---

[8] For example see Anne-Marie Kilday, *A History of Infanticide in Britain: c 1600 to the Present* (Basingstoke, U.K.: Palgrave MacMillan, 2013); Jan Kociumbas, "Azaria's Antecedents: Stereotyping Infanticide in Late Nineteenth-Century Australia," *Gender & History* 13, no. 1 (2001): 142; Daniel J.R. Grey, "'No Crime to Kill a Bastard-Child': Stereotypes of Infanticide in Nineteenth Century England and Wales," in *Intersections of Gender, Class, and Race in the Long Nineteenth Century and Beyond*, ed. Barbara Leonardi (Cham, Switzerland: Palgrave Macmillan, 2018), 41–66.

[9] Daniel J.R. Grey, "'A Hard-Working and Nice Person?' Respectability, Femininity and Infanticide in England and Wales, 1800–2000," in *The Emerald International Handbook of Feminist Perspectives on Women's Acts of Violence*, eds S. Banwel et al. (Bradford, U.K.: Emerald Publishing, 2023), 33–45.

[10] Shani D'Cruze and Louise A. Jackson, *Women, Crime and Justice in England since 1660* (Basingstoke, U.K: Palgrave McMillan, 2009), 11–12.

[11] Daniel J.R. Grey, "'The Agony of Despair': Pain and the Cultural Script of Infanticide in England and Wales, 1860–1960," in *Pain and Emotion in Modern History*, ed. Rob Boddice (London: Palgrave Macmillan, 2014).

[12] Grey, "'The Agony of Despair'," 204.

Office correspondence records, and criminal indictment registers, as well as the judge's notebooks and newspaper reports. As recommendations to mercy were occasionally found in just one of these sources, it is probable that some went unrecorded and have therefore not been captured in this process. Analysis of this data gives an understanding of who was able to recommend mercy and which defendants were able to benefit from these recommendations. It also indicates how juries were able to influence the outcome of a trial, even when defendants were found guilty, and the ways judges could show leniency in their sentencing decisions. The case studies were chosen to represent a diversity of crimes.

Mercy Riders, Partial Verdicts, and Sentencing in Western Australia

As mentioned in Chapter 3, the role of the jury is to pronounce guilt or innocence, and juries are not able to decide on the sentencing of a defendant. However, nineteenth-century juries were able to influence the outcome of a trial by the use of mercy riders or partial verdicts.[13] Juries would normally give a reason for recommending mercy, but it is to be noted that occasionally juries in Western Australia did not do so. I was able to find nine cases before 1891 in which mercy riders were given to female defendants. Reasons given included the defendant's youth, her large family, provocation, the small value of the goods stolen, or because the jury believed the witnesses held animosity towards the defendant.

Western Australian juries also used partial verdicts. In this way, juries were able to exercise considerable discretion and to influence the sentencing of the defendants they found guilty.[14] Richard Fox notes that mercy should not be mistaken for partial verdicts based on substantive justification or defences for crimes.[15] Nonetheless, it is apparent that in

[13] John M. Beattie, "Crime and the Courts in Surrey 1736–1753," in *Crime in England 1550–1800*, ed. J.S. Cockburn (London: Routledge, 2016), 170; Coen and Howlin, "The Jury Speaks," 505.

[14] Beattie, "Crime and the Courts in Surrey," 170.

[15] Richard G. Fox, "When Justice Sheds a Tear: The Place of Mercy in Sentencing," *Monash University Law Review* 25, no. 1 (1999): 8.

some cases nineteenth-century juries gave partial verdicts based less on legal reasons than on sympathy for the defendant. In this dataset, six women received partial verdicts. These included a defendant charged with aggravated assault but found guilty of common assault, a case of murder for which the verdict was concealment of birth, one of murder found guilty of manslaughter, a case of larceny from the person found guilty of common larceny, and two cases of wounding with intent to do grievous bodily harm found guilty of the lesser crime of unlawful wounding.

Judges also had discretionary powers to show mercy or leniency. The most obvious method at their disposal was the pronouncement of the sentence, but they could also show leniency in other ways. Judges could choose to give concurrent sentences to defendants guilty of separate crimes, so that the defendant served a shorter period of time, or they could back-date the commencement of the sentence to the time of arrest.[16] In the case of defendants found guilty of murder, which carried a mandatory sentence of death, judges could choose to give a sentence of "death recorded," indicating that they would recommend mercy, and a withdrawal of the death penalty, to the Governor.[17]

Of the sixty-seven women found guilty of a crime in this dataset, at least twenty-five could be said to have received some form of mercy or leniency. Some women benefited from mercy in several forms, such as receiving a mercy rider and a partial verdict from the jury. Some of these cases are explored in further detail in the following sections.

[16] Fox, "When Justice Sheds a Tear," 12; see also "Supreme Court – Criminal Side," *Perth Gazette and West Australian Times (PGWAT)*, 4 October1867, 2.

[17] David Plater, Joanna Duncan and Sue Milne, "Innocent Victim of Circumstance or a Very Devil Incarnate - The Trial and Execution of Elizabeth Woolcock in South Australia in 1873," *Flinders Law Journal* 15, no. 2 (2013): 318.

To Whom Was Mercy Granted?

Infanticide

Research by historians and criminologists has shown that, as in Britain, most defendants in Australian infanticide cases were domestic servants or unmarried daughters living at home.[18] As discussed in Chapter 2, the number of infanticides which went undetected is generally acknowledged by historians to be high, but infanticides committed by domestic servants were often discovered and reported by their employers. These women, who usually lived in their employers' houses, had little opportunity for privacy and often shared their room with a fellow servant.

Between 1830 and 1890, thirteen women were brought before the upper courts of Western Australia to answer a charge concerned with the death of an infant. While ten of these women did fit the standard narrative of a young unmarried woman in domestic service or living at home, two of the women, Mary Goodall and Catherine Smith, were married and living with their husbands and children, and one woman, Mary Allen, was widowed.[19] In addition to these cases several women were charged, or questioned, in relation to the death of an infant but were never tried before the Court of Quarter Sessions or the Supreme Court. Mary Summerland was indicted for the murder of her baby boy in 1832 but was discharged when the Grand Jury did not consider the evidence sufficient to go to trial.[20] Elizabeth Gamble, a domestic servant in the employ of James and Sarah Drummond, who was accused of setting fire to the room in which her baby slept, was also discharged when the committal hearing found the evidence not strong enough to go to trial.[21] In 1877, Susan Kain and Mary Ann Clancey were indicted separately for

---

[18] Judith Allen, *Sex and Secrets: Crimes Involving Australian Women Since 1880* (Melbourne: Oxford University Press, 1990), 30; Laster, "Infanticide," 158; D'Cruze, and Jackson, *Women, Crime and Justice*, 77.

[19] No title, *PGWAT*, 21 July 1865, 2; Government Resident Roebourne to Attorney-General, record of Quarter Sessions, 4 January 1888, S675 cons527 1888/0287, SROWA; *R v Mary Allen*, 5 October 1859, S122 cons3472 129 case 814, SROWA.

[20] *R v Mary Summerland*, October 1832, S122 cons3472 10, SROWA.

[21] William Henry Mackie to Colonial Secretary, 20 February 1830, S2941 cons36 005 65, SROWA.

concealment of birth of their respective infants but were not tried when the Attorney-General declared their cases "no true bill," and, in 1883, Celia Jackson was investigated by police over the suspected death of a newborn infant, but, as no body was found, Celia was never charged.[22]

Two of the thirteen cases of infanticide did not proceed to trial. The verdicts in the eleven cases which did proceed to trial were almost evenly divided between acquittal and conviction (Table 6.1). One defendant pleaded guilty to concealment of birth on the advice of her defence counsel and another four were found guilty by the jury.[23] Two defendants who received a conviction were recommended to mercy by the jury.[24] All of those convicted received custodial sentences ranging from seven days to two years.

Although the verdicts were evenly divided, analysis of the qualitative data suggests that this crime may have been treated leniently in Western Australian courts in a manner similar to that found in Britain. Eleven cases were concerned with neonaticide, that is the killing of a child under one day old, and two, the cases of Mary Goodall and Catherine Smith, concerned the death of children aged nine months old. Women were more likely to be indicted for the more serious charge of murder if the

Table 6.1 Verdicts of women indicted for crimes involving the death of an infant

	Guilty	Not guilty	Partial verdict	Not Fit to Stand Trial	*Nolle Prosequi*
Concealing birth	4	5			1
Murder			1	1	
Manslaughter	1				
Total	5	5	1	1	1

Data sourced from Mark Finnane, "Western Australia Criminal Trials 1830–1861"; Mark Finnane, "Western Australia Supreme Court 1862–1899"; Record of Court Convictions, S5072 cons1156 v23, SROWA

22 "No True Bill," *Western Australian Times*, 23 November 1877, 2; W.H. Timperley, 29 October 1883, S2126 cons430 1883/0937, SROWA.

23 "Quarter Sessions," *Perth Gazette and Independent Journal of Politics and News (PGIJPN)*, 7 October 1859, 3; *R v Mary Allen*.

24 Government Resident Roebourne to Attorney-General, 4 January 1888, S675 cons527 1888/0287, SROWA.

crime showed demonstrable violence and only one of the women tried in connection with a neonaticide was indicted for murder, the other ten women being indicted for the lesser charge of concealment of birth. This is significant as the charge of murder carried a mandatory sentence of death if found guilty, whereas the maximum penalty for the charge of concealment of birth was two years' imprisonment.[25]

Although inquests were not always held in the early years of the colony, and there was no inquest held on the body of Jane Green's baby in 1840, by 1856 every justice of the peace was authorised to act in a coronial capacity and it became common for an inquest to be held in cases where the cause of death was sudden or suspicious.[26] In 1887, an inquest was held on the body of an infant born to twenty-three-year-old domestic servant, Theresa Arnold, who worked for Charles and Lucy Paterson in Perth. Dr Edward Scott testified that the baby had a bruise on the back of his head but that the cause of death appeared to be suffocation and suggested that both may have occurred accidentally during childbirth.[27] In his summing up address to the court, Coroner George Walpole Leake stated that "most probably the unfortunate girl would be proceeded against and charged with concealment of birth."[28] The jury dutifully returned a verdict stating that "how and what means he [the child] came to his death is to them unknown."[29] This verdict, which left open the possibility of a still birth or accidental death, enabled the criminal justice system to indict for "concealment of birth" rather than the capital charge of murder. That the jury was aware of this was made obvious in a note to the Colonial Secretary by the Attorney-General, Charles Warton, who wrote: "The jury took the usual merciful view. The girl ought to be charged with concealment of birth."[30] For

25 *Malicious Shooting and Stabbing Act*, 43 Geo. III, c 58 1803 (UK).

26 Lenore Layman, "Investigating Sudden Death: Inquests in Early Colonial Western Australia, 1829–1840," *Early Days* 14, no. 3 (2014): 414–33; *Coroner's Inquest Act 1856* (WA).

27 Police Magistrate Perth to Colonial Secretary, 9 February 1887, S675 cons527 1887/0545, SROWA.

28 "Inquest," *ICN*, 9 February 1887, 5.

29 Police Magistrate Perth to Colonial Secretary, 9 February 1887, S675 cons527 1887/0545, SROWA.

30 Police Magistrate Perth to Colonial Secretary, 9 February 1887.

Theresa, leniency in the criminal justice system was apparent from the very beginning of the judicial process.

Not only could women be charged with the lesser crime of concealment of birth, but at least three women were indicted for concealment of birth even though originally charged with murder or wilful murder.[31] In March 1881, the body of a newborn infant was found in the room of William Hoop's domestic servant, twenty-two-year-old Mary Ann Stone, in York. The considerable violence noted to the body of the child (the baby's head was torn almost from the body and was connected only by the skin at one side) ensured that Mary Ann was charged with wilful murder rather than concealment of birth.[32] Dr James Hope gave evidence at the committal hearing and the trial.[33]

The evidence of medical experts in infanticide trials was often phrased to allow doubt in the minds of the jury. Historian Rachel Dixon argues that the uncertainty in the testimony of medical experts was a result of the imperfect, and poorly understood, forensic science involved in determining the cause of death of newborn infants.[34] To be considered murder, the child must not only have been born alive, but also to have had a "separate existence" from the mother. The hydrostatic test used by doctors to determine whether a child had breathed involved floating the lungs in water, but was subject to considerable criticism as being unreliable, and whether the child had had a separate existence was even harder to prove, as proof of respiration is not proof of a separate existence.[35]

However, it is clear that, in Western Australia, doctors called to give testimony in infanticide cases also commented on other aspects of the case that might help with the defence, such as the possibility of the defendant being unaware of her pregnancy, that injuries to the child

---

[31] No Title, *Herald*, 26 March 1881, 2; "General Intelligence," *PGIJPN*, 3 October 1862, 3; *R v Catherine Kelly*, 7 January 1863, S122 cons3473 10 case 76, SROWA; "Summary for the Mail," *Herald*, 19 April 1873, 3.

[32] Edward G. Back, 25 March 1881, S2126 cons430 30 708, SROWA; *R v Mary Ann Stone*, 6 April 1881, S122 cons3472 107 case 958, SROWA.

[33] *R v Mary Ann Stone*.

[34] Rachel Dixon, *Infanticide: Expert Evidence and Testimony in Child Murder Cases, 1688–1955* (London: Routledge, 2022), 191.

[35] Chris Milroy, "Neonatal Deaths, Infanticide, and the Hydrostatic (Floatation) Test: Historical Perspectives," *Academic Forensic Pathology* 2, no. 4 (2012): 338–45.

may have been caused during the natural course of the birth, or that the defendant became insensible, fainted or suffered from temporary insanity during the birth.[36] It seems likely that the uncertainty in the testimony of medical experts may have been prompted as much by sympathy for the defendant as by uncertainty over medical science.

Hope testified at Mary Ann's committal hearing that, although the child had breathed, there was no test available to determine whether this occurred before or after he was fully born. He stated that, despite the unusual amount of violence used, the injuries may have been caused during childbirth if Mary Ann had attempted to deliver her child herself: "It is quite within probability that she had torn the child's neck endeavouring to deliver herself." He added a common defence used in trials involving neonaticide saying that "sometimes when a woman is in labour her mental condition is such she does not know what she does."[37] This defence would have been understandable to the jury as it conformed to gendered understandings of women as frail and prone to mental instability. Hope's testimony convinced Magistrates Walkinshaw Cowan and Richard Meares to reduce the charge from wilful murder to concealing a birth.

Mary Ann was tried in Perth on 6 April. As well as Hope's medical evidence, the jury also heard him testify that Mary Ann had told him that she was in such agony that she "did not know what happened to the child" and other witnesses testified that Mary Ann had sent for her mother on the morning of the birth, although her mother did not arrive until the late afternoon.[38] When Justice Henry Wrenfordsley addressed the jury he reiterated these facts and advised them to "give the benefit of any doubt they might have of criminal intention to the prisoner."[39] Despite the horrific injuries to her baby, Mary Ann was acquitted at trial, based on the medical evidence given by Hope, and Wrenfordsley's address to the jury in which he emphasised that the act of Mary Anne in sending for her mother constituted evidence that she was not

---

[36] For examples see: *R v Mary Ann Stone*; "Supreme Court — Criminal Sittings," *ICN*, 2 October 1889, 5.

[37] *R v Mary Ann Stone*.

[38] "Law Intelligence," *ICN*, 13 April 1881, 1.

[39] "Law Intelligence," *ICN*, 13 April 1881, 1.

intending to conceal the fact of the birth. Mary Ann was described in one newspaper report as "a respectable and good-looking young woman," but there is no report of her demeanour in the court room.[40] Nonetheless, the distress that she must have felt while trying to give birth alone, and the disastrous consequences of her attempt to deliver her child by herself, can be easily imagined and must also have been obvious to the jury members.

Concealment of birth was not only a homicide offence but also a partial defence to the charge of murder. When seventeen-year-old Jane Green was tried for the murder of her newborn child in 1840, the jury instead found her guilty of the lesser charge of concealment of birth, despite the obvious violence used to effect the child's death (see Chapter 3).[41] This was the first case of infanticide to be tried in Western Australia and Jane received the maximum sentence available for the crime of concealment of birth; the only woman to do so. The partial verdict allowed the jury to show leniency to the defendant, even when, as in the case of Jane Green, intent to kill seemed clear.

Leniency in infanticide cases was also shown by the use of mercy riders. At least two cases involving the death of an infant were recommended for mercy by the jury. One, the case of Catherine Smith, was concerned with the death of her nine-month-old daughter, Mary Andia Smith, through neglect. Catherine was indicted for manslaughter and found guilty by the jury, although they included a "strong recommendation to mercy" with their verdict. The case is significant for the way in which the roles of husband and wife were gendered by the witnesses and was also treated differently in the court to cases of neonaticide. Catherine Smith had arrived in Cossack on 18 October 1887, with her three young children, having sailed from Auckland with her husband, who was the boatswain of the *Fanny Thornton*. Sixteen days later, the family moved to Roebourne. Witnesses testified at the trial that Catherine neglected her daughter, thus failing in her role as a mother. A shocked crew member, John FitzGerald, stated that Catherine shared the captain's cabin during the voyage rather than that of her husband. He testified that Catherine

[40] "Supreme Court—Criminal Sittings," *West Australian*, 8 April 1881, 3.

[41] *R v Jane Green*, October 1840, S122 cons3472 43 case 226, SROWA.

told her husband to wash the clothes and clean the cabin. When he refused, he was ordered to do so by the captain. Witnesses complained about the unwashed state of the baby and the "stench" coming from the Smith's cabin on the ship and from their room at the hotel in Cossack (Fig. 6.1). They also testified that Mary Andia was ill, unable to hold up her head, had bedsores, that they had not seen Catherine feed her, and that she often cried and was left alone without anyone to look after her. Mary Ann Bassett, whose husband owned Bassett's Private Hotel and Boarding House in Roebourne where the Smith family were staying when Mary Andia died, stated, "I never saw her [Catherine Smith] do any work at all. The mother of a family who does her duty is always at work."[42] In all, testimony given at the trial indicated that not only had Catherine failed to meet gendered expectations of the nurturing behaviour expected from mothers but that she also lacked the fidelity expected from virtuous women.

Evidence brought to light during the trial also emphasises how women who deviated from the discourse of "respectable" femininity could be considered dangerous. In the course of the trial, evidence was uncovered

Fig. 6.1 >Cossack 1882–1885. The White Horse Hotel, where the Smith family stayed for approximately two months, is the building third from left with verandah. Courtesy SLWA, BA2579

[42] *R v Catherine Smith*, 4 January 1888, S675 cons527 1888/0287, SROWA.

which showed that the Smith's oldest daughter, four-year-old Johanna Catherine Smith, had died in Cossack just four days after arrival. The cause of death was determined at an inquest to be due to convulsions. The local newspaper reported that:

> An elder daughter died within a few days of arrival at Cossack, but it was not then known to the authorities how the prisoner was carrying on, and no suspicions were entertained, but it is now evident that both children were the victims of cruel neglect.[43]

Thus, it was Catherine's "immoral" behaviour, onboard the ship that marked her out as dangerous and therefore capable of killing her child.

While witnesses clearly blamed Catherine for Mary Andia's death, Catherine's husband was not similarly blamed, most witnesses only referring to Catherine's neglect. Testimony from Dr Thomas Frizzell attributed the death to "improper food and neglect on the part of the mother."[44] Thomas Bassett stated that "I never saw her [Catherine] attend the child. Sometimes the husband did when he came home from work."[45] FitzGerald did, however, lay the blame for Catherine's infidelity squarely with her husband stating that:

> The prisoner slept with the captain. I never saw such conduct in a ship before. The husband was more to blame for it than the mother because he ought to have put a stop to it. The scandal was felt by all on board.[46]

In saying this, FitzGerald was articulating the commonly held belief that men, who were considered to be intellectually and physically superior to women, were morally responsible for their wife's behaviour, albeit that women were criminally responsible for their own illegal acts.[47] However,

---

[43] "District News," *Victorian Express*, 28 January 1888, 3.

[44] *R v Catherine Smith.*

[45] *R v Catherine Smith.*

[46] *R v Catherine Smith.*

[47] Joanne McEwan, "Negotiating Support: Women's Networks in London and Middlesex, c. 1730–1820" (PhD diss., University of Western Australia, 2008), 243; Martin J. Wiener, *Men of Blood: Violence, Manliness, and Criminal Justice in Victorian England* (West Nyack: Cambridge University Press, 2004), 174.

it is clear that witnesses did not see men's responsibility extending to the care of children, which was seen as purely a woman's duty.

Although this case was markedly different from the cases of neonaticide, leniency by the jury was still apparent. The first two juries empanelled were unable to reach a decision despite being locked up overnight, but the third jury, although pronouncing Catherine guilty of manslaughter, still included a strong recommendation to mercy. On later reading the case file Warton noted, "I cannot refrain from saying I am astounded at the jury making a strong recommendation to mercy in a case of such unnatural negligence on the part of a wicked mother."[48] There was no reason given by the jury for the inclusion of a mercy rider, but it is clear that, although this was not a neonaticide, the jury was still reluctant to convict a mother for the death of her child.

Recommendations to leniency might also come from other players in the trial process. Theresa Arnold pleaded guilty to concealment of birth at her trial under direction from her defence lawyer, Richard Haynes.[49] In the police file the name of the baby's father was given as Alexander Rankin, a draughtsman who had been in Perth for just two years before returning to Victoria before the child's birth.[50] Surprisingly, the plea for mercy in this case came from Warton, who, according to the *Inquirer*, stated:

> We can't help feeling that there is really a far more guilty one, who has fled, and who has left this girl to bear the sorrow and shame of what has happened; and I hope, therefore, that Your Honor will not visit her with very great severity.[51]

In this way, Warton aligned Arnold's case to the standard trope of a respectable woman who was seduced and abandoned by an unscrupulous male.

---

48 Charles Warton to Attorney-General, 4 January 1888, S675 cons527 1887/0287, SROWA.

49 *R v Theresa Arnold*, 4 April 1887, S122 cons3473 137 case 2179, SROWA; "Supreme Court.–Criminal Sittings," *Daily News*, 4 April 1887, 3.

50 Police Magistrate Perth to Colonial Secretary, 9 February 1887, S675 cons527 1887/0545, SROWA; Rica Erickson, *The Bicentennial Dictionary of Western Australians, pre-1829–1888*, vol. 4 (Nedlands: UWAP, 1987), 2574.

51 "Monday, April 4," *ICN*, 6 April 1887, 3.

Sentencing was another area in which leniency was shown to women in this period. Sentences for infanticidal mothers ranged from just seven days to two years. Two women, Julia Thompson and Theresa Arnold, received seven-day sentences for concealment of birth. In 1886, Julia Thompson went to stay with her married sister, Elizabeth Bransen, in Smith's Mill, complaining that she had a tumour in her stomach. On the morning of 11 April, Elizabeth found Julia's sheets stained with blood, which Julia explained as being due to her tumour bursting. Dr Scott was called for and told them that, contrary to Julia's explanation, she must have given birth and stated that he had no alternative but to inform the police.[52] Three days later Julia admitted to her sister that she had given birth and that the body of the baby was in her box of possessions, under her bed. Although the jury found Julia guilty of concealment of birth, they added a rider of a "strong recommendation to mercy" and Chief Justice Alexander Onslow subsequently sentenced her to only one week's imprisonment.[53] This extremely lenient sentence was lower than that given for any other crime by a female defendant in the upper courts, with the sole exception of the forty-eight hour sentence given to Julia Casley for "making a false statement to the Registrar."[54]

Sometimes judges might show leniency by dating the start of the sentence from the date on which the defendant was remanded. In the 1867 case of *R v Louisa Lund*, seventeen-year-old Louisa had been working for John and Mary Locke at Lockeville in Wonnerup for five months when she was charged with concealment of birth. Mary Locke told the court that although she had previously suspected the pregnancy, Louisa herself had denied it. However, when Louisa became ill, Mary did ask her if she had given birth and, although Louisa initially denied this also, she later admitted to giving birth to a premature child, which she said she had thrown into the river. Two weeks later, Edward Brown, one of Locke's workmen, uncovered the baby's body buried in sand outside the house. Dr Frederick Vines testified at the inquest that, although he could see no marks of violence on the body, the baby's cord appeared to

[52] *R v Julia Thompson*, 7 July 1886, S122 cons3473 133 case 2150, SROWA.

[53] "Supreme-Court Criminal Sitting," *Western Mail*, 10 July 1886, 15.

[54] Mark Finnane, "Western Australia Supreme Court 1862–1899" (ADA Dataverse, V2, 2020), https://doi.org/10.26193/ESI64N.

be untied. Chief Justice Archibald Burt gave a sentence of four months' imprisonment but dated it from the day Louisa was remanded, meaning that she had only twenty-two days left to serve. His decision was possibly influenced by a note which the jury at the inquest had requested to include with the depositions, which read in part:

> We wish to add that we consider Mr and Mrs Locke are both very much to blame for not keeping a vigilant watch over Louisa Lund's movements after her confinement. ... Mrs Locke is the mother of a family and could hardly fail to notice an alteration in the girl's appearance. Nothing was said on the subject of her confinement although it appears to have been well known in Mr Locke's family until the girl was taken dangerously ill when it was thought necessary to send for Mr Rossellotty [a doctor] who made the discovery and had it not been for this it is probable nothing would ever have been said about it. When the child was found by the workman Brown he was told by Mr Locke that he was a fool for making it known, that he should have covered it up and said nothing about it. Under all these circumstances we do think that Mr and Mrs Locke are to blame.[55]

These comments are consistent with society's view that the mistress of a domestic servant was responsible for her servant's morals and behaviour. By moving blame for the child's death from Louisa to her employers, the jury positioned Louisa as the victim and her employers as perpetrators. The comments also exemplify another common behaviour shown by those surrounding infanticidal mothers; by ignoring evidence of an unmarried woman's pregnancy or, where possible, of infanticide, friends, neighbours, and employers showed a tacit sympathy and understanding for the woman's plight.

While all the defendants in the cases of neonaticide were treated sympathetically in the courtroom, and by the press, it is perhaps significant that the cases in which the newspapers commented favourably on the women's appearance, their conformity to the discourse of "respectable" femininity, and their youth were also those in which the defendant was acquitted or received a nominal sentence. While all the

---

[55] *R v Louisa Lund*, 2 October 1867, S122 cons3473 37 case 262, SROWA.

women tried or convicted of concealment of birth appear to have been considered to have fitted the standard narrative of "seduced and abandoned," those who were perceived in court to be young and attractive and who could project a persona of respectability and decency, were seen to most closely fit the feminine ideal and by doing so increased their chances of lenient treatment. At her trial, twenty-year-old Julia Thompson was described in the newspapers as a "respectable looking unmarried female" and "a rather prepossessing looking young unmarried woman" while Theresa Arnold was described as "a decent-looking young woman." Both received sentences of just seven days.[56] Additionally, two of the defendants acquitted of concealment of birth were described in similar terms; Mary Ann Stone was described as "a respectable and good-looking young woman" and Sarah Benny was described as "a respectable looking young woman."[57] These women were seen as virtuous and respectable and were not considered dangerous to the moral order of society.

The *Inquirer* also indicated sympathy for Eliza Hamilton in 1847, when she was indicted for concealing the birth of her child at the house of her employers, Lionel and Fanny Samson, in Fremantle. The paper suppressed Eliza's name, stating that:

> There was one other indictment, for concealing the birth of a stillborn child; but as a verdict of acquittal was returned, we have judged it better, in a community so small as ours, to suppress the name of the party— a system which we intend to adopt as a rule on all future occasions.[58]

Their rival, the *Perth Gazette*, had no such qualms and the *Inquirer* did not continue this policy.

Despite sympathetic framing of news articles on individual cases of infanticide, the attitude of the press to the crime of infanticide in general could be quite different. By the mid-1860s articles, deploring the practice began appearing in newspapers all over Australia:

---

[56] "Supreme Court—Civil Side," *ICN*, 14 July 1886, 2; "City Police Court," *Daily News*, 1 May 1886, 3; "Police News," *ICN*, 23 February 1887, 5.

[57] "Supreme Court—Criminal Sittings," *West Australian*, 8 April 1881, 3; "Police News".

[58] "Quarter Sessions," *Inquirer*, 13 January 1847, 3.

> The nipping of the growth of children in the bud—in another word, infanticide is a fashionable crime just now. Our quiet squares, the dark corners of our streets, our door steps, and sundry other localities, and [*sic*] the public depositories selected by travailling [*sic*] maids and unnatural mothers for the abandonment and desertion of their infants.[59]

These reports echoed similar sentiments reported in English newspapers fuelled by the agitation of English Coroner Edwin Lankester. Lankester published alarming statistics in medical journals and criticised what he considered to be misplaced leniency towards infanticidal mothers, culminating in the moral panic documented by some historians of infanticide.[60] Similar attitudes were expressed in the newspapers of the Australian colonies, although individual cases in Western Australia continued to be treated sympathetically.[61]

Homicide

Leniency is less obvious in cases involving the death of an adult. Of the four women convicted on the charge of murder, or attempted murder, of an adult, only one, Cooray, received a partial verdict. In 1855, Bridget Hurford was found guilty of the murder of her husband, despite evidence indicating that her co-accused, William Dodd, had committed the actual killing. In 1872, Margaret Cody was also found guilty of murder, although it was clear that she also was not considered to be the principal in the case, and, in 1861, Louisa Garrett was convicted of attempting to poison her husband. One case, that of Louisa Garrett, received a degree of leniency in sentencing: Burt giving a sentence of death recorded, rather than death pronounced. This indicated that mercy, in the form of a commuted sentence, would be recommended and likely reflected the fact that the victim was still living. No obvious leniency was indicated in

---

59 "Miscellaneous," *PGWAT*, 29 June 1866, 3.

60 Anne-Marie Kilday, *A History of Infanticide in Britain: c 1600 to the Present* (London: Palgrave MacMillan, 2013), 119, 171; Nicola Goc, *Women, Infanticide and the Press, 1822–1922: News Narratives in England and Australia* (London: Routledge, 2016), 92.

61 Georgina Rychner, "'The Pendulum of the Public Mind': Insanity and Activism in Capital Trials, 1880–1939" (PhD diss., Monash University, 2020), 58.

the case of *R v Kullinga and Sarah*, with both defendants receiving three-year sentences for an *inter se* crime of manslaughter, which took place on the Upper Irwin.[62] The majority of these cases have been discussed elsewhere in the book, but, taken together, indicate the gravity with which the justice system regarded homicide crimes involving the death of an adult.

Assault

Two cases of assault are worth examining for the light they cast on societal understandings as to which women were considered worthy of receiving mercy. In 1872, Margaret McGhee was indicted for wounding with intent to cause grievous bodily harm with co-accused James Darkins, after they violently assaulted sixty-four-year-old Thomas Cooper.[63] Juries would sometimes issue a mercy rider if they felt that the defendant had been provoked by the behaviour of the victim.[64] In the case of female defendants, provocation might sometimes take the form of comments that disparaged a woman's honour or femininity.

At the trial, Police Sergeant William Dale testified that "James Darkins, a notorious ruffian, and Margaret McGhee, a prostitute who lives with him … very severely injured the said Thomas Cooper by blows and kicks and by jumping upon his person and striking him with a piece of shingle."[65] The fight took place in the taproom of the Freemasons Hotel in Perth on 12 March. The evidence surrounding the cause of the fight varied with Cooper stating that, although he called Margaret a "woman sod," it was not until after she had called him an "old rogue," an "old villain," and a "man sod." However, witness William Campbell, a carpenter who was also in the taproom that day, stated that McGhee was talking loudly, and Cooper told her to "shut up" and then told her

---

62 Kullinga and Sarah, whose "crime" took place near Yarragadee were probably Nhanhargardi speakers, who would be known today as Southern Yamatji people; *R v Kullinga and Sarah*, 3 July 1878, S122 cons3473 93 case 849, SROWA.

63 *R v James Darkins and Margaret McGhee*, 3 April 1872, S122 cons3473 59 case 496, SROWA.

64 Coen and Howlin, "The Jury Speaks," 520.

65 *R v James Darkins and Margaret McGhee*.

that she "got her living by prostitution." Cooper himself denied this and implied that it was his appearance in court, as a witness against two men accused of larceny that morning, that had angered Margaret and Darkins.[66] In this case, the jury showed leniency to Margaret by convicting her on the lesser charge of unlawful wounding and including a recommendation to mercy on account of provocation. Despite evidence that Margaret's behaviour and lifestyle transgressed cultural expectations of respectable femininity, and the considerable violence used by Margaret and Darkins, the slur to Margaret's honour was still considered to be a mitigating factor.

In contrast, Mary Ann McGarvie, a recidivist brought up before the Magistrate's Court on several occasions for alcohol-related offences, was convicted of unlawful wounding the following year, when she threw a glass, in the Freemasons Hotel in Fremantle, hitting John Lee on the head and causing pieces of broken glass to embed themselves in his forehead. In his deposition, Lee described losing a lot of blood and being unable to work for five days after the event, due to continued weakness. The publican, James Herbert, described having to sit with Lee all night due to Lee's loss of blood and consequent weakness. Mary Ann pleaded for mercy on the grounds of being a "single and unprotected female" and argued that Lee had attempted to take "improper liberties" with her, saying, "What I have done I'll do again," if Lee again used the same language towards her.[67] Unlike Margaret McGhee, Mary Ann was unable to produce witnesses in court to confirm her argument of provocation. Instead, the jury believed Lee and publican James Herbert, who both stated that Mary Ann was drunk and had become abusive after Herbert refused to serve her. Consequently, Mary Ann did not receive a partial verdict or a recommendation mercy.

---

66 *R v James Darkins and Margaret McGhee*.

67 "Law Intelligence," *ICN*, 14 May 1873, 3; "Supreme Court," *PGWAT*, 9 May 1873; "Supreme Court—Criminal Sittings," *Express*, 8 May 1873, 2.

Theft

Women convicted of theft could be considered worthy of mercy in some cases. Forty-two women were found guilty of theft in Western Australia prior to 1891, with sentences ranging from the fourteen days, given to Mary Woods for larceny, to the five years' penal servitude awarded to Mary Jane Hayes for stealing £5 from the pocket of Stephen Radford in the Freemasons Hotel, Perth.[68] This latter sentence, handed down by Justice Edward Stone, was particularly harsh in comparison to sentences awarded to other women convicted of similar crimes and may have reflected Hayes's previous convictions in the Supreme Court and numerous other summary convictions.[69] I was able to find four recommendations to mercy given by the jury for theft charges although only one woman received a partial verdict.

One of these was Margaret Farmer who was accused of stealing from Frederick Croft's store in 1844, and whose case was discussed in Chapter 3. In this case, the jury recommended Margaret to mercy after the Colonial Surgeon testified that her pregnancy was at an advanced stage and that childbirth in gaol would be a dangerous proceeding.[70] In later life, Margaret appears to have become known for shoplifting. In 1864 she was tried summarily for another theft and again imprisoned, but was then hospitalised suffering from "low fever, the result … of anxiety or distress of mind."[71] The medicalisation of women's crime during the latter stages of the nineteenth century meant that women were thought to be prone to mania and hysteria, which could manifest itself as

[68] Record of Court Convictions, 1861–1914, S5072 cons1156 v23, SROWA; "Supreme Court—Criminal Sittings," *West Australian*, 17 January 1885, 3.

[69] *R v Mary Jane Gallagher and Agnes Arbuckle*, 5 July 1871, S122 cons3473 56 case 451, SROWA; *R v Mary Jane Berry*, 3 October 1877, S122 cons3473 90 case 816, SROWA; Register female prisoners, cons 4186 1, SROWA; "Newspapers & Gazettes," Trove, accessed 4 March 2022, https://trove.nla.gov.au/newspaper/; Mark Finnane, "Western Australia Criminal Trials 1830–1861" (ADA Dataverse, V1, 2019), https://doi.org/10.26193/OW6SR6; Finnane, "Western Australia Supreme Court 1862–1899".

[70] "Quarter Sessions," *Perth Gazette and Western Australian Journal (PGWAJ)*, 6 July 1844, 3.

[71] John Ferguson to Colonial Secretary, 12 November 1864, S2941 cons36 541 177, SROWA.

"kleptomania."[72] On the recommendation of John Ferguson, the Colonial Surgeon, she was discharged from custody on the understanding that her family would "undertake to keep her away from the shops."[73] It is clear that the authorities felt that Margaret was unable to stop herself from stealing.

The crime of shoplifting was particularly associated with women. The voluminous clothing styles in fashion during the nineteenth century proved useful for the concealment of stolen goods.[74] Women who set out to steal from shopkeepers would often work in pairs, with one distracting the person serving while the other extracted goods.[75] Shawls and baskets could be used to hide stolen goods. In 1872 when twenty-two-year-old Elizabeth Pickett and twenty-seven-year-old Bridget Todd embarked on a shoplifting spree in Perth, Todd was wearing a large shawl, while Pickett carried her toddler in her arms. Visiting first the shop of Messrs Glyde and Son in Hay Street, they walked out with a length of fabric under Todd's shawl.[76] They then went to Henry Monger's store in the same street, where Todd added eight children's hats to the fabric already under her shawl, and finished up at Padbury's store where Picket bought a pair of children's socks and Todd added a further hat to those already hidden. At this point, Police Seargent Dale entered the shop and pulled aside Todd's shawl, exposing the stolen items. Although Picket attempted to leave, she was stopped at the door by Dale. The women were tried only for the thefts from Monger and Padbury. Pickett, who was represented in court, was acquitted but Todd was convicted on both counts and sentenced to six months for each charge. Another method judges used to show leniency was to make multiple sentences concurrent, and, in this case, Burt ordered Pickett's sentences to be served concurrently.[77]

---

72 D'Cruze and Jackson, *Women, Crime and Justice*, 39.

73 John Ferguson to Colonial Secretary, 12 November 1864, S2941 cons36 541 177, SROWA.

74 Sylvia Bombardini, "The Shoplifter's Clothes: Technologies for a Feminist Practice," Politics of Patents: Re-imagining Citizenship via Clothing Inventions 1820–2020, accessed 23 May 2023, https://www.politicsofpatents.org/2020/08/19/the-shoplifters-clothes-technologies-for-a-feminist-practice; D'Cruze and Jackson, *Women, Crime and Justice*, 37.

75 Piper, "In Bad Company," 80.

76 "Advertising," *ICN*, 1 November 1871, 2; Archibald Paull Burt, notebooks Supreme Court criminal sittings, 1872, MN 736 2850A/13, SLWA.

77 Burt, notebooks, 1872, MN 736 2850A/13, SLWA.

Although there is no record stating why Burt decided to do this, in other cases where women were charged with multiple counts of larceny, second and third counts would often be dropped if a conviction was reached on the first, suggesting that the authorities considered one punishment sufficient example.

One of the cases recommended to mercy by the jury was that of seventeen-year-old Susannah (Susan) Hitchcock. Susan was the daughter of a farming family from Jane Brook, twenty kilometres north-west of Perth.[78] In November 1844, Susan was dismissed from the service of Alexander and Sibella Taylor, of nearby Caversham Rise, after less than a month's employment and told that "she did not suit." The true reason for her dismissal may have been due to suspicions of theft, as Sibella said she had "often heard her open my drawers." After Susan's departure several items were found to be missing, Constable Welbourne was called, and the articles were subsequently found in Susan's possession at her new residence with Charles and Ann Pratt of Guildford. In her testimony Sibella stated that she told Susan that if she returned the stolen articles: "I could not forbear appearing against her, but I would recommend her to mercy."[79] Susan was indicted for the theft of fifty-two items of linen and clothing, including a baby's diaper (she was pregnant at the time of the theft).[80] Although the jury recommended mercy on account of her age, Susan was sentenced to twelve months' imprisonment and sent to Fremantle Gaol, where she was set to the arduous task of picking oakum.[81] On 8 April she gave birth to her baby, reported to be stillborn, in Fremantle Gaol and, one month later, was sent to Rottnest Island Prison.[82] As in the case of Jane Green, it is unlikely that Susan was imprisoned with the male prisoners and more likely that she worked

[78] Bob Reece, "Fremantle's First Historian: Joseph Keane Hitchcock," *Fremantle Studies* 7 (2012): 33–50.

[79] "Quarter Sessions," *PGWAJ*, 4 January 1845, 3.

[80] *R v Susan Hitchcock*, 1 January 1845, S122 cons3472 65 case 372, SROWA.

[81] Finnane, "Western Australia Criminal Trials 1830–1861"; Quarterly returns of prisoners, 1845, S270 cons3676 11–12, SROWA.

[82] Birth, unnamed female, 1845, no. 561, Fremantle Jail [*sic*], "Online Index Search Tool," Department of Justice, accessed 24 May 2023, https://www.wa.gov.au/organisation/department-of-justice/online-index-search-tool; Bradley Brooksby, Margaret P. Doust and Michael Doust, *James and Isaac Doust and Descendants* (Bunbury: Margaret P. Doust, 2015), 37; Quarterly

for Gaoler Henry Vincent and his wife. A one-year sentence may have been considered lenient for the theft of goods worth £24 but the lived experience of those twelve months would have been anything but easy.

Bridget O'Bryan was also recommended for mercy in 1854 when she was accused of stealing ten yards of calico, four pairs of stockings, and a glass bottle from her employers, Thomas and Eliza Brown of Fremantle. In what would appear to be a conflict of interest, Thomas Brown was not only the victim in this case but also the committing magistrate. Bridget admitted stealing the bottle but did not admit to the theft of the other articles. She was found guilty by the jury with a recommendation to mercy "on account of the trifling value of the property stolen."[83]

On rare occasions, recommendations to mercy might come from elsewhere in the court. In 1876, twenty-six-year-old Mary Woods was indicted for the theft of Thomas Henderson's Inverness Cape. On 26 May that year, Henderson left his horse and trap on the road in Fremantle while he paid a visit to John Simpson. When he came out, he missed his cape, which he thought had been in the trap. Mary pleaded guilty at her trial. She stated that she had found the cape, picked it up and taken it to pawnbroker George Davies, and implied that she did so because she was unable to provide food for her family.[84] Although she went on to appear in court many more times, usually for larceny, this was the first occasion in which she had appeared in the Supreme Court and may have been the first time she had been charged with a crime.[85] She was eight months' pregnant at her trial and the *Inquirer* referred to her as "a decent-looking young married woman whose husband is in gaol." The *Inquirer* reported that:

> The Crown Solicitor said this was a case in which he honestly believed that the prisoner had been misled by sheer want, and perhaps the interests of justice, as well the interests of the young woman, would be served by

returns of prisoners, 1845; Superintendent Rottnest, August 1845, S2941 cons36 143 102, SROWA.

83 "Quarter Sessions," *Inquirer*, 12 July 1854, 3.

84 *R v Mary Woods*, 5 July 1876, S122 cons3473 85 case 762, SROWA.

85 Record of Court Convictions, 1861–1914, S5072 cons1156 v23, SROWA.

> the infliction of a very moderate sentence. Moreover, the prisoner was about to become a mother, very shortly.[86]

Mary's youth, her marital status and her adherence to the feminine ideal of a caring and nurturing mother were indicators of "respectable" femininity and rendered her a worthwhile recipient for mercy from the court. Burt gave her a lenient sentence of fourteen days' imprisonment.[87]

Women's employment options during the nineteenth century, which consisted primarily of domestic service, meant that many women lived and worked in their employers' houses, placing them in a particularly advantageous position for theft. Servants were regularly entrusted with money and material goods and their cleaning duties took them into rooms normally reserved for members of the family.[88] Domestic servants were considered to be in a position of trust, making any theft not only a breach of that trust but also a threat to the social order of elite and middle-class citizens. Historically, theft by servants was considered a more serious crime than other forms of larceny and English servants were often charged with the distinct crime of larceny by a servant.[89] This does not appear to be the case for female defendants in Western Australia before 1891, where most were charged with simple larceny and only two with larceny by a servant.

Regardless of the perceived gravity of thefts by servants, historian Joanne McEwan notes that domestic servants, in particular, were likely to be recommended for mercy by their prosecutors, although noting that reasons for these recommendations were rarely recorded.[90] This was the case in *R v Ellen Sullivan*, in which Ellen was accused of theft from her employers, Emma and Thomas Allmond. On 30 June 1855, Emma, whose husband ran a general store in Howick St, Perth, found a bundle containing two loaves of bread and some buns on the ground outside the bedroom window belonging to her twenty-five-year-old servant, Ellen

---

[86] "Law Intelligence," *ICN*, 12 July 1876, 6.

[87] Record of Court Convictions, 1861–1914, S5072 cons1156 V23, SROWA.

[88] McEwan, "Negotiating Support," 51.

[89] D'Cruze and Jackson, *Women, Crime and Justice*, 38.

[90] McEwan, "Negotiating Support," 280.

Sullivan.[91] Ellen had arrived in Western Australia three years earlier as a single woman emigrant and had a young child with ticket-of leave holder Robert Holder. Thomas and Emma called in a policeman who searched Ellen's box of possessions, finding several items which they identified as theirs, including clothing belonging to Emma, children's clothing, money, and household items. Ellen appeared in the Quarter Sessions in July charged with the theft of the bread, but with no proof of the goods having been in her possession, she was acquitted. She was also charged with the theft of the other goods in a separate indictment which was to be heard in October. Ellen was released on bail, appearing for her trial in October as Ellen Holder, having married in the intervening period. This time she was found guilty of larceny but her defence counsel, George Leake, brought in a former employer to testify to Ellen's "good character" and her employers recommended her to mercy.[92] She received a relatively lenient sentence of one month's imprisonment.[93]

There could be some leniency given in cases involving disagreements between neighbours. In the case of *R v Margaret Wilson*, Margaret was accused of stealing £1 from a letter addressed to Caroline Wetherall of Newcastle, now known as Toodyay, in 1871. Caroline's son, Alfred Wells, told the court that his mother and Margaret were "very good friends."[94] Although Caroline said that she had not given Margaret permission to open her mail, defence witness, Margaret Ostler, intimated that Wells had told her that the court case was prompted by a disagreement between the women's husbands: "Wetherall and Wilson had had some argument about some wheat, and Mrs Wetherall would not have summonsed Mrs Wilson, if it had not been for Wetherall."[95] Margaret Wilson was found guilty and sentenced to nine months' imprisonment with hard labour, the *Gazette* implying that this was a lenient sentence given because of her "good character."[96]

---

91 "Classified Advertising," *PGIJPN*, 17 August 1855, 2; "Quarter Sessions," *PGIJPN*, 12 October 1855, 3.

92 "Quarter Sessions," *PGIJPN*, 12 October 1855, 3.

93 Finnane, "Western Australia Criminal Trials 1830–1861".

94 Burt, *R v Margaret Wilson*, 1871–1872, MN 2850A/12, SLWA.

95 *R v Margaret Wilson*, 5 July 1871, cons 3473 56 case 452, SROWA.

96 "Supreme Court," *PGWAT*, 14 July 1871, 3.

One category of theft which was less likely to attract a mercy rider, or other forms of leniency, was that of "larceny from the person." Thirteen women in the study period were indicted for this offence. Typically, the victims in these cases were farmers or sailors visiting Perth or Fremantle who became drunk and were therefore easy targets for the women. This type of crime was a common occurrence in both Britain and other Australian colonies and became known as "bughunting."[97] When committed by women, the crime almost always occurred in the context of sex work, and the accused were overwhelmingly recidivists. These encounters usually began by the men "treating" the women to a drink. It is probable that most victims of larceny from the person had met the defendants while searching for sexual encounters, but in only two cases was this admitted to in court by either defendants or witnesses.[98]

Defendants who were able to dispose of the stolen items before being arrested increased their chances of acquittal. In 1874, the *Herald* reported a case heard in the Perth Police Court against Bridget Joyce, a recidivist whose name had already appeared several times in news reports, where she was labelled as a "common prostitute" and a "loose" woman. Joyce had previously been charged with crimes such as drunkenness, abusive language, theft, and riotous behaviour.[99] Similarly to reports of other pickpocketing cases in the press, the *Herald* ridiculed both the defendant and the victim in their report:

> A frail nymph rejoicing in the name of Bridget Joyce, made her bow before the magistrates, charged with stealing a silver watch and chain, from a man named Rawlings, a farm laborer in the service of Mr. Middleton, on the Swan. The complainant requiring some articles of wearing apparel came to Perth to purchase them. Meeting Bridget in the

---

[97] D'Cruze and Jackson, *Women, Crime and Justice*, 37; Alana Jayne Piper and Lisa Durnian, "Theft on Trial: Prosecution, Conviction and Sentencing Patterns in Colonial Victoria and Western Australia," *Australian & New Zealand Journal of Criminology* 50, no. 1 (2017): 11.

[98] Piper, "In Bad Company," 84; *R v Christian Geary and Charles Barber*, 7 October 1874, S122 cons3473 73 case 657, SROWA; *R v Louisa Bridger and Henry Edwards*, 4 January 1882, S122 cons3473 111 case 991, SROWA.

[99] "Police Court," *PGWAT*, 12 January 1872, 3; "Police Court.—Perth," *Express*, 29 April 1872, 3; "Perth Police Court," *Express*, 12 December 1872, 3; "Police Court—Perth," *Express*, 17 April 1873, 3.

> street, and smitten by her charms, he invited her to indulge in what she herself would term a "wet", which invitation she, nothing loth [*sic*], accepted. While partaking of the drink which the good hearted fool supplied her, it was alleged by the prosecutor that she adroitly extracted his watch out of his pocket and left the house.[100]

The charge against Bridget was dismissed due to lack of evidence, but in 1877 she was again charged with larceny from the person and this time appeared in the Supreme Court with co-accused Daniel Keyte. Keyte was a convict transported for forgery, with a subsequent conviction for robbery with violence.[101] Neither defendant was represented at the trial. In this case, Alexander Samuels, who had just been released from prison, met Keyte in the John Bull Inn in Howick Street, Perth. Keyte took him to Bridget's house where he agreed to buy a flagon of ale, giving Bridget the money to do so.[102] He testified that he "turned quite stupid" after a drink and fell asleep, waking later in the day to find that his money and cheques had disappeared from his pockets. He had been woken earlier by a "tugging" at his pocket and had seen Keyte close by. Several shop-keepers were able to testify that Bridget had paid for goods with the stolen cheques. The *Western Australian Times* reported that she was given "a very bad character" by the police and the *Herald* noted disapprovingly that Samuels was a victim to "habits of debauchery and dissipation."[103] Bridget was sentenced to six months' imprisonment, but Keyte, who was not found with stolen goods in his possession, was acquitted.[104]

It was not uncommon for newspapers to report that women had appeared in court with a child in their arms. Although many women may have been unable to leave their infants and had no choice but to do this, by bringing their child with them into court women might also attempt to enhance their performance of femininity, by emphasising their roles as

100 "Our Perth Letter," *Herald*, 29 August 1874, 3.

101 "Perth Police Court," *Express*, 12 December 1872, 3.

102 "Advertising," *Herald*, 1 February 1868, 1; "Supreme Court—Criminal Side," *Herald*, 7 April 1877, 2.

103 "Law Intelligence," *ICN*, 11 April 1877, 3.

104 "Supreme Court—Criminal Side," *Herald*, 7 April 1877, 2; "Supreme Court—Criminal Sittings," *Western Australian Times*, 6 April 1877, 2.

mothers. Bridget appeared at trial holding her baby, Emelia. The *Western Australian Times* wrote: "The female prisoner made a tearful appeal to the Jury's sympathy on behalf of her baby, but the jurors were proof against it, and convicted her."[105] Although bringing a child to court may have added to a woman's narrative as a "good" wife and mother, this did not always lead to leniency when evidence in court pointed to a defendant's "bad" character.[106] In Bridget's case the evidence of stolen goods in her possession and the inference of prostitution invalidated any respectability that may have been conferred on her by her status as a mother.

No cases of larceny from the person received a recommendation of mercy from the jury, but one case, that of Christina Burkinshaw, did receive a partial verdict. Christina was the daughter of Pensioner Guard John Campbell and had arrived in the colony, in 1851, as an eight-year-old child.[107] Her husband, ticket-of-leave holder William Burkinshaw, abandoned his wife and children in 1867 to go to the eastern states, and, on his return in 1871, was sentenced to five years' imprisonment for absconding from the colony.[108] In 1873, Christina, who was in the Emerald Isle Hotel, Fremantle, asked sailor James Houghton to "shout" her a drink. While in conversation with Houghton she asked to see a gold chain and locket he had in his possession, but, after Houghton handed it to her, she refused to return it and took it home with her. The police were called, and, although Christina told her son not to let them in, they did eventually gain access and the locket was found hidden in the back of Christina's hair. As evidence showed that Christina was handed the locket to look at and did not steal it from "the person" of Houghton, the jury found her guilty of the lesser charge of "common larceny."[109]

---

[105] "Supreme Court—Criminal Sittings," *Western Australian Times*, 6 April 1877, 2.

[106] Andrew August, "'A Horrible Looking Woman': Female Violence in Late-Victorian East London," *The Journal of British Studies* 54, no. 4 (2015): 867.

[107] Frank H. Broomhall, *The Veterans: A History of the Enrolled Pensioner Force in Western Australia 1850–1880* (Carlisle, W.A.: Hesperian Press, 1989); Erickson, *The Bicentennial Dictionary*, 1:454.

[108] General register, convict registers, S5056 cons1156 R31, SROWA.

[109] *R v Christina Burkinshaw*, 3 January 1872, S122 cons3473 65 case 568, SROWA.

As juries seldom gave their reasons for issuing a partial verdict, reasons for these must be surmised from contextual data. The low rate of partial verdicts for crimes of theft may be a reflection of the many cases of simple larceny for which there was no lesser crime and a lack of public sympathy for cases of larceny from the person, with its associations to sex work and underclass culture. However, when a partial verdict was not available to the jury, as in the case of simple larceny, or not legally justifiable, the jury sometimes expressed sympathy through the use of the mercy rider and employers would also occasionally request mercy for a servant who they had prosecuted for theft.

Property Offences Other Than Theft

Mercy riders were also given in other cases of property crimes. One of these was the 1870 trial of Jane Sheridan and John Hudgson for the "rescue of cattle seized for impounding." This case appears to have arisen from a disagreement between neighbours. Sheridan and farm labourer Hudgson were tried in Geraldton for rescuing six horses from James Smith in Rudd's Valley, 355 kilometres north of Perth. Smith complained at the trial that horses belonging to Sheridan and her intimate partner, William Carr, had been "running about" and destroying his well. When he saw six horses at the well on 22 December, driven by Sheridan and Hudgson, he attempted to seize and impound them but complained that Sheridan threatened him with the butt end of her whip.[110] Before the trial, Attorney-General George Stone had written to the Resident Magistrate of Geraldton advising him that Smith's attempted seizure of the horses was unlikely to be lawful, but the trial still went ahead.[111] Both defendants were convicted and fined £2, or one-months' imprisonment, but the jury included a recommendation to mercy for Sheridan.[112] No reason was given for the rider but it seems probable that it was given on

[110] *R v Jane Sheridan and John Hudgson*, 2 March 1870, S2941 cons36 669 62, SROWA.

[111] George Stone to Resident Magistrate Geraldton, 26 February 1870, S2755 cons49 49 1554, SROWA.

[112] *R v Jane Sheridan and John Hudgson*.

the basis of Sheridan's gender combined with an understanding of the tensions existing between Smith and Carr.

One form of property offence not often seen among female defendants in this time was that of arson. Two women were charged with this crime, but only one, Mary Trubee, was convicted. Mary Kerwin had arrived in the colony around 1850. In 1851 she married Thomas Trubee who came to the colony as part of the Parkhurst apprenticeship scheme. Their child, James, was born in 1851 and the couple moved into a cottage owned by Frederick Morrell in Northam. According to Mary, they were allowed to live in this cottage rent free for a year, on the understanding that Thomas repaired it, and Morell promised that, after a year, they could rent it for a shilling a week. By the end of the year Mary and Morrell were at loggerheads and the couple had been told that they were to leave, with Morrell saying that he "would take the roof off" if they refused to do so.[113] Mary did refuse to leave initially, but eventually she packed up her things, and, taking James with her, departed from the cottage. In her unsworn statement at the trial, she stated that she returned later that day because "there was something I wanted" and took a last walk along the river. She ran back when she noticed flames and, placing James under a tree, began to move furniture from the cottage with the help of a group of Aboriginal people. Morrell stated that he also ran up to the cottage when he noticed the flames. A neighbour, William Chidlow, took Mary into custody, chaining her to a tree, where she remained overnight. Mary complained that "He kicked me and knocked me down. He dragged me about. … I was scarcely able to stand or hold my baby and he fell from my arms."[114] On hearing the evidence, the jury found Trubee guilty of arson but recommended her to mercy "as it appeared to them that all the witnesses were enemies to the prisoner."[115] In consequence of the recommendation to mercy, Mackie sentenced Trubee to fifteen years' transportation beyond the seas, stating that this was the lowest term of transportation allowed by law. He admitted, two years later, that he had the alternative of awarding imprisonment with hard labour for a term not

---

113 Mary Trubee to the Governor, 20 August 1853, S2941 cons36 271 62, SROWA.

114 *R v Trubee*, 7 April 1852, cons 3472 93 case 538, SROWA; "Quarter Sessions," *Inquirer*, 14 April 1852, 2.

115 Criminal indictment register, 7 April 1852, S49 cons3422 01, SROWA.

exceeding three years but “the case was thought too flagrant to admit of a more lenient sentence.” At the same time, he expressed the opinion that the jury may have issued the mercy rider due to compassion for Mary for having to be separated from her child.[116] It seems that Mackie was paying lip service only to the recommendation of mercy by awarding a sentence of fifteen years’ transportation.

Conclusion

This research shows that juries in Western Australia did exercise their prerogative to recommend mercy, which was often given in response to gendered assumptions of women’s role in society. Women who had large families might be recommended to mercy in recognition of the responsibilities they had in caring for their children. Likewise, women who could prove provocation in the form of an attack on their identity as “good” women might also be recommended to mercy. Juries also used mercy riders to show sympathy to women who they felt had been unfairly treated, as in the case of Mary Trubee or Bridget O’Bryan. One mercy rider was also given due to the young age of the offender. While it is clear that juries did use the mercy rider to express sympathy for the defendant, not all riders included the jury’s reasoning, and it is not possible to state whether any of the mercy riders were given as a compromise solution in situations where a minority of jurors retained doubt of a defendant’s guilt.

Although it is not always clear whether a recommendation to mercy translated to a more lenient sentence, it is possible to state that the two cases in which recommendations to mercy were voiced by the Attorney-General and the Crown Solicitor resulted in lenient sentencing. In one of the two cases where the defendant’s employer recommended mercy, the sentencing also appears to have been lenient. Cases where the jury recommended mercy clearly did not always translate to sentencing, as shown by the fifteen-year sentence of transportation received by Mary Trubee, and yet Julia Thompson, convicted of concealment of birth, received a

116 Mackie to Colonial Secretary, 22 August 1853, S2941 cons36 271 64, SROWA.

clearly lenient sentence of seven days after the jury issued a mercy rider. Likewise, recommendations to mercy issued by medical experts were not always given credence by the judiciary, as shown by the case of Margaret Farmer, whose newborn child died in Fremantle Gaol. With such a small number of cases it is not possible to reach a conclusion as to whose voice was considered significant in recommendations of mercy, but it seems clear that the voices of authorities representing the State, such as the Attorney-General and Crown Solicitor, were privileged by the judiciary when considering recommendations to mercy.

Juries also showed leniency by exercising their rights to use partial verdicts to convict defendants. Two of the women indicted for the capital crime of murder were convicted with partial verdicts. Aboriginal woman Cooray was found guilty of manslaughter and Jane Green was convicted of concealing the birth of a child. Unlike Bridget Hurford and Margaret Cody, who were both convicted of murder, neither Cooray nor Jane had exhibited behaviour associated with "unrespectability" such as drunkenness or sex work. Although juries did not give reasons for their use of partial verdicts, it was one way in which they could control the sentence and was likely used to prevent the mandatory death sentence required in cases of murder. Margaret McGhee's case shows us that partial verdicts could also be given in cases of assault where the victim's injuries were not considered severe or where provocation had been offered to the defendant.

Judges were able to show leniency through sentencing. This took the form of short sentences, concurrent sentencing, and sentences backdated to the date of the offence. While leniency might be extended for a defendant's first offence, it was also associated with cases where newspaper reports indicated that the defendant was young, respectable, or attractive. Cases like that of Mary Jane Hayes, where the defendant was known to be a recidivist, or was known by the police to be involved in sex work, were less likely to be treated leniently by the judiciary. This applied also to women whose demeanour in court did not accord with gendered understandings of femininity, as occurred in the case of Margaret Cody.

Changing models of femininity and masculinity in the nineteenth century resulted in stronger condemnation of male violence and played an important role in women being more leniently treated in the courts. Women were considered vulnerable to unscrupulous men, which meant that men were often blamed when unmarried women committed neonaticide. Mothers charged with the murder, concealment of birth, or manslaughter of their infants were considered sympathetically, and were treated leniently, by both juries and by the State, in a similar manner to patterns already discerned in other Australian colonies and in Britain. Leniency took the form of being convicted of the lesser charge of concealment of birth rather than murder, being indicted for the lesser charge of concealment of birth, being recommended to mercy by the jury, or the Attorney-General, and by lenient sentencing. All defendants indicted for a crime involving the death of their child received at least one of these forms of leniency, and some benefited by several.

In contrast, women indicted for larceny from the person were less likely to be granted mercy or leniency. This crime, with its association with sex work and the underclass culture, was considered less deserving of sympathy and, unlike murder, was not a capital crime. However, if a woman could prove that the object was not taken from the pockets of the victim, as in the case of Christina Burkinshaw, they could be convicted on a lesser charge.

While the jury clearly ignored indications of "unrespectability" to give partial verdicts based on legal grounds, such as in the cases of Christina Burkinshaw or Margaret McGhee, women could also increase their chances of benefitting from mercy or leniency if they appeared to meet gendered understandings of femininity. Performances of docility in the courtroom, and indications of nurturing or motherhood, were likely to increase a woman's chances of gaining a mercy rider or lenient sentencing. Because the mercy rider need not be based on legal factors, it could be, and often was, used purely as an expression of sympathy by the jury or to show an understanding of the pressures and difficulties for working-class women living in the nineteenth century.

7
Afterword

This book set out to explore the experiences of women who were tried, as defendants, before the Court of Quarter Sessions and the Supreme Court of Western Australia between 1830 and 1890. Specifically, it aimed to examine how legal institutions and rules affected the outcome of women's trials and to explore the ways in which the trials were racialised, classed, and gendered. In Chapter 1, I asked five questions: How did the rate of conviction of women's crimes compare to the general population of accused in Western Australia and to trials in other Australian states? How were women treated in Western Australia's criminal justice system during the nineteenth century? What effect did defendants' co-accused status and use of legal representation have on conviction rates? How, and by whom, were recommendations of mercy applied to female defendants in the upper courts of Western Australia? How did a range of social categories, including gender, class, and race, influence the understanding of women in the criminal justice system? The book addressed these questions by examining four factors in Western Australian women's trials: the use of defence counsel, multi-defendant trials, Aboriginal women defendants, and the prerogative of mercy, to determine how these factors influenced the verdict and sentencing of women's trials. By considering

C. Ingram, *Women on Trial*, Palgrave Histories of Policing, Punishment and Justice, https://doi.org/10.1007/978-3-031-98072-5_7

all participants in the trial process, particularly the defendants, through the lens of intersectionality, this study has been able to determine how a range of social and cultural constructs may have changed or mediated outcomes determined by legal rules and institutions.

The mixed-methods approach, combining analysis of the quantitative data from the Prosecution Project database with the qualitative data from the archival sources used in numerous case studies, counteracted the limitations placed on the analysis by the necessarily small dataset, and provided a richer and more contextual understanding of women's experiences in the criminal justice system. These archival sources also helped to provide context for the accounts of women's trials by illuminating conditions in nineteenth-century Western Australia that may have caused women to enter the criminal justice system and the consequences of offending, the trial process, and imprisonment, for their lives and the lives of those around them.

This research has shown that decisions given in these trials were complex and that juries and judges were likely influenced by a number of different legal, social, and cultural factors. In doing so, it has also provided new insights into the lived experience of working-class women in nineteenth-century Western Australia. I argue that, although the use of defence counsel, the co-accused status of the defendant, and the prerogative of the jury and judge to recommend mercy or to exercise leniency influenced the outcome of the trial, these factors were often mediated by, and entangled with, social and cultural understandings of gender, class, and race.

The women who appeared in court were overwhelmingly working class. Some were unmarried domestic servants or the wives of pensioner guards or labourers. Others, particularly those brought to the colony after 1850 by the imperial government, came from the poverty-stricken underclass of Britain and, once in Western Australia, became part of the underclass communities of Perth and Fremantle. Many of these women appeared in the lower courts for crimes such as drunkenness or vagrancy. Women also appeared in the upper courts charged with more serious crimes such as assault, homicide, or theft. The most common crime for which women were charged in the upper courts was that of larceny.

Women mostly stole items with which they were familiar, such as money, clothes, or food, which could be used, sold, or pawned.

Life in colonial Western Australia could be precarious for working-class women. Women's wages were much lower than those received by men and financial security was often provided by marriage or long-term cohabitation with a male partner. Once a woman had a family, she could find herself in a vulnerable situation should her intimate partner be absent either through death or because he left the marriage. Women could also find themselves in financial difficulties if their husband was imprisoned, ill, or injured, or if they left their partner, a course some women took after enduring repeated assaults. "Respectable" employment options were limited for women with children. In these circumstances, theft could be a necessary survival strategy, especially for women with families to support.

Although some women may have used theft to combat poverty and support their families, other strategies were also available to women who found themselves in precarious circumstances. Women whose husbands had died or left the marriage might take in washing, or perhaps choose the more highly remunerated option of sex work. Women in the poorer areas of Perth and Fremantle supported each other in court, minded each other's children, and looked out for their friends when they were sick or injured. If imprisoned, women could, and did, petition the Governor for leniency, often citing reasons peculiar to their gender, such as imminent childbirth or the need to care for a family.

Overall, this research shows, not only that some women were treated with a degree of leniency in the courtroom, but also how, and why, this occurred. Women indicted for property offences who were represented at trial, or who appeared with a co-accused, were more likely to receive an advantageous outcome, whether that be an acquittal, a partial verdict, or a recommendation to mercy. However, results were dependant on crime type and women indicted for interpersonal offences were less likely to gain an advantage from being defended in court or appearing with a co-accused. Women who presented a persona of respectable femininity were advantaged at trial, often receiving shorter sentences or recommendations of mercy. As in other jurisdictions, women who, following the death of their infant, were tried for murder, manslaughter, or concealment of birth, were also treated with sympathy and leniency in the courtroom. However, equity of justice was not present for women unable to secure representation, whether due to poverty or other reasons. Nor was it present for Aboriginal women who appeared unrepresented before an all-white, all-male jury, who often could not speak or understand the language in which the court case was conducted, and who were subject to discriminatory laws.

The number of Aboriginal women who appeared in the Western Australian upper courts prior to 1891 was much lower than that of non-Aboriginal women, and this may account for the lack of scholarly research on the experiences of Indigenous female defendants in Australia. Nonetheless, this research has shown that one tenth of women appearing in Western Australian colonial courts were Aboriginal. Their experience of the criminal justice system was different to that of non-Aboriginal women and was influenced by racialised attitudes and unequal laws. Aboriginal women were also disproportionately impacted by the *Courts of General Sessions Act* which meant that trials for serious crimes in regional areas were presided over by untrained magistrates, whose ignorance of the law could adversely affect the course, and the outcome, of the trial. Aboriginal women were judged by non-Indigenous male juries and sentenced by non-Indigenous male judges, who did not understand their customary obligations or recognise customary laws, and were more likely to be convicted than non-Aboriginal female defendants.

Evidence gleaned from numerous case studies shows that beneath the use of the legal rules and institutions used in the courtroom runs the continuing thread of gender. While this did not have a direct effect on the outcomes of all trials, it was certainly entangled in many and manifested itself in a variety of forms. Women's appearance and demeanour in court were scrutinised by the press, and their age, marital status, attractiveness, clothing, and "respectability" were often reported in the newspapers. Those presenting an appearance of respectable femininity through their dress, demeanour, and speech, as occurred during the case of Mary Woods in 1876, might expect leniency from the judge and jury. Defence counsel would use gendered interpretations of women's behaviour to indicate to the jury that their client was a "respectable" woman and therefore not a danger to society. To do this they would emphasise characteristics which accorded with gendered assumptions of femininity, such as frailty or being prone to mental instability. They might also use similar tactics to discredit the victim by pointing out "unfeminine" behaviours such as drunkenness or bad language. Attacks on women's honour or good name were also seen as grounds for leniency, as exemplified by the case of Margaret McGhee, who was recommended to mercy on the grounds of "provocation" after it was shown that the victim used language that called Margaret's reputation into dishonour. Judges and juries also took a sympathetic view of unmarried women who killed their newborn babies. Many of these were young women living apart from their families in domestic service situations, and juries recognised their vulnerability to the social and economic pressures of the time.

A less expected outcome of this research was the light it shines on the everyday life of working-class women in nineteenth-century Western Australia. The use of crime records has shown us where these women lived and how they earned a living. It has highlighted the pressures they faced in their daily lives and the support networks they drew upon to navigate challenges and pitfalls. It has shown some of the survival strategies women used to support themselves and their families. This book therefore not only contributes to the study of women's crime but also provides a valuable addition to the social history of Western Australia.

The legacies of this history continue to resonate today. Research in British court cases has found that, in contrast to the sentencing of men, women who commit crimes while intoxicated are sentenced more harshly than those where alcohol was not involved.[1] Aboriginal and Torres Strait Islander women are imprisoned in Australia at sixteen times the rate of the general population of women, and Western Australia has the highest rate of imprisonment of Aboriginal and Torres Strait Islander people in Australia.[2] In 2014, Chris Cunneen and Eileen Baldry argued that it

1 Carly Lightowlers, "Drunk and Doubly Deviant? The Role of Gender and Intoxication in Sentencing Assault Offences," *British Journal of Criminology* 59, no. 3 (2019): 711.

2 "Corrective Services Australia," Australian Bureau of Statistics, accessed 14 April 2025, https://www.abs.gov.au/statistics/people/crime-and-justice/corrective-services-australia/dec-quarter-2024.

is necessary to "draw upon an understanding of the dynamics of colonial patriarchy" to understand contemporary penal culture in relation to Indigenous women. They argued that the legacy of different laws and modes of punishment, which were applied to Aboriginal people on the basis of the coloniser's "superior" race and "rightful dominance" of the colonised race, continue to influence Aboriginal women's treatment in the criminal justice system and contributes to their presence in the carceral system.[3] The trope of the Aboriginal person as "thief" still exists, with First Nations people stating that they are under greater surveillance in retail areas, leading in turn to higher rates of arrest.[4] Introduced laws which unduly disadvantage Aboriginal people, such as the "three strikes" law which mandated sentencing for some repeat offenders, have been introduced in Western Australia.[5] In 2017, the Law Society of Western Australia identified a lack of interpreting services and a lack of access to legal representation for Aboriginal people in the criminal justice system, particularly for Aboriginal women, concluding that available services were "not adequate in providing full access to justice."[6] Scholars argue that the paternalistic practice of incarcerating women, particularly Indigenous women, "for their own good" continues today due to a lack of alternative welfare options.[7] By examining women in the criminal justice system during the early days of colonisation, and the factors that determined First Nations women's experience, this research contributes to an understanding of contemporary penality in relation to women, and particularly Indigenous women.

The dataset for this research has been necessarily small, as defendant numbers were influenced by the low population of Western Australia at

---

[3] Eileen Baldry and Chris Cunneen, "Imprisoned Indigenous Women and the Shadow of Colonial Patriarchy," *Australian & New Zealand Journal of Criminology* (2014): 276–98.

[4] Amy Thunig, *The Drum*, aired 17 November 2022, on ABC.

[5] Lyn Hinds, "Three strikes and You're Out in the West: A Study of Newspaper Coverage of Crime Control in Western Australia," *Current Issues in Criminal Justice* 17, no. 2 (2005): 243.

[6] "Access to Justice Issues Faced by Aboriginal and Torres Strait Islander Peoples in Western Australia," The Law Society of Western Australia, October 2017, http://www.lawsocietywa.asn.au/wp-content/uploads/2015/10/2017OCT06_LawSociety_BriefingPapers_AccessJusticeIssues_ATIPIA.pdf.

[7] Clement Ng, "Invisible Female Indigenous Offenders in the Youth Justice System: What's the Problem? An Illustration from the Northern Territory Perspective," *Australian Indigenous Law Review* 18 (2014): 24.

this time. This has meant that results from quantitative analysis were often indicative only. Additionally, other distinctive conditions existing in Western Australia, such as the low ratio of women to men and separate laws pertaining solely to Aboriginal people, mean that the findings of this study may not be indicative of conditions for female defendants in other jurisdictions. More research into women's experience in the criminal justice systems of other jurisdictions is required if we are to determine further continuities and disruptions between the colonial system of law and that we have today, particularly in regard to the advantages, or disadvantages, of legal rules and institutions, such as co-accused status and legal representation.

Although this study has answered, or in some instances suggested answers to, questions regarding women's experiences in criminal trials in colonial Western Australia, it has also opened up new directions for future research. An examination of women's trials across multiple Australian jurisdictions, from colonisation to, say, the early twentieth-century, would allow research across a much larger dataset, providing more definitive answers and a better understanding of the way in which cultural constructs of race and gender have influenced the leniency women have historically experienced in criminal trials across a range of offences. It would also highlight the instances in which women did *not* receive more lenient treatment by the courts or in which equity of justice was not present for women. Furthermore, it would allow comparisons between different jurisdictions—required due to the varying laws and circumstances prevailing in different states.

Further research into the aftermath of the trial is also indicated. Although some excellent historical research into women's imprisonment is available, the experience of women in carceral spaces Australia wide, and across multiple jurisdictions, is still lacking. This area of research opens up possibilities for exploring the criminal activities of women across a much wider range of offending as it also captures the figures for the number of women tried and convicted in the lower courts for the more commonly committed crimes, such as public order offences or petty larceny. Studies like this can help to illuminate women's pathways into crime, recidivism rates, and offence types. The breadth of offence type captured in this type of research also lends itself to longitudinal studies, which can indicate changes and continuities across time.

Further research into petitions and witness testimonies is also needed. Examination of petitions written by, or for, female offenders would add greatly to our knowledge of the gendering of these documents. Additionally, because women were considered the experts on clothing, mending, and sewing, they frequently gave evidence in court. Female witnesses were often asked to identify items of stolen clothing or the clothing of murder victims and were sometimes able to identify perpetrators by the clothes they were wearing. Research into women's petitions and the testimonies of female witnesses would provide much-needed evidence of the lives of working-class women.

In this book, I have told the stories of working-class women in the colony of Western Australia. The research examines the consequences for women when their lifestyles, or their attempts to support themselves and care for their families, brought them into conflict with the criminal justice system. It also examines the consequences for Aboriginal women whose actions were judged by a rule of law which they had not requested, and which was often in conflict with their own lore and culture. The research presented here suggests that the factors influencing the outcomes of women's trials at this time were complex. Legal rules and institutions determined some aspects of the outcome of a woman's case but so too might social and cultural conceptions of women's role in society. The findings suggest that women did gain a greater advantage from the use of defence counsel and co-accused status than did men, and that the outcome of their trials might also be affected by lenient verdicts or the jury's prerogative of mercy, and by lenient sentencing. Running as a consistent thread beneath these findings is the cultural construct of gender, often determining which women were "worthy" to gain advantage from these rules and institutions. However, this research has also shown that many women were aware of the contexts in which the criminal justice system operated. They could, and did, use the system to their advantage by employing defence lawyers and presenting an appearance of "respectable" femininity in court. Ultimately, this research suggests that the outcome of women's trials depended on a complex mix of judicial rules and institutions entangled with cultural constructs of gender, class, and race and mediated by the interactions of defendants, jurors, witnesses, victims, judges, prosecutors, and defence counsel.

Appendix 1: Plan of Fremantle, Western Australia, 1844

See Fig. A.1.

C. Ingram, *Women on Trial*, Palgrave Histories of Policing, Punishment and Justice,
https://doi.org/10.1007/978-3-031-98072-5

Fig. A.1 Plan of the town of Fremantle, 1844. Courtesy SROWA, S235 cons3868 126

Appendix 2: Plan of Perth, Western Australia, 1871–1872

See Fig. A.2

C. Ingram, *Women on Trial*, Palgrave Histories of Policing, Punishment and Justice, https://doi.org/10.1007/978-3-031-98072-5

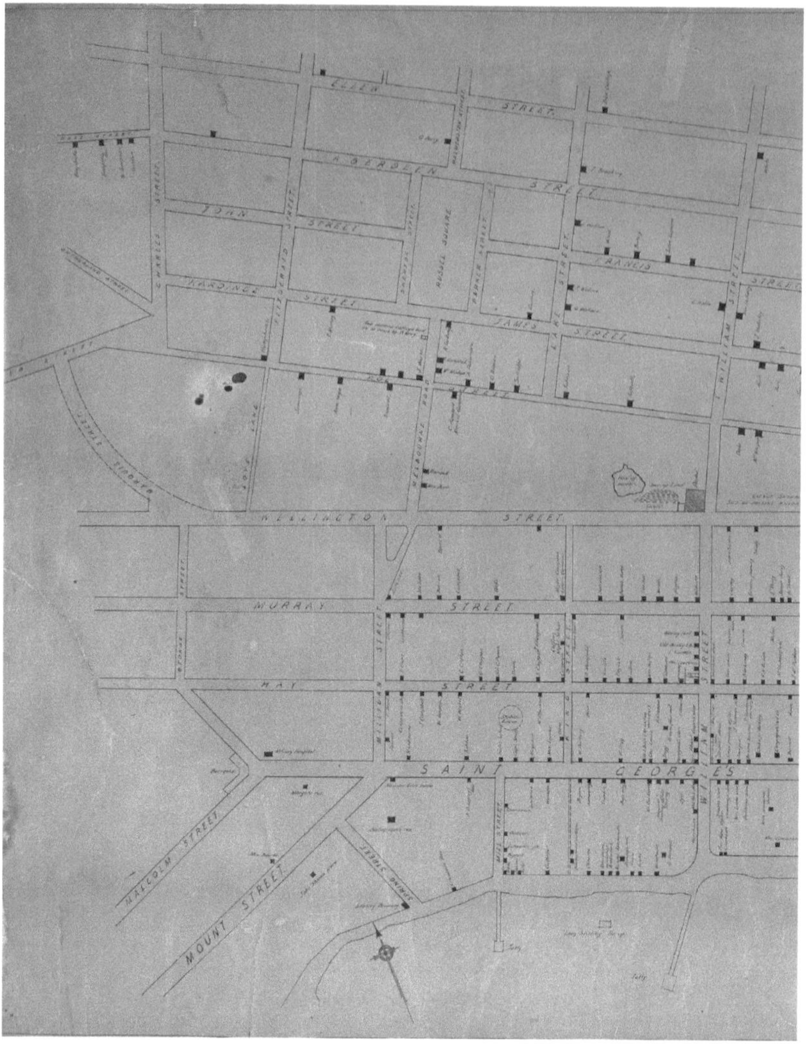

Fig. A.2 Plan of Perth (1871–1872). Compiled from memory by Jesse Hammond in 1930. Courtesy SLWA, 29/3/26 (33/1)

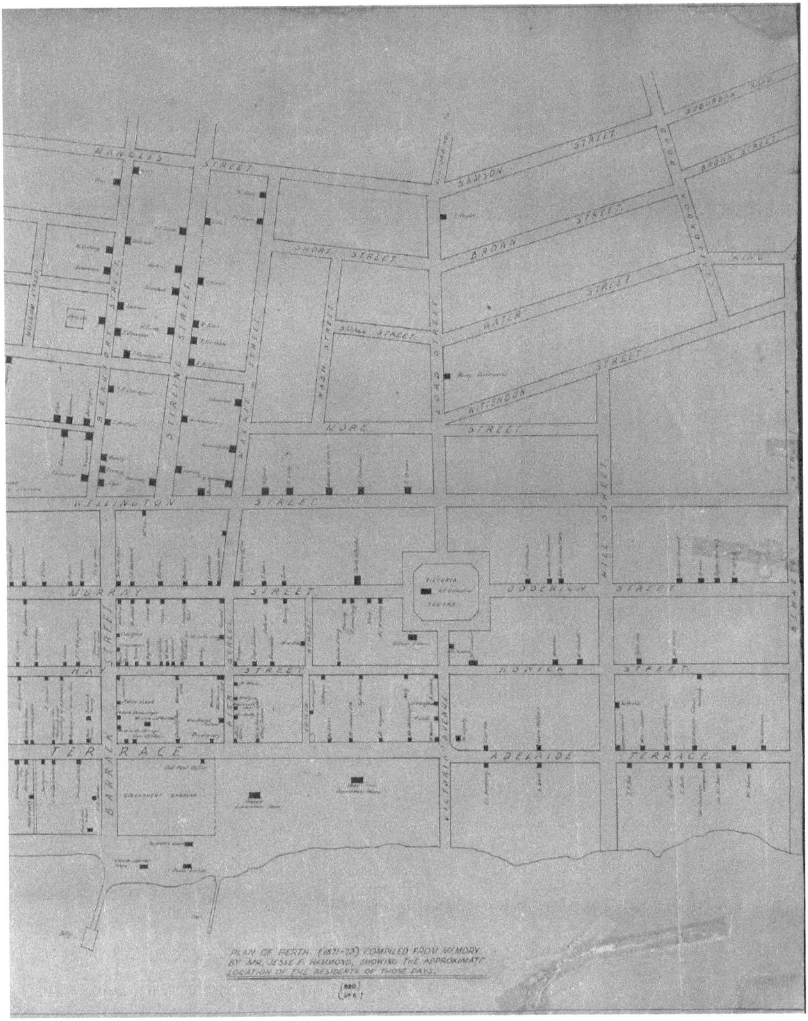

Fig. A.2 (continued)

Appendix 3: Noongar Word List

Noongar[1]	English
booka	cloak made from kangaroo skin
dowak	throwing stick
gidgie	spear
kylie	boomerang
mia	hut
wanna	women's digging stick
wonga	talk

[1] Rose Whitehurst, *Noongar Dictionary* (East Perth, W.A.: Noongar Language and Culture Centre, 1997).

C. Ingram, *Women on Trial*, Palgrave Histories of Policing, Punishment and Justice, https://doi.org/10.1007/978-3-031-98072-5

Bibliography

Primary Sources

Newspapers

Albany Advertiser
Armidale Express and New England General Advertiser
Clare's Weekly
Daily News (DN)
Eastern Districts Chronicle
Eastern Recorder
Express
Freeman's Journal
Fremantle Times (FT)
Herald
Inquirer
Inquirer and Commercial News (ICN)
Perth Gazette and Independent Journal of Politics and News (PGIJPN)
Perth Gazette and West Australian Times (PGWAT)

C. Ingram, *Women on Trial*, Palgrave Histories of Policing, Punishment and Justice, https://doi.org/10.1007/978-3-031-98072-5

Perth Gazette and Western Australian Journal (PGWAJ)
Quarterly paper / Society for the Propagation of the Gospel in Foreign Parts
South-Western News (SWN)
Truth
Victorian Express
West Australian
West Australian Times
Western Australian Times
Western Mail

Government Publications

Police Gazette Western Australia (PGWA)
Western Australian Parliament Votes and Proceedings

Archival Sources

1851 census, Class HO107 1698 116, *Ancestry.com.*
Albany Police Station, occurrence books, 1863–1922, AU WA S3240 cons364, State Records Office of Western Australia (SROWA).
Anglican Church Western Australian records, MN612 Acc. 3540A/1, State Library of Western Australia (SLWA).
Baptismal Register St Mary's Perth, accessed 16 January 2023, https://www.familysearch.org.
Browne, James. Holograph statement relating to the natives of King George's Sound, Western Australia, London, for the Aborigines Protection Society, 26 June 1839, Ak 34, Mitchell Library, New South Wales.
Burt, Archibald Paull. Letter books, MN 736 acc 2829A, SLWA.
Burt, Archibald Paull. Notebooks Supreme Court criminal sittings, MN 736 Acc. 2850A, SLWA.
Case books, AU WA S2219 cons2724 and cons5759, SROWA.
Convict Registers, AU WA S5056 cons1156, SROWA.
Correspondence files, AU WA S675 cons527, SROWA.
Correspondence inwards, AU WA S2941 cons36, SROWA.
Correspondence—letters received, AU WA S2528 cons346, SROWA.
Criminal indictment files, AU WA S122, SROWA.
Divorce files, 1864–1977, AU WA S35 cons3403, SROWA.

Evidence books, AN 17, SROWA.
Executive Council minutes, AU WA S1620 cons1058, SROWA.
Files probate, AU WA S34 cons3403, SROWA.
General files, AU WA S2126 cons430, SROWA.
Legal opinions, AU WA S1685 cons346, SROWA.
Letterbooks outwards correspondence, 1829–1900, AU WA S2755 cons49, SROWA.
Minute book Court of Quarter Sessions, 1832, AU WA S204, SROWA.
Passenger list of assisted emigrants, AN 371 acc 115, SROWA.
Patient Admission Forms, AU WA S4397 cons7543, SROWA.
Piggott, Benjamin. Accounts and farm journals 1845–1887, MN 729 Acc 2247A, SLWA.
Plaints—local court, AU WA S1686 cons348, SROWA.
Quarterly returns of prisoners, AU WA S270 cons3676, SROWA.
Receipts and discharges, AU WA S5073 cons1156, SROWA.
Record of court convictions, AU WA S5072 cons1156, SROWA.
Register of death Colonial Surgeon, 1875–1884, AU WA S4015 cons2799, SROWA.
Register of female patients, AU WA S507 cons1120 04, SROWA.
Registers criminal record books, AU WA S49 cons3422, SROWA.
Registers local prisoners, 1876–1888, AU WA S1809 cons1156, SROWA.
Registers local prisoners (male), AU WA S672 cons4173, SROWA.
Reports and Occurrences, AU WA S690 cons1156, SROWA.
Rottnest Island commitment book, 1855–1881, cons130, SROWA.
St Joseph's Orphanage register - Girls from Poorhouse, 1868–1885, Institute of the Sisters of Mercy and Papua New Guinea Archives, Sydney.
Western Australian Almanack and Directory for 1881 (Stirling Brothers: Perth, 1881), xxxix. Trove. Accessed 28 October 2021. https://trove.nla.gov.au/work/246649026.

Primary Sources—Published

Brockman, Frances Louisa. *Pioneer Daughter: The Diary of Frances Louisa (Fanny) Brockman (nee Bussell),* edited by Gillian Lilleyman. Claremont: Gillian Lilleyman, 2018.
Tanner, William, Hester Tanner, Ellen Viveash, and Pamela Statham-Drew. *The Tanner Letters: A Pioneer Saga of Swan River & Tasmania, 1831–1845.* Nedlands: University of Western Australia Press, 1981.

Wollaston, John Ramsden. *Wollaston's Picton Journal (1841–1844)*, edited by A. Burton and Percy U. Henn. Perth: Paterson Brokensha, 1955.
Wollaston, John Ramsden. *Wollaston's Albany Journals, Journals and Diaries (1841–1856)*. Nedlands: University of Western Australia Press, 1975.

Secondary Sources

Unpublished Manuscripts

Beer, Campbell. *John Bailey Pavey (1797–1882): Mariner, Sealer, Whaler and Plantagenet Pioneer*. Roleystone, W.A.: Campbell Beer, 2009.

Websites

Aboriginal History Research Services. "Walganda." Accessed 5 May 2023. https://ahwaportal.dlgsc.wa.gov.au/online-catalogue/search-wadjemup/public-view/?id=0300d033-2cbb-ea11-a812-000d3a795fc7.
AIATSIS. "Map of Indigenous Australia." Accessed 21 April 2023. https://aiatsis.gov.au/explore/map-indigenous-australia.
Ancestrylibrary. Accessed 6 June 2023. https://www.ancestrylibrary.com.au/.
Australian Bureau of Statistics. "Corrective Services Australia." Accessed 14 April 2025. https://www.abs.gov.au/statistics/people/crime-and-justice/corrective-services-australia/dec-quarter-2024.
Birman, Wendy, and Geoffrey Bolton. "Parker, Sir Stephen Henry (1846–1927)." *Australian Dictionary of Biography*. National Centre of Biography, Australian National University. Accessed 7 November 2021. https://adb.anu.edu.au/biography/parker-sir-stephen-henry-7957/text13853.
Bombardini, Sylvia. "The Shoplifter's Clothes: Technologies for a Feminist Practice." Politics of Patents: Re-imagining Citizenship via Clothing Inventions 1820–2020. Accessed 23 May 2023. https://www.politicsofpatents.org/2020/08/19/the-shoplifters-clothes-technologies-for-a-feminist-practice.
Calaby, J.H. "Preiss, Johann August Ludwig (1811–1883)." *Australian Dictionary of Biography*, National Centre of Biography, Australian National University. Accessed 21 April 2021. https://adb.anu.edu.au/biography/preiss-johann-august-ludwig-2561/text3493.

City of Fremantle. "Alma and Skinner Street Burial Records." Accessed 6 May 2022. https://www.fremantle.wa.gov.au/sites/default/files/Alma%20and%20Skinner%20Street%20Burial%20Records%201831%20-%201899.pdf.

Colonial Frontier Massacres in Australia, 1788–1930. "Ravensthorpe." Accessed 21 July 2023. https://c21ch.newcastle.edu.au/colonialmassacres/detail.php?r=895.

Department of Justice. "Online Index Search Tool." Accessed 5 May 2023. https://www.wa.gov.au/organisation/department-of-justice/online-index-search-tool.

East Perth Cemeteries. Accessed 7 May 2022. https://www.eastperthcemeteries.com.au.

Finnane, Mark. "Western Australia Criminal Trials 1830–1861." ADA Dataverse, V1, 2019. https://doi.org/10.26193/OW6SR6.

Finnane, Mark. "Western Australia Supreme Court 1862–1899." ADA Dataverse, V2, 2020. https://doi.org/10.26193/ESI64N.

Ingram, Caroline. "'How is this not murder?' Infanticide and the Law in Australian History." Australian Policy and History. Accessed 6 March 2023. https://aph.org.au/2018/10/how-is-this-not-murder-infanticide-and-the-law-in-australian-history/.

Inherit. "Butterabby Graves." Accessed 6 February 2023. http://inherit.stateheritage.wa.gov.au/Admin/api/file/9d5ab835-f51a-4276-81bc-9fd8017477bb.

Inherit. "Walebing." Accessed 21 April 2023, http://inherit.stateheritage.wa.gov.au/Public/Inventory/PrintSingleRecord/7c4ce972-2a86-4de4-acee-3aba376f28fd.

Law Reform Commission of Western Australia. "Aboriginal Customary Laws: The Interaction of Western Australian Law with Aboriginal Law and Culture, Project 94." Published September 2006, 1. https://www.wa.gov.au/system/files/2021-04/LRC-Project-094-Final-report.pdf.

Metropolitan Cemeteries Board. "Charles Woolley." Accessed 5 August 2023. https://portal.mcb.wa.gov.au/name-search/ns-detail/?id=cc789308-de1c-ec11-b6e7-00224814cbaf.

Prosecution Project. "Search Trials." Accessed 10 January 2023. https://app.prosecutionproject.griffith.edu.au/web/public-search.

Scottish Chapbooks. "The Sentimental Valentine Writer, Containing a Selection of the Best and Newest Valentine Poetry. New and Improved Series. No. 13." Accessed 22 June 2021. https://scottishchapbooks.lib.uoguelph.ca/items/show/729.

The Law Society of Western Australia. "Access to Justice Issues Faced by Aboriginal and Torres Strait Islander Peoples in Western Australia." Published October 2017. http://www.lawsocietywa.asn.au/wp-content/uploads/2015/10/2017OCT06_LawSociety_BriefingPapers_AccessJusticeIssues_ATIPIA.pdf.

Trove. "Newspapers and Gazettes." Accessed 29 August 2022. https://trove.nla.gov.au/newspaper/.

Multimedia

Amy Thunig. *The Drum*. Aired 17 November 2022, on ABC.

Theses

Ballinger, Anette. "Dead Woman Walking: Executed Women in England & Wales 1900–55." PhD diss., University of Sheffield, 1997.

Briscoe, Gordon. "Disease, Health and Healing: Aspects of Indigenous Health in Western Australia and Queensland, 1900–1940." PhD diss., Australian National University, 1996.

Chambers, Emily Jayne. "The Immigration of Domestic Servants to Western Australia in the 1850s and 1890s." Honours thesis, Murdoch University, 2017.

Clements, Nicholas Patrick. "Frontier Conflict in Van Diemen's Land." PhD diss., University of Tasmania, 2013.

Drummond, Sarah. "Exiles and Island Wives: History, Fiction and the Breaksea Islanders." PhD diss., Murdoch University, 2015.

Durnian, Lisa. "The Rise of the Guilty Plea in Australian Supreme Courts: A History." PhD diss., Griffith University, 2018.

Eluwawalage, Damayanthie. "History of Costume: The Consumption, Governance, Potency and Patronage of Attire in Colonial Western Australia." PhD diss., Edith Cowan University, 2004.

Farrell, Rita. "Dangerous Women: Constructions of Female Criminality in Western Australia 1915–1945." PhD diss., Murdoch University, 1997.

Gall, S.L. "Effects of Joint Trials on the Proportion of Guilty Verdicts Assigned to Defendants." Master's thesis, Edith Cowan University, 1999.

Groves, Joan. "The Camfields: 'The Comforts of Civilisation' in Early Colonial Western Australia." Honours thesis, Edith Cowan University, 2006.

Lanman, Emily. "Prisoners, Power and Panopticon: Investigating Fremantle Gaol, 1831–1841." Master's thesis, University of Notre Dame Australia, 2021.

McEwan, Joanne. "Negotiating Support: Women's Networks in London and Middlesex, c. 1730–1820." PhD diss., University of Western Australia, 2008.

Owen, Chris. "'Weather Hot, Flies Troublesome...': Police in the Kimberley District of Western Australia 1882–1901." PhD diss., University of Western Australia, 2013.

Piper, Alana Jayne. "In Bad Company: Female Criminal Subcultures in Brisbane and Melbourne, 1860–1920." PhD diss., University of Queensland, 2013.

Roscoe, Katherine Ann. "Island Chains: Carceral Islands and the Colonisation of Australia, 1824–1903." PhD diss., University of Leicester, 2018.

Rychner, Georgina. "'The Pendulum of the Public Mind': Insanity and Activism in Capital Trials, 1880–1939." PhD diss., Monash University, 2020.

Stasiuk, Glen. "Wadjemup: Rottnest Island as Black Prison and White Playground." PhD exegesis, Murdoch University, 2015.

Tilbrook, Lois. "Shadows in the Archives: An Interpretation of European Colonization and Aboriginal Response in the Swan River area." PhD diss., University of Western Australia, 1987.

Wallis, Alexandra. "Hysterical Women: Moral Treatment of Female Patients in the Fremantle Lunatic Asylum, 1858–1908." PhD diss., University of Notre Dame, 2020.

Journal Articles

Andrews, J. A. "Joint Trials." *Modern Law Review* 30, no. 6 (1967): 645–58.

August, Andrew. "'A Horrible Looking Woman': Female Violence in Late-Victorian East London." *Journal of British Studies* 54, no. 4 (2015): 844–68.

Baldry, Eileen, and Chris Cunneen. "Imprisoned Indigenous Women and the Shadow of Colonial Patriarchy." *Australian & New Zealand Journal of Criminology* 47, no. 2 (2014): 276–98.

Ballinger, Anette. "Masculinity in the Dock: Legal Responses to Male Violence and Female Retaliation in England and Wales, 1900–1965." *Social & Legal Studies* 16, no. 4 (2007): 459–81.

Barrington, Robin. "A Race War: Tracing Emotions on the Murchison Frontier in Western Australia 1880–1915. *Studies in Western Australian History* 32 (2018): 95–117.

Bartels, Lorana. "Painting the Picture of Indigenous Women in Custody in Australia." *Queensland University of Technology Law and Justice Journal* 12, no. 2 (2012): 1–17.

Bartels, Lorana, Patricia Easteal, and Robyn Westgate. "Understanding Women's Imprisonment in Australia." *Women & Criminal Justice* 30, no. 3 (2019): 204–19.

Bolton, Geoffrey. "Who Were the Pensioners?" *Studies in Western Australian History* 4 (1981): 84–89.

Bond, Christine E.W., and Samantha Jeffries. "Sentencing Indigenous and Non-Indigenous Women in Western Australia's Higher Courts." *Psychiatry, Psychology and Law* 17, no. 1 (2010): 70–78.

Brock, Peggy. "Protecting Colonial Interests: Aborigines and Criminal Justice." *Journal of Australian Studies* 21, no. 53 (1997): 120–29.

Callahan, Kathy. "On the Receiving End: Women and Stolen Goods in London 1783–1815." *The London Journal* 37, no 2 (2012): 106–21.

Calo, Robert R. "Joint Trials, Spillover Prejudice, and the Ineffectiveness of a Bare Limiting Instruction." *American Journal of Trial Advocacy* 9, no. 1 (1985): 21–42.

Carter, Michael J. "The Hermeneutics of Frames and Framing: An Examination of the Media's Construction of Reality." *SAGE Open* 3, no. 2 (2013): 1–12.

Choo, Christine, and Chris Owen. "Deafening Silences: Understanding Frontier Relations and the Discourse of Police Files Through the Kimberley Police Records." *Studies in Western Australian History* 23 (2003): 129–56.

Coen, Mark, and Niamh Howlin. "The Jury Speaks: Jury Riders in the Nineteenth and Twentieth Centuries." *American Journal of Legal History* 58 (2018): 505–34.

Crenshaw, Kimberlé Williams. "Demarginalising the Intersection of Race and Sex: A Black Feminist Critique of Anti-Discrimination Doctrine, Feminist Theory and Anti-Racist Politics." *University of Chicago Legal Forum* 1, no. 8 (1989): 139–67.

Curthoys, Ann. "The Beginnings of Transportation in Western Australia: Banishment, Forced Labour, and Punishment at the Aboriginal Prison on Rottnest Island before 1850." *Studies in Western Australian History* 34 (2020): 59–77.

Curthoys, Ann, and Jeremy Martens. "Serious Collisions: Settlers, Indigenous People, and Imperial Policy in Western Australia and Natal." *Journal of Australian Colonial History* 15 (2013): 121–44.

Drury, Michael. "Infant Mortality in Perth Western Australia, 1870–1914: A Preliminary Analysis." *Studies in Western Australian History* 5 (1982): 62–71.

Esteal, Patricia, Lorana Bartels, Noni Nelson, and Kate Holland. "How Are Women Who Kill Portrayed in Newspaper Media? Connections with Social Values and the Legal System." *Women's Studies International Forum* 51 (2015): 31–41.

Evans, Ray. "Don't You Remember Black Alice, Sam Holt? Aboriginal Women in Queensland History." *Hecate* 8, no. 2 (1982): 7–21.

Finch, Lyn, and Jon Stratton. "The Australian Working Class and the Practice of Abortion 1880–1939." *Journal of Australian Studies* 12, no. 23 (1988): 45–64.

Finnane, Mark, and Andy Kaladelfos. "Race and Justice in an Australian Court: Prosecuting Homicide in Western Australia, 1830–1954." *Australian Historical Studies* 47, no. 3 (2016): 443–61.

Fox, Richard G. "When Justice Sheds a Tear: The Place of Mercy in Sentencing." *Monash University Law Review* 25, no. 1 (1999): 1–28.

Gardiner, Amanda. "Can Historical Infanticide Investigations Help Us Understand Embodied Experiences of the Past?," *Australian Feminist Studies* 36, no. 109 (2021): 352–76.

Godfrey, Barry, and David J. Cox. "'The Last Fleet': Crime, Reformation, and Punishment in Western Australia After 1868." *Australian & New Zealand Journal of Criminology* 41, no. 2 (2008): 236–58.

Godfrey, Barry, Stephen Farrall, and Susanne Karstedt. "Explaining Gendered Sentencing Patterns for Violent Men and Women in the late-Victorian and Edwardian Period." *The British Journal of Criminology* 45, no. 5 (2005): 696–720.

Haebich, Anna. "Murdering Stepmothers: The Trial and Execution of Martha Rendell." *Journal of Australian Studies* 22 (1998): 66–81.

Handford, Peter. "Criminal Prosecutions in Western Australia: A View from the Nineteenth Century." *University of Western Australia Law Review* 43, no. 1 (2018): 143–71.

Heppingstone, I. D. "The Story of Alfred and Ellen Bussell: Pioneers of the Margaret River." *Early Days* 6, no. 3 (1964): 33–45.

Hetherington, Penelope. "Baby-Farming in Western Australia: The Case Against Alice Mitchell." *Studies in Western Australian History* 25 (1907): 75–97.

Hinds, Lyn. "Three Strikes and You're Out in the West: A Study of Newspaper Coverage of Crime Control in Western Australia." *Current Issues in Criminal Justice* 17, no. 2 (2005): 239–53.

Hunter, Ann. "The Origin and Debate Surrounding the Development of Aboriginal Evidence Acts in Western Australia in the Early 1840s." *University of Notre Dame Australia Law Review* 9 (2007): 115–46.

Hyland, Joanne. "The Vilest and Most Degraded of Human Beings': An Investigation into why Female Convicts were not Transported to Western Australia." *Studies in Western Australian History* 34 (2020): 147–63.

Ingram, Caroline. "'There not being any place to keep her': Incarcerating Women in Nineteenth-Century Western Australia." *Australian Historical Studies* 55, no. 1 (2024): 158–77.

Jeffries, Samantha, and Christine E.W. Bond. "Gender, Indigeneity, and the Criminal Courts: A Narrative Exploration of Women's Sentencing in Western Australia." *Women & Criminal Justice* 23, no. 1 (2013): 19–42.

King, Peter. "Female offenders, Work and Life-cycle Change in Late-eighteenth-century London." *Continuity and Change* 11, no. 1 (1996): 61–90.

Kociumbas, Jan. "Azaria's Antecedents: Stereotyping Infanticide in late Nineteenth-Century Australia." *Gender & History* 13, no.1 (2001): 138–60.

Langbein, John H. "Shaping the Eighteenth-Century Criminal Trial: A View from the Ryder Sources." *The University of Chicago Law Review* 50, no. 1 (1983): 1–136.

Langbein, John H. "Historical Foundations of the Law of Evidence: A View from the Ryder Sources." *Columbia Law Review* 96, no. 5 (1996): 1168–202.

Laster, Kathy. "Infanticide: A Litmus Test for Feminist Criminological Theory." *Australia and New Zealand Journal of Criminology* 22, no. 3 (1989): 151–66.

Layman, Lenore. "Investigating Sudden Death: Inquests in Early Colonial Western Australia, 1829–1840." *Early Days* 14, no. 3 (2014): 414–33.

Leipold, Andrew D., and Hossein A. Abbasi. "The Impact of Joinder and Severance on Federal Criminal Cases: An Empirical Study." *Vanderbilt Law Review* 59 (2006): 349–404.

Lightowlers, Carly. "Drunk and Doubly Deviant? the Role of Gender and Intoxication in Sentencing Assault Offences." *British Journal of Criminology* 59, no. 3 (2019): 693–717.

Lydon, Jane. "Racial Punishment from Slavery to Settler Colonialism: John Picton Beete in Demerara and Swan River." *Slavery & Abolition* 44, no. 1 (2023): 1–25.

McKenna, Mark. "Yukun's return." *The Monthly* (2022). Accessed 10 May 2023. https://www.themonthly.com.au/issue/2022/december/mark-mckenna/yukun-s-return.

Merry, Kay. "The Cross-Cultural Relationships Between the Sealers and the Tasmanian Aboriginal Women at Bass Strait and Kangaroo Island in the Early Nineteenth Century." *Counterpoints* (2003): 80–88.

Milroy, Chris. "Neonatal Deaths, Infanticide, and the Hydrostatic (Floatation) Test: Historical Perspectives." *Academic Forensic Pathology* 2, no. 4 (2012): 338–45.

Moreton-Robinson, Aileen. "Towards an Australian Indigenous Women's Standpoint Theory: A Methodological Tool." *Australian Feminist Studies* 28, no. 78 (2013): 331–47.

Nettelbeck, Amanda. "Equals of the White Man: Prosecution of Settlers for Violence against Aboriginal Subjects of the Crown, Colonial Western Australia." *Law and History Review* 31, no. 2 (2013): 355–90.

Nettelbeck, Amanda, "'Keep the Magistrates Straight': Magistrates and Aboriginal Management on Australia's North-west Frontiers, 1883–1905," *Aboriginal History* 38 (2014): 19–37.

Ng, Clement. "Invisible Female Indigenous Offenders in the Youth Justice System: What's the Problem? An Illustration from the Northern Territory Perspective." *Australian Indigenous Law Review* 18, no. 2 (2014): 19–28.

Pearn, John. "Emigrating to Queensland: Medical Advice for Intending Colonists." *Queensland History Journal* 22, no. 10 (2015): 765–74.

Piper, Alana Jayne. "'A Growing Vice': the *Truth* about Brisbane Girls and Drunkenness in the Early Twentieth Century." *Journal of Australian Studies* 34, no. 4 (2010): 485–97.

Piper, Alana Jayne. "Victimization Narratives and Courtroom Sexual Politics: Prosecuting Male Burglars and Female Pickpockets in Melbourne, 1860–1921." *Journal of Social History* 51, no. 4 (2018): 760–83.

Piper, Alana Jayne. "'I Was a Man of Honour': Masculinities and Theft in Early Twentieth-Century Western Australia." *Australian Historical Studies* 51, no. 3 (2020): 282–98.

Piper, Alana Jayne, and Lisa Durnian. "Theft on Trial: Prosecution, Conviction and Sentencing Patterns in Colonial Victoria and Western Australia." *Australian & New Zealand Journal of Criminology* 50, no. 1 (2017): 5–22.

Piper, Alana Jayne, and Mark Finnane. "Defending the Accused: The Impact of Legal Representation on Criminal Trial Outcomes in Victoria, Australia 1861–1961." *Journal of Legal History* 38 (2017): 27–53.

Piper, Alana Jayne, and Mark Finnane. "Access to Legal Representation by Criminal Defendants in Victoria, 1861–1961." *University of New South Wales Law Journal* 40, no. 2 (2017): 638–63.

Piper, Alana Jayne, and Victoria Nagy. "Versatile Offending: Criminal Careers of Female Prisoners in Australia, 1860–1920." *Journal of Interdisciplinary History* 48, no. 2 (2017): 187–210.

Piper, Alana Jayne, and Victoria Nagy. "Risk Factors and Pathways to Imprisonment Among Incarcerated Women in Victoria, 1860–1920." *Journal of Australian Studies* 42, no. 3 (2018): 268–84.

Piper, Alana Jayne, and Lauren Vogel. "Co-Offenders Before the Court: The Joinder Effect in Victoria, 1861–1961." *Law&History* 5, no. 2 (2018): 111–36.

Plater, David, Joanna Duncan, and Sue Milne. "'Innocent Victim of Circumstance' or a 'Very Devil Incarnate' - The Trial and Execution of Elizabeth Woolcock in South Australia in 1873." *Flinders Law Journal* 15, no. 2 (2013): 315–80.

Plater, David, and Victoria Geason. "'The Prisoners Could Not Have That Fair and Impartial Trial Which Justice Demands': A Fair Criminal Trial in 19th Century Australia." *Canterbury Law Review* 25 (2019): 161–203.

Plater, David, and Sue Milne. "'All That's Good and Virtuous or Depraved and Abandoned in the Extreme'? Capital Punishment and Mercy for Female Offenders in Colonial Australia, 1824 to 1865." *University of Tasmania Law Review* 33, no. 1 (2014): 83–140.

Plater, David, and Sue Milne. "'Assuredly There Never Was Murder More Foul and More Unnatural': Poisoning, Women and Murder in 19th Century Australia." *Canterbury Law Review* 25 (2019): 53–94.

Plomley, Brian, and Kristen Anne Henley. "The Sealers of Bass Strait and the Cape Barren Island Community." *Tasmanian Historical Research Association Papers and Proceedings* 37, no. 4 (1990): 37–127.

Reece, Bob. "The Revd George King." *Studies in Western Australian History* 20 (2000): 35–48.

Reece, Bob. "Fremantle's First Historian: Joseph Keane Hitchcock." *Fremantle Studies* 7 (2012): 33–50.

Reece, Bob. "Richard McBryde Broun: Fremantle's Government Resident, 1834–1858." *Early Days* 101 (2017): 25–42.

Roscoe, Katherine. "'Too Many Kill 'Em. Too Many Make 'Em Ill': The Commission into Rottnest Prison as the Context for Section 70." *Studies in Western Australian History* 30 (2016): 43–57.

Roscoe, Katherine, and Barry Godfrey. "Postcolonial Churn and the Impact of the Criminal Justice System on Aboriginal People in Western Australia, 1829–2020." *Journal of Criminology* 55, no. 4 (2022): 532–49.

Russell, Lynette. "'Dirty Domestics and Worse Cooks': Aboriginal Women's Agency and Domestic Frontiers, Southern Australia, 1800–1850." *Frontiers: A Journal of Women Studies* 28, nos 1 and 2 (2007): 18–46.

Saunders, Kay. "The Study of Domestic Violence in Colonial Queensland: Sources and Problems." *Australian Historical Studies* 21, no. 82 (1984): 68–84.

Schmidt, Leigh Eric. "The Fashioning of a Modern Holiday: St. Valentine's Day, 1840–1870." *Winterthur Portfolio* 28, no. 4 (1993): 209–45.

Stevens, Simon. "A Social Tyranny: The Truck System in Colonial Western Australia, 1829–99." *Labour History*, no. 80 (2001): 83–98.

Strange, Carolyn. "Masculinities, Intimate Femicide and the Death Penalty in Australia, 1890–1920." *British Journal of Criminology* 43, no. 2 (2003): 310–39.

Strange, Carolyn, and Les Hetherington. "Murderess or Miscarriage of Justice? A Case of Husband Poisoning in Early Federation New South Wales." *Australian Historical Studies* 51, no. 3 (2020): 299–323.

Straw, Leigh S.L. "'The Worst Female Character': Criminal Underclass Women in Perth and Fremantle, 1900–1939." *Journal of Australian Studies* 37, no. 2 (2013): 208–24.

Stubbs, Julie. "Indigenous Women in Australian Criminal Justice: Over-represented but Rarely Acknowledged." *Australian Indigenous Law Review* 15, no. 1 (2011): 47–63.

Swain, Shurlee. "Maids and Mothers: Domestic Servants and Illegitimacy in 19th-century Australia." *The History of the Family* 10, no.4 (2005): 461–71.

Wallis, Alexandra. "The Disorderly Female: Alcohol, Prostitution and Moral Insanity in 19th-Century Fremantle." *Journal of Australian Studies* 43, no. 3 (2019): 333–48.

Watson, Katherine D. "Medical and Chemical Expertise in English Trials for Criminal Poisoning, 1750–1914." *Medical History* 50 (2006): 373–90.

Weinberg, Mark. "Joint Trials – the Problem of Reciprocal Blame." *Criminal Law Journal* 8, no. 4 (1984): 197–216.

Young, Denise. "Layers of Visibility: Convict Discipline, Crime and Punishment, King George's Sound, Western Australia, 1826–1831." *Studies in Western Australian History* 34 (2020): 41–57.

Zedner, Lucia. "Women, Crime, and Penal Responses: A Historical Account." *Crime and Justice* 14 (1991): 307–62.

Books

Allen, Judith. "Octavius Beale Reconsidered: Infanticide, Babyfarming and Abortion in NSW 1880–1939." In *What Rough Beast?: The State and Social Order in Australian History*, edited by Sydney Labour History Group, 111–29. Sydney: Allen & Unwin, 1982.

Allen, Judith. *Sex and Secrets: Crimes Involving Australian Women Since 1880.* Melbourne: Oxford University Press, 1990.

Appleyard, R.T. "Western Australia: Economic and Demographic Growth, 1850–1914." In *A New History of Western Australia*, edited by C. T. Stannage, 211–36. Nedlands: University of Western Australia Press, 1981.

Arnold, Murray. *A Journey Travelled: Aboriginal-European Relations at Albany and the Surrounding Region from First Contact to 1926*. Crawley, W.A.: UWA Publishing, 2015.

Barrie, David G., and Susan Broomhall. *A History of Police and Masculinities, 1700–2010.* London: Routledge, 2012.

Beattie, John M. *Crime and the Courts in England, 1660–1800.* Princeton: Princeton University Press, 1986.

Beattie, John M. "Crime and the Courts in Surrey 1736–1753." In *Crime in England: 1550–1800,* edited by J.S. Cockburn, 155–86. London: Routledge, 2016.

Berryman, Ian ed., *A Colony Detailed: The First Census of Western Australia 1832.* North Perth: Creative Research, 1979.

Bignall, Merle. *First the Spring: A History of the Shire of Kojonup, Western Australia.* Nedlands: University of Western Australia Press, 1892.

Blackburn, Geoff. *The Children's Friend Society: Juvenile Emigrants to Western Australia, South Africa and Canada, 1834–1842.* Northbridge, W.A.: Access Press, 1993.

Blackstone, William. *Commentaries on the Laws of England* vol. 2. Oxford: Clarendon press, 1765–1769.

Bolton, Geoffrey. *Land of Vision and Mirage, Western Australia Since 1826.* Crawley: University of Western Australia Press, 2008.

Bolton, Geoffrey, and Geraldine Byrne. *May it Please Your Honour: A History of the Supreme Court of Western Australia from 1861–2005.* Perth: The Supreme Court of Western Australia, 2005.

Bolton, Geoffrey, and Prue Joske. *History of the Royal Perth Hospital.* Perth, W.A.: Royal Perth Hospital, 1982.

Brooksby, Bradley, Margaret P. Doust, and Michael Doust. *James and Isaac Doust and Descendants.* Bunbury: Margaret P. Doust, 2015.

Broomhall, Frank H. *The Veterans: A History of the Enrolled Pensioner Force in Western Australia 1850–1880.* Carlisle, W.A.: Hesperian Press, 1989.

Budrikis, Stella. *The Edward Street Baby Farm.* Fremantle: Fremantle Press, 2020.

Burton, Antoinette. "Introduction: Archive Fever, Archive Stories." In *Archive Stories: Facts, Fictions and the Writing of History,* edited by Antoinette Burton, 1–24. Durham, NC: Duke University Press, 2005.

Cannon, Michael. *The Woman as Murderer: Five Who Paid with Their Lives.* Mornington: Today's Australia Publishing Company, 1994.

Castles, Alex C. *An Australian Legal History.* Sydney: The Law Book Company, 1993.

Collins, Patricia Hill, and Sirma Bilge. *Intersectionality.* Oxford: Polity Press, 2016.

Conor, Liz. *Skin Deep: Settler Impressions of Aboriginal Women.* Perth, W.A.: UWA Publishing, 2016.

Creswell, John, W., and J. David Creswell. *Research Design: Qualitative, Quantitative, and Mixed Methods Approaches.* Thousand Oaks, California: SAGE Publications, 2018.

Curthoys, Ann, Shino Konishi, and Alexandra Ludewig. *The Lives and Legacies of a Carceral Island: A Biographical History of Wadjemup/Rottnest Island.* London: Routledge, 2023.

Cushing, Nancy. *A History of Crime in Australia: Australian Underworlds.* London: Routledge, 2023.

Damousi, Joy. *Depraved and Disorderly: Female Convicts, Sexuality and Gender in Colonial Australia.* Cambridge, U.K.: Cambridge University Press, 1997.

Daniels, Kay. *Convict Women.* Sydney: Allen & Unwin, 1998.

D'Cruze, Shani, and Louise A. Jackson. *Women, Crime and Justice in England since 1660.* Basingstoke, U.K.: Palgrave McMillan, 2009.

D'Cruze, Shani, Sandra Walklate, and Samantha Pegg, eds. *Murder: Social and Historical Approaches to Understanding Murder and Murderers.* London: Routledge, 2011.

Dixon, Rachel. *Infanticide: Expert Evidence and Testimony in Child Murder Cases, 1688–1955.* London: Routledge, 2022.

Douglas, Heather, and Mark Finnane. *Indigenous Crime and Settler Law: White Sovereignty After Empire.* Basingstoke, U.K: Palgrave McMillan, 2012.

Erickson, Rica, ed. *Dictionary of Western Australians,* vol. 2. *Bond, 1850–1868.* Nedlands: University of Western Australia Press, 1979.

Erickson, Rica, ed. *The Bicentennial Dictionary of Western Australians, pre 1829–1888*. 4 vols. Nedlands, W.A.: UWAP, 1987–1988.

Erickson, Rica. *The Bride Ships: Experiences of Immigrants Arriving in Western Australia 1849–1889*. Carlisle, W.A: Hesperian Press, 1992.

Erickson, Rica. "T.N. Yule Esq.: A Gentleman of Misfortune." In *Rica's Stories*, edited by Lenore Layman, 63–81. Nedlands, W.A.: The Royal Western Australian Historical Society, 2001.

Fall, Victor George. *The Mills of Jarrahdale, a Century of Achievement 1872–1972: A History.* Nedlands, W.A: Royal Western Australian Historical Society, 1972.

Finnane, Mark. "Indigenous Peoples and Settler Criminal Law." In *The Cambridge Legal History of Australia*, edited by Peter Cane, Lisa Ford, and Mark David McMillan, 629–50. Cambridge: Cambridge University Press, 2022.

Fitch, Valerie J. *Eager for Labour: The Swan River Indenture, 1829–1832.* Carlisle, W.A.: Hesperian Press, 2003.

Frances, Raelene. *Selling Sex: A Hidden History of Prostitution.* Sydney: University of NSW Press, 2017.

Gilchrist, Catie. *Murder, Misadventure and Miserable Ends: Tales from a Colonial Coroner's Court*. Sydney: HarperCollins, 2019.

Goc, Nicola. *Women, Infanticide, and the Press, 1822–1922: News Narratives in England and Australia.* London: Routledge, 2016.

Gothard, Jan. *Blue China: Single Female Migration to Colonial Australia.* Carlton South: Melbourne University Press, 2001.

Green, Neville. *Broken Spears, Aboriginals and Europeans in the Southwest of Australia.* Cottesloe: Focus Education Services, 1984.

Green, Neville, and Susan Moon. *Far From Home: Aboriginal Prisoners of Rottnest Island 1838–1931.* Nedlands: University of Western Australia Press, 1997.

Grellier, Margaret. "Women and the Family." In *Westralian Voices: Documents in Western Australian Social History,* edited by Marion Aveling, 275–358. Nedlands: University of Western Australia Press, 1979.

Grey, Daniel J.R. "'The Agony of Despair': Pain and the Cultural Script of Infanticide in England and Wales, 1860–1960." In *Pain and Emotion in Modern History*, edited by Rob Boddice, 204–19. London: Palgrave Macmillan, 2014.

Grey, Daniel J.R. "'No Crime to Kill a Bastard-Child': Stereotypes of Infanticide in Nineteenth-Century England and Wales." In *Intersections of Gender,*

Class, and Race in the Long Nineteenth Century and Beyond, edited by Barbara Leonardi, 41–66. Cham, Switzerland: Palgrave MacMillan, 2018.

Grey, Daniel J.R. "'A Hard-Working and Nice Person?' Respectability, Femininity and Infanticide in England and Wales, 1800–2000." In *The Emerald International Handbook of Feminist Perspectives on Women's Acts of Violence,* edited by S. Banwel, L. Black, D. K. Cecil, Y. K. Djamba, S. R. Kimuna, E. Milne, L. Seal, and E. Y. Tenkorang, 339–45. Bradford, U.K.: Emerald Publishing, 2023.

Haebich, Anna. *Murdering Stepmothers: The Execution of Martha Rendell.* Crawley, W.A.: UWA Publishing, 2009.

Hallam, Sylvia. "Aboriginal Demography in Southwestern Australia census lists." In *Aborigines of New Norcia, 1845–1914*, edited by Neville Green and Lois Tillbrook, 174–201. Nedlands: University of Western Australia Press, 1989.

Hallam, Sylvia. "Aboriginal Population." In *Historical Encyclopedia of Western Australia,* edited by Jenny Gregory and Jan Gothard, 22–34. Crawley: University of Western Australia Press, 2009.

Hallam, Sylvia, and Lois Tilbrook. *Aborigines of the Southwest Region 1829–1840*. Nedlands: University of Western Australia Press, 1990.

Harding, Sandra. "Conclusion: Epistemological Questions." In *Feminism & Methodology: Social Science Issues*, 181–190, edited by Sandra Harding. Milton Keynes: Open University Press, 1987.

Hasluck, Alexandra. *Royal Engineer: A Life of Sir Edmund DuCane.* Sydney: Angus and Robertson, 1973.

Hay, Douglas. "Property, Authority and the Criminal Law." In *Albion's Fatal Tree: Crime and Society in Eighteenth-Century England*, edited by Douglas Hay, Peter Linebaugh, John G. Rule, E. P Thompson, and Cal Winslow, 17–63. London: Penguin, 1975.

Heidensohn, Frances. *Women and Crime.* London: Macmillan Press, 1985.

Heidensohn, Frances. *Crime and Society.* London: Macmillan Education, 1989.

Henderson, Graeme. *The Wreck of the "Elizabeth."* Sydney: Australian Society for Historical Archaeology, 1973.

Hetherington, Penelope. *Paupers, Poor Relief and Poor Houses in Western Australia, 1829 to 1910*. Crawley, W.A.: UWA Publishing, 2009.

Hetherington, Penelope. *The Marriage Knot: Marriage and Divorce in Colonial Western Australia 1829–1900*. Crawley, W.A.: UWA Publishing, 2013.

Hitchcock, Joseph Keane, and J. W. B. Stevens. *The History of Fremantle: The Front Gate of Australia, 1829–1929.* Fremantle City Council, 1929.

Hunter, Ann. *A Different Kind of "Subject": Colonial Law in Aboriginal-European Relations in Nineteenth Century Western Australia 1829–61.* North Melbourne: Australian Scholarly Publishing, 2012.

James, M. S. *A Superior Body of Men.* Bloomington: Authorhouse, 2014.

Kilday, Anne-Marie. *A History of Infanticide in Britain: c 1600 to the Present.* London: Palgrave MacMillan, 2013.

Klein, Dorie. "The Etiology of Female Crime." In *The Criminology of Deviant Women,* edited by Freda Adler and Rita James Simon, 58–81. Boston: Houghton Mifflin Company, 1979.

Langbein, John. *The Origins of Adversary Criminal Trial.* Oxford: Oxford University Press, 2005.

Langton, Marcia. *"Well I Heard It on the Radio and I Saw It on the Television": An Essay for the Australian Film Commission on the Politics and Aesthetics of Filmmaking by and about Aboriginal People and Things.* Sydney: Australian Film commission, 1993.

MacDonald, Robert. "Dangerous Youth and the Dangerous Class." In *Youth, the "Underclass" and Social Exclusion,* edited by Robert MacDonald, 1–25. London: Routledge, 1997.

MacRae, Damien. *Encyclopaedic Australian Legal Dictionary.* Sydney: Butterworths, 2002.

Muurling, Sanne, Marion Pluskota, and Manon van der Heijden. "Introduction: Women and Crime in History." In *Women's Criminality in Europe, 1600–1914,* edited by Manon van der Heijden, Marion Pluskota, and Sanne Muurling, 1–25. Cambridge: Cambridge University Press, 2020.

Naffine, Ngaire. *Female Crime: The Construction of Women in Criminality.* Sydney: Allen & Unwin, 1987.

Nagy, Victoria. *Nineteenth-Century Female Poisoners: Three English Women Who Used Arsenic to Kill.* Basingstoke: Palgrave Macmillan, 2015.

Nettelbeck, Amanda. "Intimate Violence in the Pastoral Economy: Aboriginal Women's Labour and Protective Governance." In *Intimacies of Violence in the Settler Colony: Economies of Dispossession Around the Pacific Rim,* edited by Penelope Edmonds and Amanda Nettelbeck, 67–88. Cham, Switzerland: Palgrave Macmillan, 2018.

Nettelbeck, Amanda, L. A. Knafla, R. Smandych, and R. Foster. *Fragile Settlements: Aboriginal Peoples, Law, and Resistance in South-West Australia and Prairie.* Vancouver, Canada: UBC Press, 2016.

Owen, Chris. *"Every Mother's Son Is Guilty": Policing the Kimberley Frontier of Western Australia 1882–1905.* Crawley: UWA Publishing, 2017.

Palk, Deidre. *Gender, Crime and Judicial Discretion, 1780–1830.* Woodbridge, U.K.: Boydell Press, 2006.

Palmer, Kingsley. *Noongar People, Noongar Land: The Resilience of Aboriginal Culture in the South West of Western Australia.* Canberra, ACT: Aboriginal Studies Press, 2016.

Pollak, Otto. *The Criminality of Women.* Philadelphia: University of Pennsylvania Press, 1950.

Reece, Bob. "Glimpses of Fremantle." In *Voices from the West End: Stories, People and Events That Shaped Fremantle,* edited by Paul Longley Arthur and Geoffrey Bolton, 8–19. Perth: Western Australian Museum, 2012.

Rose, Lionel. *Massacre of the Innocents: Infanticide in Great Britain 1800–1939.* London: Routledge, 2016.

Russell, Enid. *A History of the Law in Western Australia.* Nedlands: University of Western Australia Press, 1980.

Ryan, Jan. *Ancestors: Chinese in Colonial Australia.* Fremantle: Fremantle Arts Centre Press, 1995.

Saunders, Kay. *Deadly Australian Women.* Sydney, N.S.W.: ABC Books, 2013.

Seal, Lizzie. *Women, Murder and Femininity: Gender Representations of Women Who Kill.* Basingstoke: Palgrave MacMillan, 2010.

Shoemaker, Robert. "Streets of Shame? The Crowd and Public Punishments in London, 1700–1820." In *Penal Practice and Culture, 1500–1900: Punishing the English,* edited by Paul Griffiths and Simon Devereaux, 232–57. Basingstoke: Palgrave Macmillan, 2003.

Smart, Carol. *Women, Crime and Criminology: A Feminist Critique.* London: Routledge and Kegan Paul, 1976.

Smith, Woodruff D. *Respectability as Moral Map and Public Discourse in the Nineteenth Century.* London: Routledge, 2018.

Statham-Drew, Pamela. *James Stirling: Admiral and Founding Governor of Western Australia.* Crawley: University of Western Australia Press, 2003.

Stephenson, Lyn, and Tom Stannage. "Law and Order." In *Westralian Voices: Documents in Western Australian Social History,* edited by Marion Aveling, 65–105. Nedlands: University of Western Australia Press, 1979.

Straw, Leigh S. L. *Drunks, Pests and Harlots: Criminal Women in Perth and Fremantle, 1900–1939.* Kilkerran: Humming Earth, 2013.

Thomas, James, and Alex Stewart. *Imprisonment in W.A.: Evolution, Theory and Practice.* Crawley: University of Western Australia Press, 1978.

Tilbrook, Lois. *Nyungar Tradition: Glimpses of Aborigines of South-Western Australia 1829–1914.* Nedlands: University of Western Australia Press, 1983.

Toussaint, Sandy. "Western Australia." In *Contested Ground: Australian Aborigines Under the British Crown,* edited by Ann McGrath, 240–68. London: Routledge, 2020.

Whitehurst, Rose. *Noongar Dictionary.* East Perth, W.A.: Noongar Language and Culture Centre, 1997.

Wiener, Martin J. *Men of Blood: Violence, Manliness, and Criminal Justice in Victorian England*. West Nyack: Cambridge University Press, 2004.

Williams, Lucy, and Barry Godfrey. *Criminal Women 1850–1920: Researching the Lives of Britain's Female Offenders.* Havertown: Pen & Sword Books Limited, 2018.

Wilson, H. Margaret. *Sarah Theodosia and the Hall Family.* Perth, W.A.: Margaret Wilson, 1994.

Zedner, Lucia. *Women, Crime and Custody in Victorian England*. Oxford: Clarendon Press, 1991.

Index

C. Ingram, *Women on Trial*, Palgrave Histories of Policing, Punishment and Justice, https://doi.org/10.1007/978-3-031-98072-5

D

FSC
www.fsc.org
MIX
Papier | Fördert
gute Waldnutzung
FSC® C083411

Kolibri 360 GmbH
Ferdinand-Jühlke-Straße 7
99095 Erfurt, Deutschland
produktsicherheit@kolibri360.de